PUNCH AND JUDY

AND OTHER ESSAYS

PUNCH AND JUDY
& OTHER ESSAYS

BY

MAURICE BARING

Essay Index Reprint Series

BOOKS FOR LIBRARIES PRESS, INC.
FREEPORT, NEW YORK

First Published 1924
Reprinted 1968

LIBRARY OF CONGRESS CATALOG CARD NUMBER:

68-16904

PRINTED IN THE UNITED STATES OF AMERICA

TO

Desmond   MacCarthy

PREFACE

THE following essays have been collected from the back numbers of reviews, magazines, and newspapers. The earliest of them was published in 1899, the latest in 1923.

I have not attempted to make any radical alterations in the earlier essays, nor to rewrite them in the light of later experience, and I am fully conscious that in those articles which deal with theatrical matters there are repetitions. The same thing is said over and over again. It is a good thing to do this in journalism. There is little excuse for it in a printed book, but I did not notice it until it was too late.

My thanks are due to the editors and proprietors who have so kindly and so courteously allowed me to reprint these articles.

The article on Taine appeared in the ninth edition of the *Encyclopædia Britannica*, and I have slightly abridged it. The article on Sully-Prudhomme came out in the same book. It was not signed when it first appeared. In later editions, by a strange tangle of circumstances, it came to be attributed, through nobody's fault, to initials more illustrious than my own : namely, E. G.

"Punch and Judy" and La Fontaine's *Fables* came out first in the *London Mercury*; the papers on Mrs. Campbell and on Gilbert and Sullivan in the *Fortnightly Review*; "Racine" in the *National Review*; "Sarah Bernhardt" in the *Illustrated Review*; "A Place of Peace" in the *Evening News*; "Crabbe" in the *Saturday Review*; "The Return of Eleonora Duse" in *Vanity Fair*, New York; "Tolstoy's Last Play" in the *Daily Mail*; "Chaliapine" in *St. Martin's Magazine*. Nearly all the remaining papers appeared either in the *Morning Post* or the *New Statesman*; one is new, and one came out in a Review that no longer exists : *The Speaker*.

My thanks are also due to the scholar who kindly corrected the proofs and whose name I will not mention, lest any lapse of mine be attributed to his oversight.

MAURICE BARING

3 GRAY'S INN SQUARE
April 1924

CONTENTS

MISCELLANEOUS ESSAYS

AUTHORS AND BOOKS

MISCELLANEOUS ESSAYS

PUNCH AND JUDY

(A Paper read to the Newman Society at Oxford)

"*R*ACINE," said Madame de Sévigné, in one of
her letters, "*passera comme le café.*"[1] She
said this because she thought Racine was a new-
fangled person, a kind of Cubist, and she was being
loyal to Corneille. She will no doubt be ultimately
right. A day will come when there will be no more
Racine and no more coffee, only an *Ersatz* for each.
But relatively she was wrong.

She thought Racine and coffee belonged to that category of heresies of which a living poet has said : " The
wind has blown them all away."

Nevertheless when you hear a statement of that
kind made by a person of intelligence, such as
Madame de Sévigné, you cannot help feeling a little
bit alarmed.

I remember when I was a small child feeling a cold
chill come over me when I heard my father say that nearly
all the most characteristic and seemingly permanent of
the street denizens of London, whom he remembered,
had vanished, except the muffin-man, who seemed to
have elements of eternity about him, and that even
Punch and Judy would pass away.

For all practical purposes the Punch and Judy show
has almost passed away. Almost, but not quite. A

[1] It appears she did not. Some one else said she did. (But she
thought it.)

3

few weeks ago, outside Harrods' Stores, I saw a performance of Punch and Judy. The Pan-pipes played ; Toby barked ; Punch's high falsetto rang through the fog ; Judy's querulous remonstrances were quickly smothered ; and the drama marched, from logical step to logical step, to its tragic and inevitable close. Punch foiled the policeman, murdered the doctor, fooled the hangman, was baffled by the clown, and finally met with the doom of Doctor Faustus. Terrified, he went into the night, crying out the Cockney equivalent for

" O lente, lente, currite, noctis equi."

In the street, looking on at this rollicking comedy, this terse tragedy, this intoxicating melo-drama — I mean melo-drama (counting Toby and the Pan-pipes) and not melodrama—a mixed crowd had assembled. There was an errand-boy, oblivious of his mission, a butcher's cart pausing in its brisk career, a wistful nursery-maid and a crowded, vocal perambulator, several school children, several grown-up people, a policeman, a clerk, a postman, a bookmaker—in fact, a representative audience. Not one of them could withdraw his or her attention from the spectacle until it was over, and even the more parsimonious, who were determined to see the show for nothing and pretended to go away when the bag came round, sneaked back again when that dangerous moment was tided over. It was a great success. The audience laughed ; a small child in front of me enjoyed the coffin ecstatically ; and several minor members of the audience, especially the baby in the perambulator, screamed when the devil came for Punch. There was a sigh of disappointment when it was all over.

The same week I witnessed a spectacle of a different

kind. A drama called *Atlantide*, at Covent Garden, on the film. It was the cinematograph version of a French romance : the collision of two French officers with a French " She-who-must-be-obeyed." In rapid succession we witnessed rides on the desert ; the arrival of some officers in a forgotten and unspoiled corner of the continent of Atlantis ; the palace of Antinea (an Atlantean), in which former intruders, who one and all had hung their harps on weeping willow-trees to signify they died of love, were embalmed in bronze, by a process peculiar to Atlanteans, and were kept in the library and labelled and card-indexed by the librarian ; we saw the apartments of Antinea herself, rich with Moorish fretwork, plentifully stocked with Benares bowls, a little overcrowded perhaps, possibly a trifle too reminiscent of an international exhibition ; and finally Antinea herself unveiled. So great was her charm—we learn from the book, and the marginal notes of the film corroborated the fact—that a man at her bidding kills his best friend with a small hammer. The trouble is there is no one from Atlantis to play this tremendous part. And the audience, face to face, not with a mask, or with the unfettered fancy of its imagination, but with a concrete European lady, who obviously had experience of the movies, could hardly help feeling a shade disappointed.

Then came an escape ; more desert scenes, a mirage, in which a vision of the Crystal Palace suddenly lent a cosy touch to an otherwise unfriendly landscape of waste and arid desolation.

Then a final scene in which the escaped officer feels the call of Antinea, and sets out for Atlantis once more.

On paper what could be more thrilling ? The spectacle

seemed to offer all that the eye and the imagination could ask for :—adventure, gorgeous landscape, love-interest, terror, pity, excitement, suspense, a marvellous and poisoned camel perishing in its pride, a forgotten continent ; slaves, palm-trees, the *Illustrated London News* arriving punctually at the city of Antinea, the false lure of the mirage, the conflict between love and duty, the clash of wills, love, death ; all the elements of tragedy and romance, and yet . . . the spectacle, judging from its effect on an audience, which was certainly interested and amused, but at the end a little tired, " and pale, as it seemed, at last," was less successful than Punch and Judy as performed in the Tottenham Court Road.

But why, it may be asked, compare the two at all ? Cannot both be enjoyed separately and differently by a reasonable person ?   Well, this is why I want to compare them : Punch and Judy and the cinematograph represent, I think, between them the ultimate possibilities, the complete range and scope of the drama of yesterday, to-day, and of the future.

This occurred to me the first time I saw a movie. I at once followed the advice of the wise man who said : " Directly I get a new idea I look up and see which Greek author has expressed it best."   I found my idea expressed more fully, more concisely, and more skilfully than I could ever have expressed it in a book of critical articles written in the 'sixties and the 'seventies by the poet Théodore de Banville, which were collected and republished in 1917, under the title of *Critiques*.

In June 1878, Théodore de Banville made an astonishing prophecy. Talking of the magic of the dramatic poets he said it was indeed a wondrous feat to silver a whole sky, and to make the shadow twinkle with diamonds, by the happy manipulation of twelve syllables. He was thinking of two famous lines of Corneille. Our poets have done it over and over again in the manipulation of *ten* syllables. For instance :

" How sweet the moonlight sleeps upon this bank."
Or,
" The moon is up and yet it is not night."
Or,
" Far over sands marbled with moon and cloud."

But these miracles, said Théodore de Banville, will happen no more, because they no longer serve any purpose. To see, he says—I will transpose his French allusions into their English equivalents—to see, he says, the dawn in russet mantle clad, walking o'er the dew of yon high eastern hill, or the floor of Heaven thick inlaid with patines of bright gold, is now the business of the electrician and the limelight lighter ; and magic will be paid for, just as heating and sweeping, monthly. The Muse of poetry, he said, who needs nothing to aid her to establish her dominion, will, in her pride, go back to the Ode and to the Epic. As to the stage, it will diverge into two widely different currents. On the one hand, into spectacular pantomime, aided by all the latest improvements in mechanism, lighting, and scenery, and, on the other hand, into realistic drama, modern bourgeois drama, which will go straight to the point, and indulge more and more in the shorthand business of an age of hustle and the style of the Morse code.

This was written in 1878, and not only did Théodore de Banville thus foresee the cinematograph, but his prophecy about the future of the drama came literally true. The drama diverged into the two currents he foreshadowed : the movies and the realistic drama. Ibsen all over the world, with his herd of hysterical shopkeepers wrangling over an antimacassar : the Théâtre Antoine in Paris, the Art Theatre in Moscow, the Court Theatre in London ; Mr. Shaw, Mr. Galsworthy, Mr. Granville Barker, etc. Théodore de Banville forgot one thing—he forgot Punch and Judy. He forgot Guignol ; he was spared the vision of the Grand Guignol.

My object in writing this paper is to point out that in the bare existence of Punch and Judy, in the mere fact that Punch and Judy is not yet dead and can still be seen, there is not only still a lingering hope of something else, but there actually exists something else which is akin to Punch and Judy and founded on the same tradition.

In another page, from the same book, Théodore de Banville tells us what led him to the conclusion that something like the cinematograph was bound to evolve.

He quotes what he calls a terrible and decisive aphorism : " When the stage attains to material perfection dramatic poetry will cease to exist." He adds the reason of this, namely, that *the human eye tires of any spectacle that lasts a quarter of an hour*.

I don't know whether Théodore de Banville ever assisted at an exhibition of *tableaux vivants*, but if he did, he surely would have said one minute instead of a quarter of an hour. No human being can behold a *tableau vivant*, however beautiful, for more than a minute, if for so long. If the spectacle is prolonged, he will scream. And it is this which proves the inanity of elaborate scenery in the mounting of Shakespeare and of all poetical drama.

Once more, we find Théodore de Banville speaking

to the point. In talking of Racine's plays, he says that Racine was right to have them performed, in contemporary costume, on a stage crowded with noblemen, without giving a thought to local colour or historic verisimilitude. The day, he says, when Talma, in the name of progress, mounted Racine with a pretence of physical and pictorial probability, the intimate atmosphere (*le sens intime*) of the plays was lost for ever. Racine's plays were meant to be played in a drawing-room, and his verse was meant to be recited in the earshot of an eager, inquisitive, receptive crowd of people. What is true about Racine is true in a different way and for different reasons about Shakespeare.

Théodore de Banville, about the mounting of Shakespeare, says this : " Very little furniture, extremely simple scenery, straight wings, and a frieze, which is in reality the continuation of a curtain, are the real accessories you need for Shakespeare, and they allow his changes of scene to take place in sight of the audience. When *Hamlet* was played here," he continues (he is writing in 1869), " the drama was killed by pretentious scenery which was heavily dumped down in front of us, by changes of scene and the noise of scene-shifting, by the constant fall and rise of the curtain, and, above all, by the *entr'actes* which unduly interrupted the action."

How true this used to be about the Shakespearean productions at the Lyceum ; how terribly true about all modern productions of *Hamlet*, with the exception of those at the " Old Vic." It is a tragic situation : all this trouble and expense, all the thousands of pounds spent on scenery, mounting, and electrical effects, is so much money wasted, and makes the production of many plays impossible. It has killed the production of poetical drama in England, but it has never satisfied the patrons of the drama, because you cannot get over the initial fact, which I have already mentioned, that the human eye tires of any scenic effect after a minute. Therefore, if the public need scenic effect, it must have something more than *static* scenic effect. *It must have scenes that move* : the movies. Hence the cinematograph ; and hence Théodore de Banville's prophecy of the cinematograph. Well, if that is what the public wanted, they have got it. But I maintain that given the finest cinematograph in the world, and a great actor or actress performing either in tragedy or comedy against a bare curtain, in a real play, with spoken words, the play would have the greater success, granted, of course, that the opportunities for seeing either performance were equal. It would not be fair to pit a cinematograph that can go on all day and all night (Sundays included) against an actor who cannot speak for more than three hours at a stretch, six nights in the week and at two matinées.

I have often heard it said : " That is all very well, but now the public is used to elaborate scenery, it will always insist on having it." My point is that the public, after the curtain has risen, does not notice the scenery at all, nor even look at it after the first minute of the action. It looks at the actors. It is following the play ; and as the whole essence of drama is action, and rapidity of action, a play of Shakespeare's, for instance, which is divided into a multitude of scenes, suffers from a forcible lowering of the pulse, and its stride is impeded, retarded, and checked if the action is suspended while the scene is being changed, especially if the change involves either a long wait, or a deafening noise of hammering behind a swaying back cloth.

Any one who has had the good fortune to witness a

performance of *Hamlet* without scenery, with merely a curtain in the background, will probably have been surprised to find how little he missed the scenery ; how completely any thought of it vanished directly the actors held the attention. It is on record that one of Garrick's greatest triumphs happened in a French drawing-room. He acted the dagger scene from *Macbeth*, and moved a small and elegant audience to terror. It is obvious that they did not feel the need of limelight or of an artificial thunderstorm in the foreground.

But one need not drag in Garrick to make the point. Children's charades and Punch and Judy prove it. Supposing there was a long wait between each successive episode in Punch and Judy, while the scene was being changed and lighting effects were being prepared, the audience would melt away.

The recent revival of *The Beggar's Opera*[1] is another proof that scenery is waste of money, for in recent times no play has been more simply mounted or more success-ful : and the first run[2] of *The Beggar's Opera* lasted ninety-five years longer than that of *Chu Chin Chow*.

Another point is this : stage scenery, however elaborate, however realistic ; stage lighting, however complicated and ingenious, is always, and must always be, a compara-tive failure. A tree on the stage can never look like a real tree ; a stage bird never sings as well as a real bird ; a tea-tray is never quite as realistic as a real thunder-storm, although once at a rehearsal of *Macbeth* I heard the late Sir Herbert Beerbohm Tree tell a real thunder-storm that he had warned it a thousand times to mind its cue and not to break in on his soliloquy : to be less in-tempestive. Stage scenery can neither compete with

---

[1] It ran for four years.
[2] It ran for one hundred years.

Nature nor with the camera. That being so, why waste money on it ? Why not learn a lesson from Punch and Judy ?

The lesson is beginning to be learnt. There is a theatre in Paris, the *Vieux Colombier*, where Shakespeare's plays are produced with the minimum of pageantry and the maximum of effect ; there is the " Old Vic." in London, where Shakespeare is enjoyed by the same kind of people he wrote his plays for. Since this paper was spoken, there has been a revival of Shakespeare at the Kingsway on the very lines I have here advocated. Two years ago the revival of the *Yellow Jacket* proved that two actors sitting on a table could give the illusion of a boat floating down a river. There are others, but what I should like to see is not only a wholesale revival of Punch and Judy, not only State-endowed Punch and Judys, and pensions for retired Codlins and Shorts, and homes for decayed Tobys, but a host of puppet-shows all over the country, for which poets such as Mr. Bridges, Mr. Chesterton, Mr. Yeats, Mr. Hardy, Mr. de la Mare, Mr. Kipling, Mr. Belloc, Miss Sitwell, and in fact all the poets (old and young) should write plays.

These plays could be produced at once, without any bother. There would be no long heart-searchings as to whether or not the public could stand them. If the public couldn't stand them, you could instantly change the bill and produce *King Lear* or *The Comedy of Errors*. There would be no delicate debate about the casting ; no manipulating of the play to suit the actor-manager, no rivalry between various actors, no question of any one of the puppets saying : " Very well, then, I shan't play."

No rivalry as to the space between the names of the

actors on the play-bills, which even in Paris is a source of
trouble. I remember the plight of a French academician
who was found measuring a playbill outside a theatre
with his umbrella. When he was asked what he was
doing, he said : " I am measuring the space between
the name of my leading actress and her subordinates,
and that between the name of my leading actor and his
subordinates, as she says unless she is given as much
interspace as he is enjoying she will throw up her part
in my play." There would be none of these unforeseen
obstacles, and the drama would go back to what it was
originally meant to be, what the French still call it : *Le
Spectacle*, and what in England, alas ! now survives only
in the all too rare revivals of the incomparable drama of
Punch and Judy.

Le Spectacle. The Show. That is what we want. And
that is what we get neither at the movies nor in the
theatre nowadays, and hardly anywhere, except in Punch
and Judy. Just before the war, I was in Russia, and I
met a poet who is now famous, calm, and dead. He died
of scurvy in St. Petersburg, during the revolution. He
is famous now for a poem about Bolshevism (not a
Bolshevik poem) called *The Twelve* ; but he was well
known before this in Russia, as a writer of exquisite
verse, and of plays which were performed by living
puppets. His name was Alexander Blok. I spent an
evening in the winter of 1912 with him and some other
Russian poets and men of letters, whose names I have
forgotten ; but I remember that Blok spoke of nothing
but the disappearance of the show, the *spectacle*, and
he used the French word. He said on the modern stage
there was no *spectacle*. Greek plays and Shakespeare
were not allowed to be spectacles, in the French sense
of the word *spectacle*, in the sense that children's charades,

the Passion Play at Ammergau, *The Beggar's Opera*, and Punch and Judy are spectacles. The Chinese, he said, still had the right spectacle. Their plays are not, indeed, played by puppets, but by human beings ; human beings, nevertheless, who are so perfectly trained in movement, facial play, and facial contortion, that on a diminutive stage two men, without any accessories, save weapons, can give by hardly moving their bodies a realistic representation of a battle.

I had another Russian friend who once described to me one of these mimic battles, and he told me that two impassive Chinamen, with their wonderfully disciplined muscles and their obedient, elastic grimaces and facial contortions, had for the first time brought home to him what *alarums and excursions* meant on the stage. Alexander Blok denied that there was any spectacle left in modern drama. He thought Chekov's plays were penny-readings of a gloomy kind ; Gorky's plays short stories gone wrong ; Bernard Shaw's plays overgrown pamphlets ; the whole of the modern French stage intolerable, with the exception of Rostand. What he wanted was Molière, Shakespeare, Punch and Judy ; and he wrote one excellent play of the kind himself, in which the heroine was made of cardboard. In talking thus he was unwittingly sowing a seed : the seed of expressionism.

But now let us listen for one moment to the voice of common sense, to the man who may reasonably ask : " But what do you suggest should be done ? Punch and Judy is great fun, and we know that actor-managers sometimes spoil Shakespeare. The movies are a living fact. You need not like them, but you can't get rid of them. They are there, and Punch and Judy is not there. The movies may be as undramatic, in spite of all their elaborate thrills, as Mrs. Jarley's waxworks, but the sad fact remains that Mrs. Jarley has won and Codlin and Short have lost the battle. When Mrs. Jarley tried to explain to little Nell the quality of her waxworks, little Nell asked a dangerous question : " I never saw waxworks, madam," she said. " Is it funnier than Punch ? " " Funnier ? " said Mrs. Jarley in a shrill voice, " it is not funny at all, it is calm and classical."

Nothing at first sight could appear less calm and less classical than the movies, especially those films that deal with classical subjects ; but as drama, as a spectacle, they are, compared with Punch and Judy, tame and pseudo-classical. They tire the eye, and I don't believe the sight of Dr. Jekyll turning into Mr. Hyde, in sight of the audience, thrills a schoolboy as much as the appearance of the coffin and the skeleton in Punch. I know it doesn't. I have put the matter to the test. Either drama happens or it does not happen ; and if it is not happening, not all the runaway trains, not all the motorbicycles leaping over express trains, in the world, not all the mirages in the Sahara, will make it happen. *A railway accident is not drama.*

Again the voice of common sense breaks in and says : " What do you suggest ? What is your alternative ? " Matthew Arnold said : " Organise the theatre, the theatre is irresistible." Very well, then, how would you organise it ? Do you suggest the mounting of plays being put in the hands of artists ? Do you suggest that every play should have Gordon Craig screens, Cubist scenery, and Scriabin effects of sound mixed with colour ? (God forbid !) Well, if not, if you simply want charades and Punch and Judy, the stage cannot be reformed without being reformed altogether—reformed out of existence.

Well, what I want is not the impossible. All I ask is that the play may be allowed to do its own work, with the help of actors, and that it should not be stifled by accessories, scenery, properties, incidental music, limelight effects, dances, alarums, and excursions, which fail to convince and merely succeed in retarding the action because they are not a part of it. They are ruinously costly, and—this is my main point—the public, if they only knew it, and if only the managers knew it, do not want them at all, and in reality pay no attention to them. I can give a good example of this. Some years ago the late Sir Herbert Beerbohm Tree produced *Macbeth* at His Majesty's Theatre. Beerbohm Tree was a man of imagination and a dreamer of dreams. His imagination sometimes found adequate expression in the rendering of character parts such as Svengali, but this did not satisfy him. He saw and thought big, and expressed his dreams in grandiose Shakespearean productions, which were enormously expensive, and sometimes extremely beautiful, as pageants, but they rarely allowed *le spectacle* any free play. While he was rehearsing *Macbeth*, I attended several of the rehearsals. One afternoon, he was rehearsing the last act. There was a scene at the back, and an embryo portcullis somewhere. Macbeth's army was being played by private soldiers of the Coldstream Guards. They stood dotted about on the stage in their red tunics, carrying light canes. In the foreground stood Beerbohm Tree in his ordinary clothes, and wearing, I think, a jewelled helmet. Nothing could have been more incongruous than the outward appearance of that act as it was played that afternoon to an empty theatre. In the stalls there were a few friends. And yet no sooner did the actors begin to speak their words, than the attention of the scant audience, of the supers on the stage, of the scene-shifters in the wings, was held ; and when Tree, hardly raising his voice, spoke the speech which begins : " To-morrow and to-morrow and to-morrow," and which I have always imagined Shakespeare was made to write in at the actor's bidding, the effect was overwhelming. He was making no effort, and the verse was allowed to do its own work.

A few nights later, I was present on the first night, but there was so much dancing, so much music, so many floating ghosts and whirling witches, so many changes of scene, so much startling illumination, and such a wealth of unexpected detail and business, that one had not time to listen to the words, and the play seemed the whole time to be standing still. One felt all that wealth of colour and change had been a waste of money, and that the audience would have been held in a far tighter grip had they been able to witness the play in the undress clothes of rehearsal. I realised once and for all, not only how little accessories, how little all *that is not the play* matters ; not only this, but also that in a play, *everything that is not the play is an obstacle*, a cause of delay, a retarder. I don't mean I want all the supers in a play to be dressed in the clothes they wear in everyday life ; on the contrary, the more gorgeous the dresses the better. But I know that often one super will do quite as well as ten supers, and that incidental music has a damping effect on drama, that to be effective it must be an integral part of the drama, as in Wagner, or in Debussy's *Pelléas et Mélisande*.

My answers to the objections of common sense are, I think, the essence of common sense. I don't want the stage to be turned into something else ; an æsthetic electrocution chair, or a gallery of living waxworks, or a

2

hall of conjuring tricks, or a palace of reflectors. I
want it to be restored to what it originally was : a home
of illusion. The cart of Thespis, the Miracle Plays, the
Tréteau de Tabarin, the *Hôtel de Rambouillet*, the Globe
Theatre, Punch and Judy, the Italian puppet-shows, all
of them had this in common : they provided *the opportunity of make-believe* : and with the minimum of effort
they achieved the maximum of effect. They had another point in common : they let their actors *dress up*.
A man, or a woman, or a child, they knew, could
dress up enough like something else to create the
necessary illusion. But not all the painters, photo-
scenists, stage-managers, and lime-lighters in the world
can make a scene that is unreal in itself, and deprived
of the aid of human action, give the illusion of reality.
Not long ago I saw a version of *Macbeth* played by a
little boy and a little girl. It was an abridged version,
in prose, and in three acts. Lady Macbeth was left out ;
but the whole story was told, and a little more than
Shakespeare told us, for the last act, which was called
"Judgement," happened in Hell, and Macbeth was brought
up before Satan. Now, the little girl who played Satan,
by twisting a red shawl round herself, managed to convey
as good a *picture* of a stage Satan as any I have seen ;
indeed far better than many. And this brings me to my
point, to my common-sense answer to the objections of
common sense. The stage is an artificial thing. Let it
remain artificial, and do not let it try (and fail) to be as
natural as Nature, because the thing is impossible. The
best electric light is not in the least like sunlight ; the
most skilful artificial flowers are not in the least like
almond blossom ; the best painted and the best lighted
stage sunset or dawn is not comparable with a real sunset
or dawn. But a frankly artificial stage tree is effective ;

behind footlights an impossible stage sky is effective, because instead of trying to emulate sun and air it is making the most of gas or gauze.

So far from wishing to abolish scenery, all I want is for scenery to resume its proper place ; to abound in its own sense, and no longer to be ashamed of itself ; not to be snobbish, or to aspire to a rank above its station. I want the stage to remain the stage, and not to try to encroach on the domain of painting, sculpture, music, and photography. I want the attention of the audience to be concentrated on the actors ; and if the play and situations demand and require it, I should like the costumes to be never so gorgeous, as long as they are appropriate. Nothing could be better than the costumes in Punch and Judy. They create a complete illusion. Nothing could be better than the costumes in the Italian puppet-shows and in *The Beggar's Opera*. The princess in the puppet-show looks like a princess, and the clown looks like a clown, and we are satisfied. But when the Art Theatre at Moscow spent an infinity of labour in trying to set before us, on the stage, an old Russian country-house, at dawn, with windows opening on to a large cherry orchard in full blossom, with the birds singing, the audience admired the pains that had been taken, but were no more convinced of the reality of the cherry-blossom and the larks than they would have been by the birds in a toy symphony. In fact my answer to the objection of common sense is this : " The play's the thing " ; write and act the play, the rest will take care of itself. And as we have got beyond the cart of Thespis and the *Tréteau de Tabarin*, let us make the footlighted stage as effective as it can be, but let us take care that our effects do not neutralise the action of the play. Let us, above all, remember that everything on the stage is sham and make-believe, and that the more artificial it is, the greater will be its poetic reality. A crown of tinsel on the stage is more effective than the purest gold ; stage jewels are more brilliant behind footlights than the most authentic pearls and diamonds ; a Bengal light on the stage is more satisfying than the subtlest shades of photo-scenery.

If you read reminiscences of the great plays and great acting of the past, who is there who ever recollects or even gives a passing word to the scenery or to the mounting ?

Wagner spent a lot of time and trouble in trying to make some mechanical ravens fly across the stage when the *Valkyrie* was first produced at Bayreuth. The ravens broke down, sideslipped, and crashed in mid-flight ; but what if they had flown ? What if they had been intrinsically or automatically stable ? Would their accurate flight have increased by one iota (twice iota is, I believe, the minimum angle of glide) the effect of ravens and winged steeds that the music was giving from a hundred instruments, in spite of rotund tenors and massive prima donnas ?

But in the music dramas of Wagner there is an excuse for elaborate scenery ; there is more than an excuse, there is a *reason* for it. Wagner's idea was to act on the senses by every possible means ; and scenery was just as integral a part of his music drama as Zeppelins or gas were of German warfare. The trouble is that elaboration and multiplication of means does not necessarily produce an increase of effect ; and in the long-run it is the *sound* and the song of Wagner that either casts or does not cast a spell, and not the scenery.

When we read of the great acting, the great actors and plays of the past, the records tell us of Mrs. Siddons gliding, swiftly as a ghost, through the sleep-walking scene in *Macbeth*. The recorder (Hazlitt) certainly had no eyes for the back-cloth. Or, Keats tells of the gusto in the voice of Kean as he said : " Be stirring with the lark to-morrow, gentle Norfolk." Charlotte Brontë writes of the stamp of doom on Rachel's brow, and sorrow striking that stage-empress ; and we remember Sarah Bernhardt as the guilty queen, broken by unwilling guilt and Christian remorse, and saying in the stately accents of the Court of Louis the Fourteenth that she was slowly going to hell. Or, as I remember her at a concert I attended in the Hotel Ritz at Paris, during the South African War, moving a stiff, stodgy, and depressed audience to tears by an evocation of dawn and spring and dew, of the babble of April's lady and her lord in May, as she recited a lyric of Victor Hugo's. Or people remember Irving, as Becket, facing the murderers in Canterbury Cathedral. No amount of stage architecture could have added an inch of dignity to his carriage, or a spark of fire to the serene and confident courage of his gaze.

It is not necessary to invoke the past. Not longer ago than in February 1922, Chaliapine held a whole tightly-packed Albert Hall audience breathless, although he had a bad cold ; and here once and for all was a final proof of the needlessness of scenery. Here was a man with laryngitis, acting in a foreign language few of the audience could understand, and acting in a way that moved this audience to tears or laughter, as he pleased ; whether he sang the tragedy of *Boris Godounov* or a ditty about the Provincial governor's daughter in which he expressed the fatuous, drunken, sleepy, half-articulate, meandering, maudlin, infatuated, fond fancy of a minor government official.

Chaliapine did and does what the great actors of all
time did and do. They move us by their utterance,
and by their gestures, and not by the devices of the
surroundings nor the colour of the backgrounds. But
the question remains whether modern plays, even granted
all the achievements of actors and actresses of genius,
can move us as much as the plays in which the actors
are subordinate to the play itself, and sunk in it ; in
which the play, and the play only, is the thing.
That is to say, in the Greek Tragedy and in Punch
and Judy.

If you come to think of it, the most successful, and,
indeed, often the most striking, parts of great actors
and actresses are generally to be found in inferior plays.
It is in such plays that the mimes can make the most
of their mimicry. But in very great plays no mimicry
is necessary at all. The *Agamemnon* and *Œdipus Rex*
can do without expression. No amount of facial play
could add or detract from the situations or the words
in which and by which they are expressed. Shakespeare
can be badly acted, but the best acting of Shakespeare
adds little to the majesty of the spoken word, which
subsists even if it is being recited by a school-child.

Not long ago I heard two scenes from *Macbeth* played
by schoolboys aged eight, nine, and ten, at a day school
in London. As the magnificent words came through
their piping trebles, and the action was intimated by
their ingenuous and unsophisticated gestures, I felt that
I was hearing *Macbeth* for the first time. I understood
why Shakespeare's heroines were played by boys ; why
the Greek tragedians played with masks and spoke
through a pipe ; for these children acted with the mask
of innocence, and spoke through the pipe of childhood ;
and the play, Shakespeare's play, came to you direct

without any admixture of art o
was nothing to detract from it. T
thing.

To go back to Punch and Judy, what
anything to that tremendous drama ?
it is to think that the audience which I s
Tottenham Court Road did not go away
was very good, but that's not my idea
" Punch underacted in the scene with th
or " So-and-so was very good, but
Punch."

In Punch and Judy, the play and nothing
is the thing. That is perhaps why it is the
plays, although the various versions of t
story of Dr. Faustus, which is so obviously in
tradition, run it close. Here, again, how
effective any version of Dr. Faustus would be
by puppets. If Helen of Troy were a doll, w
be spared the doubt of wondering when Marlo
into Faust's mouth the lines : " Is this the fa
launched a thousand ships ? " whether he did not
" Is *this* the face that launched a thousand ships ?
doubt that so often assails us when we see the H
the Cleopatras, the Shes-whom-we-could-so-
imagine-might-be-disobeyed, on the modern s
and on the films.

For all these reasons, I return to my initial p
I wish that the poets and playwrights of the prese
and the future would go back to Punch and Judy, an
to the puppet-show, and learn of it. There is no plac
like a puppet-stage for Jonson's learned sock and Shakespeare's wood-notes wild ; and there, more easily than
in the cinematograph, or on the vast Reinhardt circuses
of Germany, Gorgeous Tragedy can come sweeping

SARAH BERNHARDT

I

" *SANS doute il est trop tard pour parler encor d'elle* "
So Alfred de Musset began his beautiful
poem to La Malibran, in which he said almost
all there is to be said about the death of one of
the queens of the stage. Only, in the case of La
Malibran, the world's regret, which found so lovely an
echo in the song of the poet, was all the more poignant
because La Malibran died in the flower of her youth.

Sarah Bernhardt, according to standards which we
should apply to any one else, was an old woman when
she died ; old, and full of glory, " having seen, borne, and
achieved more than most men on record," and yet when
the news of her death flashed through the world it seemed
an incredible thing, and the blackness and the void that
the disappearance of her presence left behind were felt
by the whole world. The world seemed a duller and a
greyer place without her :

> " She, she is dead ; she's dead : when thou knowst this,
> Thou knowst how wan a ghost this our world is."

That was the feeling we had when the news of her
death came. It came with the shock, as of something
living, vital, and actual leaving us, and not as the final
vibration of an echo of the past. For Sarah Bernhardt

never grew old. She remained young because her spirit was able to serve the novitiate which, La Rochefoucauld tells us, awaits the human being at every stage of his life, and she was ready at each revolution to face the possibilities of the new phase. So that death caught her acting for the cinematograph.

Many years ago, in 1882, after her first performance of Sardou's *Fédora*, Jules Lemaître, bidding her farewell as she was starting for America, in one of the most graceful tributes to her genius ever written, advised her, when she was weary of travel, adventure, and struggle, to come back and find a final home at the Théâtre français and to rest in the admiration and sympathy of " ce bon peuple Parisien," who, he said, would forgive her anything, as it owed her some of its greatest pleasures. And then, he added : " Un beau soir, mourez sur la scène subitement, dans un grand cri tragique, car la vieillesse serait trop dure pour vous." No doubt he was right, if he thought of Sarah retiring, as others have done, to some quiet suburb, living in the company of a parrot and an old servant, and weeping over old Press cuttings, a living ghost, and only a name to the present generation. Only that was just what did not and what could not happen. Although she had lost a leg, and though she was over seventy, she was still finding new things to do, and things which she, and she only, could do, and till the hour of her death she continued to adjust new means to a fresh end, and never gave the world the chance of saying " What a pity ! "

Indeed, one of the triumphs of her career was the twelve performances she gave of *Athalie* after the war, for one of which all the theatres of Paris closed to give the whole theatrical profession the chance of witnessing this example of her incomparable art.

II

What remains of it all ? What idea will future generations have of the art and the power of Sarah Bernhardt ? What will they believe ? Will they just think of her as an old-fashioned catchword brandished to check the enthusiasm of the young as they swing their censers to a new idol ? No, she will be more than that : the very photographs that exist of her, from her early days at the Comédie française, when she was as slender as a sylph, and a puff of wind seemed sufficient to blow her away, until the other day, when she embodied the sumptuous malignity of Athalie, bear witness to the feline grace, the exotic poetry, the electric power, the enigmatic expression, the strange splendour, as baffling to analysis as the scent of an aromatic herb, that emanated from her personality.

I believe there are cinematograph films which reveal at least some of the most telling of her gestures, some of the most poignant of her silences, and I used myself to have a gramophone record which held a poor ghost of her voice ; but all that is nothing, for Sarah Bernhardt's art was a complex whole, a combination of rhythmical movement, gesture, look, speech, hands, hair, body, and spirit ; and those who never saw her will only be able to guess at it, but it will be one of the beautiful and permanent guesses of mankind ; one of the lasting dreams of poets, one of the most magical speculations of artists and of all smokers of " enchanted cigarettes," like the charm of Cleopatra, the voice of the masters of the *bel canto*, the colours of Greek paintings and the melodies of Greek music. The record of her struggles, her efforts, her achievements, and her triumphs, exists in full and analytical detail. We can find it in the collected writings of Sarcey, Jules Lemaître, T. T. Weiss, and in the articles of Jacques de Tillet, Faguet, and others. I have lately been reading a number of the articles that Sarcey wrote on the various plays in which Sarah Bernhardt appeared, from the outset of her career, and I feel as if I had been watching the long and crowded panorama of her artistic destiny.

It was a difficult career from the start. She did not want to be an actress. She once told me herself, that her ambition had been to be a painter, but since she was forced to go on the stage she decided that if she had to be an actress, she would be the first. *Aut Cæsar, aut nullus.* There should be no question about it. I enjoyed her friendship for many years, and that was one of the few remarks I ever heard her make on the subject of acting or the stage. She never theorised about her parts, or the plays she acted in. They were to her, I think, so much plastic material that she kneaded and moulded and shaped with all the skill and force at her command. In kneading them she was guided by instinct, and she made herself perfect in execution by unremitting, relentless practice.

When, as a little girl, she was taken by her mother to face the entrance examination for the Conservatoire before a jury headed by Auber, she recited, instead of a tirade from Corneille or Racine, La Fontaine's Fable, " Les Deux Pigeons " (just as Trilby sang, " Au clair de la Lune ").

Scarcely had the lines, so says a contemporary record,

> " Deux pigeons s'aimaient d'amour tendre,
> L'un d'eux s'ennuyant au logis,"

passed her lips, when Auber interrupted her, spoke to her and told her she was admitted. The story has often

been told, but it has always struck me that the recitation
of those two lines probably contained, as in a microcosm,
the whole of Sarah Bernhardt's genius, just as in some
early lines of a poet written in the April of his genius
you sometimes find the blossom that foretells the whole
majesty and all the golden fruits of the tree. Such a
poem is the short sigh written by the boy D'Annunzio
and beginning :

> " O falce di luna calante,"

or Keats's sonnet on Chapman's Homer.

When Sarah Bernhardt played Adrienne Lecouvreur
she used to recite the opening of that fable, and one felt
as one heard it that for the perfect utterance of beautiful words this was the Pillars of Hercules of mortal
achievement, that it was impossible to speak verse
more beautifully.

III

The sighing of La Fontaine's Fable by this little girl
at the Conservatoire was the prelude, the prophecy,
and in one sense the epitome of all her long and glorious
career ; but the career was far from being one of roses,
roses all the way. The whole of Sarah Bernhardt's
artistic life was a fight against apparently insurmountable
difficulties—obstacles from the moment when she was
handicapped by her frailty, the delicacy of her constitution, the weakness of her lungs and her vocal organs,
until the moment she had to face, first the inability to
move, owing to invading rheumatism, and then the loss
of a leg. She prolonged the wrestle until she was on
her death-bed. It was a long time before she won the
suffrages of the critical. She made her début at the
Théâtre français in 1862, but all that Sarcey, who as a

conscientious and hard-working critic expressed for so
many years the opinion of the play-going world of Paris,
said of her on this occasion was that she held herself
well and spoke her lines distinctly.

It is interesting in following her career as it is revealed
in his articles to note the gradual crescendo of his appreciation. When she played *Le Passant*, by Coppée, at
the Odéon in 1869, he noted the delicate charm with
which she spoke the verse. The performance made her
famous. In 1872 she left the Odéon, returned to the
Théâtre français and played in *Mademoiselle de Belle-Isle*.
Sarcey notes her delicious diction, but doubts whether
she will ever find those strong and vibrating accents
that carry an audience away. Nature had, he said,
denied her that, otherwise she would be a complete
artist, and such a thing, he added, did not exist on the
stage. She followed this up by playing the part of Junie
in Racine's *Britannicus*. Sarcey notes that she has " Je
ne sais quel charme poétique, elle dit le vers avec une
grâce et une pureté raciniennes." In 1873 she plays the
small part of Aricie in *Phèdre*, and Sarcey says of her
voice that it is music itself and of an unimaginable purity
and transparency. In 1876 she had belied Sarcey's
prophecy that she would never have the strength to
move an audience, by her performance of the Roman
Vestal's mother in Parodi's tragedy, *Rome Vaincue*. In
this tragedy she played an old woman, Posthumia, who
is blind, and who, at the end of the tragedy, stabs her
daughter to save her from being buried alive ; the
daughter is bound and cannot stab herself, and the
mother, being blind, has to fumble for the place of her
heart.

" Elle était admirablement costumée et grimée,"
wrote Sarcey, " un visage amaigri, ridé, et d'une majesté

extraordinaire ; des yeux vagues et ternes, un manteau qui, tombant des deux côtés quand les bras se soulevaient, semblait figurer les ailes immenses de quelque gigantesque et sinistre chauve-souris. Rien de plus terrible et de plus poétique ensemble . . . ce n'était plus là une comédienne ; c'était la nature même, servie par une intelligence merveilleuse, par une âme de feu, par la voix la plus juste, la plus mélodieuse, qui jamais ait enchanté les oreilles humaines. Cette femme joue avec son cœur et ses entrailles. Elle hasarde des gestes qui seraient ridicules chez tout autre et qui emportent une salle. . . ."

No completer criticism of the art of Sarah Bernhardt is to be found than in these lines. Many have thought her rendering of this old woman, Posthumia, one of the two greatest triumphs of her career, and it is doubtful whether she ever excelled it ; she chose an act of this play together with an act of *Phèdre* for the celebration of her jubilee in Paris.

It must have been about this time that she first appeared in *Phèdre*, for in 1877 Sarcey talks of her success in *Andromaque* as exceeding that of her *Phèdre*, and he notes the number of shades she can indicate by the simple modulation of her voice in three lines of verse, without any seeming search after effect or time-taking effort, and also the continuous tremor that thrilled the audience as she spoke her lines ; she was interrupted by unstiflable bravos, as happens sometimes to great singers.

In the same year, she played Doña Sol in *Hernani*, and from that time forth she was recognised not only as an actress of genius, but as a personality that counted not only in the life of the world of art, but in life in general. She became henceforth to France something as well known as the Arc de Triomphe, and more than that, an object of unceasing interest and curiosity, the theme of poets, the godsend of gossips and paragraph makers, the centre of a legend.

In 1879 she went to London with the Comédie française and she appeared in *Phèdre, Hernani, Andromaque, L'Etrangère, Le Sphinx*, and *Zaïre*. The London public went mad about her, and Sarah Bernhardt having tasted blood, in the shape of the conquest of London, determined on the conquest of the world. She abandoned the Théâtre français after a quarrel, and went to America.

That was the first great break in her career.

IV

All this time, her travels, her adventures, her extravagances, her tantrums, her quarrels, her facile successes, her cheap victories, never prevented her from continuing, at the same time, as if on a parallel line, her personal battle and wrestle with the angel of art, and from every now and then discovering and achieving a new victory, conquering a fresh province.

In 1880, she plays Adrienne Lecouvreur for the first time, and in London, and reveals to Sarcey, who goes to London to hear her, what were to him unsuspected stops of pathos and passion. In the same year she plays *Froufrou* in London, and she has to compete with memories of Aimée Desclée. She must succeed or die. " Eh, bien ! " says Sarcey, comparing them in the scene which was Desclée's greatest triumph, " elle en est venue à bout. C'est tout autre chose et c'est aussi puissant. . . . Au quatrième acte, il n'y a pas de discussion possible, Mad^{elle} Sarah Bernhardt s'est montrée supérieure à sa devancière."

Then came more journeys and more world-tours, and, in 1882, the beginning of her association with Sardou, her production of *Fédora*, the first of those ingenious and powerful melodramas which were cunningly constructed in order to bring out her especial qualities, garments which were cut tightly to her measure, and which no one else has been able to wear since. *Théodora, La Tosca, Gismonda, La Sorcière*—she toured the world with these, and no plays brought her louder applause, and in no plays could she produce a more certain and sometimes a more stunning effect. But although her performance in them was certainly a unique phenomenon, which nobody since has been able to imitate or to emulate, they were for her easy triumphs, and it was not in them that she reached anywhere near the high-water mark of her art. She could sometimes content herself by merely imitating herself in them, and by letting the strong situations do the business, with the minimum effort on her part, although I can bear witness that there was often a vast difference between Sarah Bernhardt playing listlessly in a part of Sardou's, and any one else playing the same part with all their might.

The wrestle with art went on in spite of Sardou. Again she moved Sarcey to an ecstasy of surprise when she first plays in *La Dame aux Camélias* in Paris in 1883 : " I have seen something perfect ! " he exclaims. She continues to experiment. She plays Lady Macbeth. At one time she has the idea of playing it in English, and takes lessons from Madame de Guythères, an inhabitant of Versailles, who told me of the first lesson. When she arrived for the second lesson, Sarah Bernhardt was selling her furniture and starting for America. The facts of life had intervened. She plays in Richepin's *Nana Sahib* ; she plays Cleopatra in an adaptation of

3

Shakespeare by Sardou ; she plays Joan of Arc. She visits London every year. She still tours the world. Then there comes to her a moment when she instinctively feels that the public is tired of her repertory and irritated by her producing stuff that is inferior to her, so on her return from a prolonged tour in South America she turns over quite a new leaf. She takes the Renaissance Theatre in Paris, either in 1892 or 1893, and produces a delicate play by Jules Lemaître, *Les Rois*. " The Sarah of the 'seventies has come back to us," said the critics. In 1893 she plays Phèdre, and Sarcey says that in the part she is younger and more beautiful than she was at the Théâtre français in the 'seventies, when her powers were not quite ripe enough for the part.

" Chose étrange, inouïe, inexplicable, mais qui est vraie cependant, Mme Sarah Bernhardt est plus jeune, plus éclatante et, tranchons le mot, plus belle qu'elle n'a jamais été, d'une beauté artistique qui fait passer dans tout le corps un frisson d'admiration comme à l'aspect d'une belle statue." Lemaître speaks in the same note. With one voice the French critics agreed that never was anything finer seen. It was here she reached the high-water mark of her genius. She does not stop ; she brings into prominence Rostand, and produces *La Princesse Lointaine*, *La Samaritaine*, D'Annunzio's *Ville Morte*, and Sudermann's *Magda*. She takes a theatre of her own. She plays in *Hamlet* and *L'Aiglon*, and from this moment till the day of her death her artistic career alternates between hazardous experiments likely to be caviare to the general, such as Tristan Bernard's *Jeanne Doré*, and revivals of popular plays such as *La Dame aux Camélias*, or new productions calculated to please the crowd. She injures her leg, and her leg has to be amputated. No matter, she will appear in plays where it is not necessary for her to walk. The European war breaks out, she plays to the *poilus* in the trenches. And still the experiments continued ; still the wrestle with great art continued, and culminated in her production of *Athalie* in 1920. Finally, while she was rehearsing a new play by Sacha Guitry, she fell ill from the malady from which she was destined never to recover. But she spent her last illness in rehearsing for the films, until, after the long contention, the moment for the final *recueillement* came and she received the last Sacraments.

V

She spent her life in making discoveries and in surprising the public and her critics by finding out what she could not do, and in immediately doing it. She began by surprising herself in 1873 when playing in *Zaïre* ; she thought she was dying, and she determined to die in real earnest, to spite the manager, with whom she had quarrelled. She gave a cry of real pain when the stage dagger struck her, and she thought she could never recover ; but to her astonishment she found herself, after the tremendous effort, exertion, and nervous expenditure, as fresh as a daisy. After this experience she knew she could draw when she liked on her physical resources. Her energy, the amount of hard work she accomplished, were frightening to think of. Her recreation was change of work. She could command sleep when she wished, but she never rested. Yet she was fundamentally sensible. She made the best of the inevitable, and from the beginning to the end of her career she turned her limitations into virtues.

She had a weak voice by nature and a delicate constitution, yet she succeeded by self-training, practice, management, and tact, in achieving so great a mastery of modulation, pitch, and tone that she could express anything from the fury of the whirlwind to the sigh of a sleepy stream.

VI

What was the secret of her art, and what were the main characteristics of her genius ?

I believe that the secret of her art was that of all great art : that she was guided by an infallible instinct, and that whatever she did she could not go wrong. When what she did was done, it seemed simple, inevitable, and easy ; and so swiftly accomplished, that you had no time to think of the *how* ; nor was your sense sharp enough, however carefully you watched, to detect the divine conjury. It was the same whether she spoke lines of La Fontaine ánd Racine, or whether she asked, as she poured out a cup of coffee, as she did in one play : " Du sucre, deux morceaux ? " She was artistically inerrant. It is this gift which was probably the secret of the great actors of the past : Garrick, Siddons, Talma, and Salvini. It is certainly to be seen in the work of the great singer of the present, Chaliapine, whether he is portraying Satan holding his court on the Brocken, or a foolish, good-natured Chinovnik, half-fuddled with drink after a night out. When such a gift is at work, the greater the material it is interpreting, the greater, of course, the effect.

The greater the play Sarah Bernhardt appeared in, the greater the demand on her instinct, which *was* her genius ; the swifter and the fuller the response. As the occasion expanded, so did her genius rise to it.

Her Hamlet was and is still hotly discussed, and quite lately several eminent English writers have expressed opinions that are completely at variance with one another on the subject. But every critic when he reads *Hamlet* creates a Hamlet in his own image, and when he sees it acted, the more vivid the impersonation, the more likely it is to be at variance with his own conception. One critic finds her Hamlet an unpardonable Gallic liberty to take with Shakespeare; another, that she electrified Hamlet with the vigour of her personality. I remember a cultivated philosopher, who was a citizen of the world, telling me that he thought her Hamlet the only intelligible rendering he had seen of the part, just because it rendered the youthful inconsequence of the moods of the moody Dane. But whether you thought it justifiable or unjustifiable, true or untrue to Shakespeare, in witnessing it you were aware of the genius of the interpreter answering the genius of the dramatic poet. Deep was calling to deep.

When Hamlet looked into the guilty King's face at the end of the play within the play, or thought for one second that the King and not Polonius had blundered into death behind the arras; when Hamlet concealed his forebodings from Horatio, and when Hamlet looked at Laertes during the duel and let him know that he knew the swords had been exchanged and that one of them had been poisoned, all thought of the part—the rendering, tradition, the language, the authorship—went to the winds: you knew only that something which had been invented by one great genius was being interpreted by another great genius, and that the situation had found an expression which was on its own level. That, at least, was the impression of many.

A brilliant Irish essayist (whose essays appeared during the war) arrived at just such a conception of Hamlet as Sarah Bernhardt did, and it should always be remembered that she was the first to give to the French stage a plain and accurate translation of *Hamlet* in which the play was allowed to speak for itself, and was neither "adapted" nor dislocated by being put into romantic French verse.

A French friend of mine, an English scholar, who was a friend of M. Marcel Schwob, the translator of this version of *Hamlet*, assisted at some of the rehearsals, and once or twice, he told me, Sarah Bernhardt consulted him as to the meaning of a passage. He said what he thought, and she answered in a way which showed she had completely misunderstood him, had perhaps not even listened. Then, he said, she went on to the stage and played the passage in question, not only as if she understood the words that he had explained, but as if she had had access to the inner secrets of the poet's mind. This, again, was an instance of her instinct at work. If you pressed her for a theory about any part or passage she might invent something ready-made to please you, but it would have been an afterthought and not a pre-conceived plan. She acted by instinct and left the theory to others.

Her performance in Musset's *Lorenzaccio* was thought by some to be the most subtly interesting of all her achievements—nothing she ever did received greater praise from the critical in Paris (it received but little in London). M. Camille Mauclair speaks of " ce magni-fique ' Lorenzaccio ' dont elle faisait une des merveilles de sa carrière." It is true that Musset's work was mangled to make an acting play, but as it was written it would probably be unactable, and given the nature of Sarah Bernhardt's performance it was worth it. But there was one part which, great as it was, needed no readjustment or alteration when she assumed it, and that was the part of Phèdre.

Of all the parts she played it demanded the greatest

effort and exertion, and that is why, during her long
career, she played it comparatively seldom. Here, at
any rate, she was beyond discussion. When she played
it for the first time in London in 1879 she was so overcome with nervousness that she had to be pushed on to
the stage, and as she began to speak she pitched her
voice too high. Whenever she played it afterwards,
she told me herself that she went through an agonising
period of anguish, wondering whether she could bear
the heavy load, and I remember seeing her between the
acts of one performance in London, reading over her
part, which was copied out in a large copy-book, mur-
muring the lines and saying to herself, with tears in her
eyes : " Quel rôle, quel rôle," fearful even then of
succumbing !

In reading the play again and conjuring up the visions,
the sounds, of the harmonious, rhythmical, architectural
symphony which was her Phèdre, the moments I remember most vividly were firstly her look, as of a
frightened hunted animal suddenly caught in a trap,
when in the first act Oenone first mentions the name of
Hippolyte and Phèdre cries out, as if stabbed by a
poisoned arrow, or feeling the fangs of a steel trap close :

" C'est toi qui l'as nommé ! "

Then I see her sitting rigid with horror on her golden
throne as she reflects that her Father is Judge in Hell
and there is no refuge for her, the guilty, either on the
earth, in the sky, or under the earth :

" Minos juge aux enfers tous les pâles Humains."

As she said the line her eyes reflected the visions of
Virgil and Dante :

" Terribiles visu formae ! Letumque, Labosque ! "

There was a line she charged with so great a sorrow

and so grave a load of beauty that one thought Racine
must have stirred in his tomb as she said it :

> " On ne voit pas deux fois le rivage des morts."

And the note of pathos was almost unbearable when
she said :

> " Est-ce un malheur si grand que de cesser de vivre ? "

But perhaps most beautiful of all, and as striking in
its restraint as the explosions of the preceding acts were
formidable by their fury, was her utterance of Phèdre's
final speech.

> " J'ai voulu, devant vous exposant mes remords,
> Par un chemin plus lent descendre chez les morts.
> J'ai pris, j'ai fait couler dans mes brûlantes veines
> Un poison que Médée apporta dans Athènes.
> Déjà jusqu'à mon cœur le venin parvenu
> Dans ce cœur expirant jette un froid inconnu.
> Déjà je ne vois plus qu'à travers un nuage,
> Et le ciel, et l'époux que ma présence outrage.
> Et la mort à mes yeux dérobant la clarté
> Rend au jour qu'ils souillaient toute sa pureté."

After all the passion and the paroxysms, the storm
and stress, the exultations and the agonies, she breathed
out her final confession with that calm and harmonious
unity of tone and absence of gesture and of facial expression which the quiet close of a great tragedy demands.
She spoke as if she were already dead, with the im-
personality and aloofness of what was no longer mortal.
Her voice seemed to come from a distance, from the
sunless regions ; the chill of Cocytus was upon it, and
as her head fell on the shoulder of the attendant slave,
visions of the masterpieces of Greek sculpture were
evoked, and all that the poets have said so briefly and so
sweetly about the mowing down of beautiful flowers,
and broken blossoms and ruined rhymes.

It was in moments such as these that Sarah Bernhardt

enlarged rather than interpreted the masterpieces of the
world. But praise of her now is no longer a living thing
that might prove an incentive to others to go and see
and hear for themselves. It is only a dirge of regret
and a procession of melancholy shadows. Nevertheless,
it is fitting to weave a few words, however idle and
inadequate, and to honour her imperishable name with
a perishable wreath.

VII

When in the future people will say, " But you
should have heard Sarah Bernhardt in the part ! " the
newcomers will probably shrug their shoulders and say,
" Oh, we know all about that ! "

But they will not know, nor will anybody be able to
tell them or explain to them what Sarah Bernhardt could
do with a modulated inflexion, a *trait de voix*, a look,
a gesture, a cry, a smile, a sigh, nor what majesty, poetry
and music she could suggest by the rhythm of her
movements and her attitudes, what it was like to hear
her speak verse, to say words such as :

> " Songe, songe, Céphise, à cette nuit cruelle,"

or,

> " Si tu veux faisons un rêve."

Nobody will be able to tell them, because, in spite of
the gramophone and the cinematograph, the actor's
art dies almost wholly with the actor. It is shortlived,
but only relatively shortlived ; and nobody understood
that better than Sarah Bernhardt, one of whose mottoes
was " Tout passe, tout casse, tout lasse."

(It was tempered by another : " Quand même.")

On the loom of things the poems of Homer are only
a little less ephemeral than a leading article, and the art

of a Phidias is, after all, as perishable as the sketches of a " lightning " music-hall artist.

> " Le temps passe. Tout meurt. Le marbre même s'use.
> Agrigente n'est plus qu'une ombre, et Syracuse
> Dort sous le bleu linceul de son ciel indulgent."

The most enduring monuments, the most astounding miracles of beauty achieved by the art and craft of man, are but as flotsam, drifting for a little while upon the stream of Time ; and with it now there is a strange russet leaf, the name of Sarah Bernhardt.

1923.

GILBERT AND SULLIVAN

(A Lecture given at the Royal Institution, 2nd June 1922, with Musical Illustrations by Major Geoffrey Toye.)

THE late Arthur Strong, who was librarian of the House of Lords, and not only a scholar of encyclopædic knowledge, but who also had a rare appreciation of all the arts, and an appreciation based on knowledge, used to say that the greatest English composer England had produced since the days of Purcell was Arthur Sullivan, the Sullivan of *Pinafore* and *Ruddigore*, and not the Sullivan of the *Golden Legend*, and that compared with him most of our modern composers were but the grammarians of music. He may have been right or wrong about modern composers ; he may have been unjust ; he was not speaking on oath. But it is certain that Sullivan carried on the true tradition of English music, or rather that in his work the English musical genius that produced tunes like " The Girl I Left Behind Me " and " The Bailiff's Daughter of Islington " was born again and flowered once more in a glorious springtide. The melodies in Sullivan's comic operas are as English as those older tunes, that is to say, as English as a picture of Constable, a lyric of Shakespeare, as English as eggs and bacon.

No foreigner, however painstaking, or however assimilative, can cook eggs and bacon, just as no Englishman can make French coffee. No nation can learn to make something which is peculiar to the genius of another nation. The most striking instance of this I can recall was the case of aeroplane manufacture during the war. When the French made English machines from English designs, and the English made French machines from French designs, the results were never satisfactory. A French-designed machine made by Englishmen was never the same as a French machine, and an English-designed machine made by a Frenchman was never quite like an English machine. And when the Germans copied either, the copy though accurate and faithful was Teutonic.

It is perhaps because Sullivan's lighter music is so essentially English that it has taken years to obtain serious recognition. The tunes achieved instant popularity because they were English, but it was probably because of this instantaneous and widespread success that people failed to perceive the rarity and the value of the gifts which were being so freely bestowed upon them. They knew the tunes were catchy. They kept on humming them. They admitted them to be pretty; but they did not realise their inestimable, their unique artistic price. They felt as people feel when they see the work of a great water-colourist, or, indeed, of any great artist. " Oh, any one could do that! We could do it ourselves if we knew how to paint or to compose." It seemed so simple, so easy. The essentially English quality of the stuff made them feel this all the more strongly.

The tunes seemed as easy to produce as the improvisations of a schoolboy playing with one finger. It was only when Sullivan was dead, and after many years of experience of the barren fruits of English musical comedy, that the public began to wonder whether after all the matter was quite as simple as they had thought.

And when, after many years, there was two years ago a
revival on a large scale, in London, of the greater number
of the operas, many of us experienced a shock of surprise.
The tunes were as catchy as ever, but the daintiness, the
elegance, the finish, the workmanship, the beautiful
businesslike quality of the work, its ease and distinction,
its infinite variety, forced themselves upon the attention
of everybody. The large public recognised at once
that here was something which not every one could do ;
and that nothing at all like it was being done, or had been
done, by any one else for years. The revival of *The
Beggar's Opera* underlined the fact. That garden of
English melody enhanced the authenticity of Sullivan's
gift. It endorsed the credentials and the lineage of his
music and of his charm. It proved that he was no
bastard, and no pretender, but a rightful heir of Purcell,
and a lawful representative of Merry England. What
a joy it was, we all felt, when Gilbert and Sullivan and
The Beggar's Opera were revived, to hear real English
music once more ! Not the slosh of ballad concerts,
nor the jangle and rattle of ragtime and of modern revues,
with their grating metallic tang and twang, their exas-
perating hesitations and their alien languor, but the
music of the English soil ; so noble, so gay, so debonair,
so beautiful. The music that grew in England like
wayside flowers, of which Purcell wove garlands, which
the cavaliers put in their velvet hats, and the soldiers
of the Georges wore as a cockade or flung to the girls
they left behind them ; flowers which were then neglected for many years, until Sullivan planted his rollicking
border ; flowers which were forgotten, buried under
rubbish, and artificial and tawdry exotics, until the war
at moments cleared those weeds away, and the soldiers
in Flanders and France marched once more to the old

rhythms, and invented preposterous but entirely English words to the native airs of their country. Now it is extremely doubtful whether we should ever have been enriched with this precious legacy of English music if Sullivan had never met Gilbert. It is to this marvellously fortunate conjunction and collaboration that we owe this exuberant and entrancing revival of English dance, rhythm, and song.

It was Gilbert's rhythms, Gilbert's wit and fancy, Gilbert's fun and quaint mockery, Gilbert's whimsical poetry that played the part of the blue-paper packet of the composite Seidlitz powder, and when mingled with the white-paper packet of Sullivan's music produced the enchanting effervescing explosion. It is this which makes it impossible in talking of these operas to dissociate Gilbert from Sullivan, and to judge either, as far as the comic operas are concerned, separately.

The Gilbert of the operas has been compared to Aristophanes ; and the comparison has been said to be a wild one. To place Gilbert in the same rank as Aristophanes, it is said, would mean he should have written lyrics as beautiful as those of Shakespeare. But to compare Gilbert and Sullivan with Aristophanes is not, I think, a wild comparison, for the lyrical beauty which is to be found in the choruses of the Greek poet, is supplied, and plentifully, by the music of Sullivan. I once heard Anatole France say that, speaking in an exaggerated way, the texts we possessed of the plays of Aeschylus were in reality librettos of operas of which the music was lost, as if, for instance, we only had an operatic libretto of *Hamlet* or *Faust*. If the Greek music was as good as the words, we must have lost a good deal ; but we can't tell. It has perished. Fortunately, Sullivan's music has not perished and Gilbert's text is complete. It does not for its purpose need to be any better. For its purpose not even Aristophanes could have improved on it, because the point about Gilbert's lyrics and Gilbert's verse is that it is just sufficiently neat, lyrical and poetical, besides being always cunningly and incomparably rhythmical, to allow the composer to fill in the firm outline he has traced with surprising and appropriate colour.

Take these four lines of a trio from the first act of *The Mikado* :

> " To sit in solemn silence in a dull dark dock,
> In a pestilential prison with a life-long lock,
> Awaiting the sensation of a short, sharp shock
> From a cheap and chippy chopper on a big black block."

There is nothing very remarkable about this happy jingle, but Sullivan's handling of it makes one think of Bach.

If Gilbert had been a great verbal poet, a poet like Shelley or Swinburne, there would have been no room for the music ; the words would have been complete in themselves ; their subtle overtones and intangible suggestions would have been drowned by any music, however beautiful. As it is, the words have just enough suggestive beauty, and are always unerringly rhythmical, and this is just the combination needed to enable the composer to display his astonishing musical gift. I don't pretend to any musical knowledge whatever, but it is not necessary to be a trained musician to re-cognise and to feel the amazing powers of musical and rhythmical invention which Sullivan displays through-out these operas. His rhythmical invention seems to be inexhaustible and infinitely various.

You have exquisitely funny and appropriate rhythm

like his setting to Ruth's song in the first act of *The Pirates of Penzance* :

" When Frederic was a little lad he proved so brave and daring,
His father thought he'd 'prentice him to some career seafaring.
I was, alas ! his nurserymaid, and so it fell to my lot
To take and bind the promising lad apprentice to a pilot.
A life not bad for a hardy lad, though surely not a high lot.
Though I'm a nurse, you might do worse, than make your boy a
    pilot.

I was a stupid nurserymaid, on breakers always steering,
And I did not catch the word aright, through being hard of hearing ;
Mistaking my instructions, which within my brain did gyrate,
I took and bound this promising boy apprentice to a pirate.
A sad mistake it was to make and doom him to a vile lot,
I bound him to a pirate—you—instead of to a pilot."

Or the lilt of the rollicking duet in *Ruddigore*, " Oh, happy the lily when kissed by the bee " ; or, perhaps most surprising of all, the sad, endless tangle of the Lord Chancellor's nightmare in *Iolanthe*, as delirious as Tristan's fever :

" When you're lying awake
With a dismal headache,
And repose is tabooed with anxiety,"

with its transition at the end, in which the notes seem to smell of dawn and dew :

" But the darkness has passed,
And it's daylight at last,
And the night has been long,
Ditto, ditto, my song,
And thank goodness, they're both of them over ! "

But one need hardly say that the most salient and supreme of Sullivan's gifts is that of *tune* ; the gift of pouring out a stream of beautiful bubbling melodies. Most of these tunes are part of the permanent furniture and limbo of our minds. They are on the mouths of all, and chiefly on the lips of the young. They rise in the heart and gather on the lips unbidden. Let those who

are inclined to think Sullivan's melodies too facile listen
on the gramophone to the duet in *Ruddigore*, " The Old
Oak Tree," or turn up the score of *Princess Ida* and play
the quartette, " The World is but a Broken Toy," or
" Free from his Fetters Grim " in *The Yeomen of the
Guard*. This is such a beautiful tune that the public,
when Mr. Derek Oldham sang it during the recent
revival, never even encored it. They were too greatly
moved to do so, too satisfied even to applaud.

Sullivan has another gift which is the hall-mark of
great art, the gift of discretion, of leading up to an effect
in such a way that the effect when it comes seems as
sudden as an April shower and yet as inevitable as a
flower opening.

For instance, the way a famous song is led up to in
Pinafore :

> " I am an Englishman, behold me.
>   He is an Englishman :
>   For he himself has said it," etc.

Or more striking still, in *The Mikado*, the music that
precedes the phrase :

> " For he's going to marry Yum-Yum."

Gilbert's favourite opera is said to have been *The
Yeomen of the Guard*, and certainly he never wrote more
beautiful words than :

> " Is life a boon ?
>   If so, it must befall
>   That Death, whene'er he call,
>   Must call too soon.
>   Though fourscore years he give,
>   Yet one would pray to live
>   Another moon !
>   What kind of plaint have I
>   Who perish in July ?
>   I might have had to die,
>   Perchance, in June !

4

Is life a thorn ?
    Then count it not a whit !
    Man is well done with it ;
Soon as he's born
    He should all means essay
    To put the plague away ;
And I, war-worn,
    Poor captured fugitive,
    My life most gladly give—
I might have had to live
Another morn ! "

And Sullivan never wrote anything more exquisite than the music to this, nor than the duet, " I have a Song to Sing, O," and the unaccompanied quartette, " Strange Adventure," in the same opera. But here both the poet and the composer enter into successful rivalry with other composers of the past. The lyric " Is Life a Boon ? " might have come from an Elizabethan song-book ; the duet, " I have a Song to Sing, O," from an Italian opera. I would like to give one instance of something which only Gilbert could have written and only Sullivan could have composed. An instance of the kind is, I think, the quintette in the Second Act of the *Sorcerer* :

" I rejoice that it's decided,
    Happy now will be his life,
For my father is provided
    With a true and tender wife.
She will tend him, nurse him, mend him,
    Air his linen, dry his tears,
Bless the thoughtful fates that send him
    Such a wife to soothe his years."

No poet except Gilbert would ever have thought of the phrase, " Air his linen, dry his tears." No composer could have clothed the words more appropriately or more exquisitely. But it is, perhaps, in *Iolanthe* that Gilbert and Sullivan display, if not their highest, their most peculiar qualities. *Iolanthe* is, I think, the most Gilbertian of all the operas, and the music is peculiarly characteristic of Sullivan. Nobody but Gilbert could have imagined the Arcadian shepherd, who is half a fairy—a fairy down to the waist ; but his legs are mortal—and is engaged to a ward in Chancery ; the susceptible Lord Chancellor ; the chorus of peers ; the philosophical sentry who thinks of things that would astonish you, and the final departure of peers and fairies to fairyland :

> " Up in the sky
> Ever so high
> Pleasures come in endless series.
> We will arrange
> Happy exchange,
> House of Peers for House of Peris."

In this opera we are in the centre and capital of the cloud-cuckoo-land of Gilbert's invention, the head-quarters of his fantastic fairyland. That Gilbert lived in fairyland, or rather that he created a fairyland of his own, is a fact that is often overlooked. He is credited with the honours, the supreme honours, of topsy-turvydom, so that whenever anything peculiarly contrary to common sense happens in the public life or the Government of the country, we call it Gilbertian, but he is not as a rule credited with the glamour of magic. And yet that he possessed the secret key which unlocks the doors of that tantalising country is proved by the verdict of those who are the sole and only judges, namely, children. Children know that the land of *Ruddigore*, of *The Gondoliers*, of *The Mikado*, *Iolanthe*, and *Patience* is fairyland—the real thing. Only a few months ago I had the opportunity of comparing the opinions of some children who had been taken to see first *Jack and the Beanstalk* at the Hippodrome and then *Iolanthe*. Their verdict was that *Iolanthe* was a real pantomime, and that *Jack and the Beanstalk* in its modern shape, interlarded with political allusions and music-hall tags, was not. In Gilbert's world the impossible is always happening. The Arcadian shepherd does marry the ward in Chancery. Private Willis, of the Grenadier Guards, does sprout little red wings, and the Fairy Queen sees to it that he is properly dressed. The pictures come down from their frames in *Ruddigore*, and the picture that hangs at the end of the gallery in a bad light comes to life in obedience to Gilbert's inflexible and impossible logic, and marries his old love. Even in the operas where there are no actual fairies and no element of the supernatural, no pictures coming to life, no dapper salesman brewing love-philtres as in the *Sorcerer* ; even in a plain satire such as *Patience*, we look at things through a coloured glass, or a glass that reveals hidden colours, such as that which the wizard gave to the Prince in the fairy tale, and through which, when he looked at the stars, he saw that they were many-coloured instead of all of them being white. They would be many-coloured looked at through such a glass, of course. And constantly throughout this opera we hear the horns of elfland faintly blowing, especially when the twenty lovesick maidens languish vocal in the valley, or when they lead Bunthorne " like a heathen sacrifice with music and with fatal yokes of flowers " to his (and to their) eternal ridicule.

Or again, when the Gondoliers embark on board the *Xebeque* and set sail for the shores of Barataria :

> " Away we go
> To a balmy isle,
> Where the roses blow
> All the winter while."

That is one of the most important factors in the power of

Gilbert, who here again was able to find a purveyor of fairy music in Sullivan, and I think that *The Mikado* has, perhaps, more than all the other operas, the quality of a fairy tale, although there are no fairies in it.

Another important factor in Gilbert's work is the quality of his satire. Some people detest it. It affects them like bitter aloes. But it owes its enduring permanence, not to bitterness, for it is never really bitter, but to a certain breadth and force which have two cardinal merits. Firstly, that of being dramatic, of getting over the footlights, of appealing to the component parts of a large and mixed audience, so that the stalls will smile at one line and the gallery be convulsed at another, and all will be pleased ; and, secondly, of being general enough to apply to the taste and understanding of succeeding generations. Gilbert's satire, although directed at the phenomena of his own time, had a Molière-like quality of broad generalisation, which applied not only to the fashions and follies of one epoch, but to the eternal weaknesses of unchanging human nature.

So that when the First Lord in *Pinafore* sings :

> " Stick close to your desks and never go to sea,
> And you may all be rulers of the Queen's Navee,"

or when Private Willis says that every boy and every girl that is born into the world alive is either a little Liberal or else a little Conservative, the words go quite as straight home to a modern audience as they did to the public which first heard them.

But although Gilbert's satire is not bitter, it is undeniable that it sometimes has an element, not only of downrightness, but of harshness in it. It is not savage, like that of Juvenal or Swift, but it is not too squeamish for a knock-out blow. This may sometimes, and does sometimes, ruffle and jar upon the sensitive. But these easily ruffled persons should remember that Gilbert's harshness is an ingredient which is to be found in all the great comic writers ; in Aristophanes, in Cervantes, in Molière, and indeed in any comic writer whose work endures for more than one generation. It is a kind of salt which causes the soil of comedy to renew itself ; and in Gilbert's case it arises from his formidable common sense. He never took his paradoxes seriously as so many of his successors did. He is as sensible as Dr. Johnson, and sometimes as harsh. Gilbert has often been blamed for gibing at the old. It is true that his jokes on the subject of the loss of female looks are sometimes fierce and uncompromising. But they are mild indeed compared with those of Aristophanes, Horace, and Molière ; and on closer inspection, we find it is not really at the old he is gibing, but at the old who pretend to be young ; at Lady Jane's infatuation for Bunthorne ; at Katisha's pursuit of Nanki Poo. Such things exist, and if they exist we must not be surprised if satirists laugh at them, and laugh loud. What is exceptional in Gilbert's satire is that he combined with this downright strong common sense and almost brutal punching power a vein of whimsical nonsense and ethereal fancy which generally goes with more gentle and flexible temperaments.

The third cardinal quality of Gilbert's work is almost too obvious to dwell upon, namely, his wit, both in prose and in rhyme ; his neat hitting of the nail on the head, his incomparable verbal felicity and dexterity ; and the peculiar thing about Gilbert's verbal felicity is its conversational fluency. He uses the words, the phrases, and the very accent and turn of ordinary everyday conversation and yet invests them with a sure, certain, and infectious rhythm, the pattest of rhythm ; and rhymes that are always inevitable, however fantastic and far-fetched.   For instance :

> " When the coster's finished jumping on his mother,
>   On his mother,
> He loves to lie a-basking in the sun,
>   In the sun.
> Ah, take one consideration with another,
>   With another,
> The policeman's lot is not a happy one,
>   Happy one."

Or again :

> " But when it begins to blow,
> I generally go below,
> And seek the seclusion that a cabin grants,
> And so do his sisters and his cousins and his aunts."

We find the same pat neatness in his prose.   Take Ko-Ko's explanation to the Mikado :

" When your Majesty says ' Let a thing be done,' it's as good as done—practically it *is* done—because your Majesty's will is law.   Your Majesty says, ' Kill a gentleman ! ' and a gentleman is told off to be killed. Consequently that gentleman is as good as dead— practically, he *is* dead—and if he is dead, why not say so ? "

Another remarkable fact about Gilbert's satire is this : Just those subjects which, when he treated them, were thought to be the most local and ephemeral, have turned out, as treated by him, to be the most perennial and enduring.   Take *Patience*, for instance.   *Patience* was a satire on the æsthetic craze of the 'eighties.   It was produced in 1881.   It was aimed at the follies and ex-aggerations of the æsthetic school—the greenery-yallery, Grosvenor - gallery, foot-in-the-grave, hollow - cheeked, long-necked and long-haired brood of devotees of blue china and peacocks' feathers and sunflowers, who were the imitators, the hangers-on, and the parasites of a group of real artists and innovators, such as Whistler, Burne-Jones, and Rossetti.

Punch started the campaign of ridicule, and Du Maurier's pictures of the adventures of Maudle and Postlethwaite towards the end of the 'seventies are amongst the most entertaining and delightful of his drawings. *Patience* is said to have killed the phase ; but outside the pages of *Punch* it is doubtful if æsthetes were really very plentiful, and *Patience* was based on the legend of a few, of a very few, people. But in writing this satire, Gilbert, if he magnified the follies of his contemporaries, hit the bull's-eye of a wider target. He struck at the heart of artistic sham, so that his satire is appropriate to any time and any place.

Wherever there is real art there is always exaggerated imitation, and wherever there is real admiration there is false admiration too. In Bunthorne and Grosvenor, Gilbert drew two types which sum up between them the whole gamut of artistic pretension and humbug. In every false world of art there is always a Bunthorne who has discovered that all is commonplace, and the burden of whose song is " Hollow, Hollow, Hollow." There is always, too, a Grosvenor, the apostle of simplicity, who is ready to write " a decalet, a pure and simple thing, a very daisy—a babe might understand it. To appreciate it, it is not necessary to think of anything at all." There is always a rapturous maiden ready to say " not supremely, perhaps, but oh so all-but."

In the great flood of latter-day verse the School of Bunthorne still exists :

> " Oh to be wafted away
> From this black Aceldama of sorrow,
> Where the dust of an earthy to-day
> Is the earth of a dusty to-morrow."

That is Bunthorne's " little thing of his own," called
" Heart Foam."

I will not quote from a modern Bunthorne—that
would be far too dangerous—but this is how the brilliant
parodist of *Punch* who signs himself " Evoe " travesties
the modern Bunthorne :

> " Now while the sharp falsetto of the rain
> Shampoos the bleak and bistre square,
> And all seems lone and bare,
> A crimson motive floats upon the breeze."

I think Bunthorne would have been proud to sign
these lines. Grosvenor's poem began :

> " Gentle Jane was as good as gold,
> She always did what she was told."

And this school of elaborate simplicity still has
disciples. The twenty lovesick maidens are with us
still. They read Freud and they paint cubes, and listen
with rapture to the music of Scriabin, and the more
unintelligible they find it the better they like it. This
doesn't at all mean that the art they admire is really
sham, any more than the art of Whistler and Rossetti
was sham in the 'eighties ; but it means that every
school of art has always had, and always will have, foolish
disciples who imitate and exaggerate the faults of the
master without being able to emulate his excellences.

But there always comes a moment in the world of
make-believe, whether it is the world of the *Précieuses
Ridicules* or the world of the Dadaists, when the voice of
common sense will come breaking in, like the chorus
of Gilbert's heavy dragoons. The entry of these
dragoons in *Patience* is one of those effects which show
Gilbert's sure instinct for stage effect, his consummate

stagecraft, his profound knowledge of the theatre. The sudden crash of the brisk music of common sense and its clash with the Della-Cruscan world of vaporous nonsense is not only comic but dramatic and *scenic*. It appeals to the eye as well as to the ear and the mind. It is comic and dramatic by the contrast it affords, by the shock of surprise it gives, and the incongruous situation it creates ; and it is scenic by the picture it presents. The very uniforms conspire, with their brilliance and unabashed primary colours, to, as Henry James would say, " beautifully swear " with the Whistlerian and pre-Raphaelite colours and arrangements in pink and mauve and sage-green of the rapturous maidens.

To some people the chorus of those heavy dragoons will recall a picture of an epoch that is as far away now as Nineveh and Tyre. The picture of London in the 'eighties ; the bands playing " A Magnet hung in a Hardware Shop " in the streets in the morning ; the Park in the afternoon, crowded with elegant carriages, barouches, and victorias, a high-perched dowager waving a small gloved hand ; Rotten Row in the morning, crowded with top-hatted cavaliers and ladies witching the world with horsemanship and faultless habits ; the photographs of Mrs. Langtry and the professional beauties in shop windows ; the perfumed, padded, silken missives of St. Valentine's Day ; the little flat bonnets with bows ; the Du Maurier ladies, haggard from adoration, green with love and indigestion at the classical concerts ; and the Princess of Wales driving past in an open carriage as beautiful and as graceful as Queen Alexandra. And before leaving the subject of *Patience*, I should like to end with one quotation which contains, I think, the whole essence of Gilbert and Sullivan, so that if this song alone survived we should know what was the best they could do, both of them :

> " Prithee, pretty maiden, will you marry me ?
>   Hey, but I'm hopeful, willow willow waley.
> I may say at once I'm a man of propertee,
>   Hey willow waly O.
> Money I despise it,
> Other people prize it,
>   Hey willow waley O."

Gilbert never wrote anything better than that, and Sullivan, as usual, rose to the occasion, and clothed these tripping syllables with a most delicate vesture of melody, in which a fairy-like pizzicato accompaniment falls on the thread of tune, like dewdrops on gossamer. If this song had had German or Italian words, and had reached us from Vienna or Milan, the critics would have made as much fuss over it as over any tune in Mozart.

Cannot you imagine it being warbled by an Italian welter-weight prima donna and a luscious Italian tenor ?

> " Non del mio amore, Donna, ti scordar,
>   Deh ! esperanza, sorgi in cuore mio,
> Dai miei soldi non c'è da dubitar;
>   O salice senza Addio ! "

Or in German something like this :

> " Willst Du, hübsche Jungfer, nicht mein Weibchen sein?
>   Bin ich doch hoffnungsvoll, O Weide Wehe !
> Will es Dir gleich sagen hab' ein Schloss am Rhein,
>   O Weide ! Wehe ! "

Or in French :

> " Charmante bergère, Je demande ta main !
>   (Douce espérance, miron, mirontaine)
> Sache sans mystère, je possède un moullin,
>   (Oh, mirontaine)."

Or in Russian :

Хочу быть твоимъ мужемъ, душенька моя,
Ахъ мнѣ скучно и грустно, Верба !
Я тебя одѣну въ шелка и въ соболя,
Ахь ! ты Верба моя, моя Верба !

Or words to that effect. I don't pretend that they are correct. That tune, when *Patience* was first produced, was whistled in the streets and taken for granted as one of the popular airs of the day ; but how few people at the time recognised its rarity as a gem.

You have only to look at the back numbers of *Punch* to see how niggardly critical opinion of all shades was of its praise of these masterpieces when they were first produced. And I remember myself hearing grown-up people talking of them as if they were so much scaffolding for the display of the actors of the day, who, we must not forget, were then, as their successors are now, quite unusually remarkable.

It is seldom that one cast included two such exceptional artists as George Grossmith and the great baritone who lately left us, Rutland Barrington. They did more than perfectly fill their parts. They inspired Gilbert and Sullivan to create new characters : Grossmith with his perfectly natural fantasy, and Barrington with his suave imperturbable gravity.

It must be a comforting thought for modern musicians that it takes about thirty years for people to appreciate their music at its true value, even when, as not always happens, it wins instantaneous popularity. But when *Princess Ida* was first produced the verdict of *Punch* and of the public was : " No Grossmith part," just as they now might say : " No Leslie Henson or no Nelson Keys part."

Sometimes history repeats the case of Bizet, whose masterpiece *Carmen*, which was to prove one of the most popular of operas, was kept for years, unacted, in the drawer of a manager.

I remember once during Holy Week at Moscow, when there was a fair going on at the Kremlin, seeing a little old man hawking about some goldfish in a very small bottle.

He kept on piping out in a high falsetto :

" Fish, fish, fish, fish, little goldfish,
Who will buy ? "

" Who will buy ? " he piped as he walked up and down between the bookstalls and the booths. But the people bought toys and sugar-plums, clothes and books, boots and old odd volumes of *Punch* and John Stuart Mill and Mrs. Humphry Ward—but no goldfish.

No one would buy the little goldfish ; for men do not recognise the gifts of Heaven, the magical gifts, when they see them. In the case of Gilbert and Sullivan they bought at once ; but they thought that the goldfish were as common as dirt. It was only when the sellers were dead that they recognised that what they had been buying so easily and so cheaply was magical merchandise from fairyland ; that there was nothing to match it, and nobody else to provide anything of that kind any more.

Even now, it is doubtful whether Sullivan's music has received the serious recognition it deserves. Critical people, the serious that is to say, are always prone to despise a goldfish because it is gold and looks pretty, and they are sometimes inclined to patronise tunes if they are gay, light, and joyous. Anything in art that is ponderous, serious, complicated, and unintelligible is at once respected ; but if a tune is gay and easy, a pqem rhythmical and well rhymed, a picture pleasantly coloured, with a subject that is perfectly plain, so that if it represents a field the field looks like a field, and not like the forty-second proposition of Euclid, the serious are inclined to look at it askance. I remember in 1914 some academicals wrote indignantly to the newspapers because " Tipperary " was a popular tune, and this roused Dr. Ethel Smyth, a judge of tune if ever there was one, to wrath ; and she wrote to say she was certain that the tune of " Tipperary " would have delighted Schubert.

Some people will never forgive Sullivan for being popular, and never admit that a tune which can be as infectious as small-pox in a slum should be taken seriously. But the whole point of really great art is that while it satisfies the critical it pleases the crowd, that while children can enjoy it, it fills the accomplished craftsman with despair at being unable to emulate it : Bunyan's *Pilgrim's Progress*, *Alice in Wonderland*, Gray's *Elegy*, and *The Midsummer Night's Dream* are instances in point.

But there is no reason to be despondent. Gilbert and Sullivan's operas, always popular, are now receiving the best kind of recognition, although there are still some dissentient voices and still some implacable high-brows. And they are as popular with the young generation as they were with the old. About this there is no possible doubt whatever ; when they are given at the Universities now, they are even more popular than lectures on relativity, and the undergraduates crowd to them. About their popularity in London there can be little doubt when people are ready to sit outside the theatre for twenty-four hours to be present at the last performance of the season.

At the Prince's Theatre, during the recent admirable revival of the operas, there was something in the atmosphere of the theatre which was different from that at all other theatres in London, except the " Old Vic." You felt at once you were forming part of an audience that definitely knew what they liked. They were there to enjoy themselves, and they knew they *would* enjoy themselves. This in itself is to some people unpardonable.

The operas were enjoyed by the old who saw them through mists of many memories, and who were not disappointed with their present-day interpretation. They were enjoyed by the young, and they came as a revelation to those who had never seen them before. Children found in them the most magical of pantomimes; politicians, the keenest and the most actual of satires; musicians, a treasure-house of skill and invention; writers and playwrights, an ideal of verbal felicity and stage-craftsmanship far beyond their reach.

One night, during the recent revival of *Iolanthe*, I was sitting next to a celebrated modern author and an extremely accomplished manipulator of words. When the chorus sang :

> " To say she is his mother is a bit of utter folly !
>   Oh, fie ! Strephon is a rogue !
>   Perhaps his brain is addled and it's very melancholy !
>   Taradiddle, taradiddle, tol lol lay ! "

he said to me, " That's what I call poetry," and he added that he thought that the most permanent and enduring achievement of the Victorian age would be neither that of Tennyson, Browning and Swinburne, nor of Gladstone, Disraeli and Parnell, nor of Darwin, Huxley and Ball, but the operas of Gilbert and Sullivan. I am inclined to agree with him ; and I should not be in the least surprised if, in ages to come, people will talk of the age of Gilbert

and Sullivan as they talk of the age of Pericles. Perhaps
they will confuse fact with fiction, and the children of the
future will think that trials by jury in that amusing age
were conducted to music ; that pirates and policemen
hobnobbed at Penzance ; that Strephon, the Arcadian
Shepherd, brought about the reform of the House of
Lords ; that the Bolshevik Revolution took place in
Barataria ; and the Suffragist movement happened at
Castle Adamant.

In thinking of the triumph and the permanent popularity of these operas, and the excellent manner in which
they are produced and interpreted at the present day,
it is impossible not to regret that we should only be able
to hear them during a short season at intervals of two
years.

What we want is a permanent Opera House, where not
only Gilbert and Sullivan, but all other English music,
such as *The Beggar's Opera*, and foreign music too,
should be done all the year round.

What a grand opportunity is here for a model millionaire such as Gilbert would have invented, to create a
permanent Gilbert and Sullivan House, at which other
operas might be acted, new operas produced, and old
operas revived. Perhaps such a man will turn up one
day ; for although all millionaires are not model, some
of them are musical.

1922.

MRS. PATRICK CAMPBELL [1]

THERE is nothing quite like the excitement of the rise of a new star in the theatrical firmament. It grows from day to day, it thrives, not only on the increasing discussion, the multitudinous comparing of notes, the sometimes conflicting but ever-vibrating impressions of the daily increasing crowd of the spectant and the expectant, as the ripples caused by the fall of the stone of talent on the stagnant waters spread daily in widening circles, but also on the hopes and dreams for the future that the startling success and triumph of the present evoke and inspire.

These hopes and dreams are infinite, and often fantastic ; many of them are doomed either never to be realised, or to be violently shattered in a partial realisation, again to turn to ashes in disappointment and disillusion ; but something comes of it all, however short it may fall of what we expected, and for that something, whatever it is, let us be duly thankful.

When the new star first emerges we forget for the moment what a spendthrift Nature is, as Matthew Arnold said, talking of Byron and Heine ; and how the ruby is almost bound to have a flaw ; or to put it the other way, what a strict housekeeper she is, and how carefully she mixes the chicory with the coffee ; we forget the thousand and one circumstances that are necessary

[1] *My Life and Some Letters*, by Mrs. Patrick Campbell. London : Hutchinson & Co.

5

for the subsistence of good acting, apart from the acting
of the actor or the actress in question ; the taste, and the
want of taste, and not only the taste, but the mood of the
public ; the harmony or discord between the actor
and the authors, and between the actor and the cast ;
the financial difficulties and opportunities and necessities of production, and all the thousand and one problems
of theatrical demand and supply.

We forget all this as we gape and wonder at the rays
of the new star, and we say to ourselves, if she or he can
make so much of this part, then what will her Lady
Macbeth be ? what her Cleopatra ? or what his Hamlet,
what his Othello ?

And often there is no Lady Macbeth, and the Hamlet
turns out to be much like the other Hamlets. We
dream of possibilities in Aeschylus, Euripides, Shakespeare, Schiller, Racine, Ibsen, D'Annunzio, and we get
a long course of Sardou, or a leading part in a Drury
Lane spectacular play. If we are philosophers we realise
that it must be so, saying to ourselves : " Le mieux
est l'ennemi du bien," and we give thanks for what
we get.

When Mrs. Patrick Campbell appeared in *The Second
Mrs. Tanqueray* in May 1893, the excitement caused
by her acting was the most incandescent factor in that
hot and radiant summer. I was in Florence at the time,
and I remember getting an imperative letter saying I
must come home at once and see Mrs. Patrick Campbell.
I had been seeing many plays at the charming out-of-
door theatre, the Arena Nazionale, in Florence, where
a company of Italians acted every kind of play in the
repertory, from Tolstoy's *Powers of Darkness* to *The
Private Secretary*, with incomparable ease and natural-
ness and unabashed prompting ; and I remember the

first time I went to the play on arriving in London (I could not get places for *Mrs. Tanqueray* till a few nights later) that the English actors (and they were good actors) seemed to me stilted, slow, affected, and artificial in their utterance and their movements.

A few nights later I got places at the St. James's Theatre. The first half of the admirably constructed first act of *The Second Mrs. Tanqueray* (and I know of no better " exposition," no surer *entrée en matière*) I still felt was being played in what, after the Italian ease, seemed to me more like a foreign language than Italian, and then Mrs. Patrick Campbell came on to the stage, and her slowest gesture and her most deliberate note were made and struck before one had time to know how it had been done. Instead of seeing nothing but mechanism, one could not believe in the existence of any mechanism at all. One was face to face with nature and truth ; and as the play went on one forgot to think about it at all ; one was merely conscious of " infinite passion and the pain of finite hearts that yearn."

I remember saying to my companion, " What a Hedda Gabler she will be, and why not Lady Macbeth ? and why not, even, Swinburne's Mary Stuart in *Chastelard* ? " My companion assented to the Hedda Gabler, but not to the Lady Macbeth ; and I remember building a castle in the air out of the kind, a new kind, of Lady Macbeth that Mrs. Campbell could give us ; and how defensible and welcome such a Lady Macbeth would be. But the next phase which occurred in the progress of the new planet was neither a Shakespearean triumph, nor an interpretation of Ibsen, nor an experiment in the poetic drama, but a leading part in a modern drama, *The Masqueraders*, one of the less interesting of Mr. Henry Arthur Jones' plays. One of those little exterior factors

which are inseparable from stage life, which I alluded
to just now, and which although small, are so vitally
momentous, had come into play ; Mrs. Campbell and
Mr. George Alexander, owing to an unfortunate misunderstanding, were no longer on speaking terms.
" One foolish anecdote of this time has clung to me,"
Mrs. Campbell tells us. " Mr. Alexander in this play
by Mr. Jones had to look into my face and tell me I
was beautiful, and that he adored me, or some such
words, and one night he said it with such a look in his
eyes, as though he would willingly have wrung my
neck, that I burst out laughing." It is hardly necessary
to say that when such things happen there is for the
moment no more question of art. There followed a
drama by Mr. Haddon Chambers at the Haymarket,
John-a-Dreams, in which Mrs. Campbell had little to
do but to look beautiful, and in March 1895 the star
blazed out again with great lustre and more triumphant
than ever in *The Notorious Mrs. Ebbsmith*.

" The rôle of Agnes Ebbsmith and the first three acts
of the play filled me with ecstasy," she writes. This
ecstasy was contagious. Mrs. Campbell's triumph on
that first night, at which I was present, was as great as,
perhaps greater than, it had been in *The Second Mrs.
Tanqueray*. She displayed not only grace, charm,
pathos, and poetry, sarcasm and passion, but a deep
vibrating note of serious power, and she let loose a storm
of emotion in the third act. " Now," said every one,
" she has entered into her kingdom. Now she has the
ball at her feet." They might also have added :

" Now hangeth all on one tremendous if——"

The first thing that happened was that circumstances
and the hard necessities of theatrical life stepped in even

to interrupt the run of this most successful play, and to interrupt its success for good.

Mr. Beerbohm Tree's tour in America had not been a financial success, and he returned and claimed Mrs. Campbell for a production of *Fédora* at the Haymarket. She was bound to him by her contract.

" I played Agnes Ebbsmith eight times a week for a fortnight while rehearsing *Fédora*. It was an impossible feat. I had only time to study the last act, the death-scene, of this more than exacting rôle. After a fortnight the work told on my voice, and I was dumb." The dreams, and the high hopes which seemed now on the verge of realisation, were sacrificed for the time being on the altar of Sardou, and as the effort resulted in a complete breakdown on the part of Mrs. Campbell, nobody was any the better for it. I never saw Mrs. Campbell in the part of Fédora, and although the photograph of her in the death-scene, which is in her book, leaves one guessing at something beautiful, Fédora is not really a character at all ; Fédora is a machine for exploiting Sarah Bernhardt, and I have never seen any other actress play the part who could set that intricate piece of machinery in complete motion, interesting as their performances might be for other reasons. For the problem before the actress in playing Fédora is not that of portraying a Russian Princess, who is not really there, but of filling a part which has been cut to the exact requirements and measure of a unique personality and temperament.

But Fate was ready with a compensation. In September 1895, Mrs. Campbell went from the Haymarket to the Lyceum, and opened with Mr. Forbes-Robertson in *Romeo and Juliet*. The critical had clamoured for her to play Shakespeare, and when she did so they were not all of them as grateful as they might have been. Some of them complained that her rendering was not traditional. Mr. Archer wrote in the *World* : " What was my astonishment to find that the majority of critics went into unmeasured and evidently heartfelt raptures over an impersonation in which after the balcony scene I have been unable to discover a single luminous ray or thrilling moment." We have here no ordinary difference of opinion over which one can only shrug one's shoulders and say : " There's no accounting for taste ! "

In *Romeo and Juliet* we saw another side of the star. " The poetry of mortals is their daily prose," is a phrase of Meredith's in recounting the tragic idyll of Richard Feverel and Lucy. It needs a great artist to make us realise how profoundly true the saying can sometimes be ; and Mrs. Campbell had achieved this very feat in her interpretations of Agnes Ebbsmith and Paula Tanqueray. She had invested the part of Paula Tanqueray, which belongs to the soil of hard and bitter reality, with poetry, without making the part unreal. She had heightened the poignancy of the part without impairing its truth. She had humanised Paula Tanqueray without unduly magnifying her. When Eleonora Duse played the part, it was difficult to think of her Paula living in the prosaic neighbourhood created for us without, as Mr. Walkley said at the time, setting the whole country-side aflame. Mrs. Campbell gave us a Paula who at times was almost unbearably probable ; the scene when she receives the neighbour, Mrs. Cortelyon, made one turn cold with discomfort by its stinging, icy insolence ; at the same time she made us feel that Paula Tanqueray had another side, a background of sorrowful beauty in her soul. And there is nothing in such an interpretation that is incompatible with the part as it is written.

In Agnes Ebbsmith some people said, and I agree with
them, that she transcended the part, and interpreted
the ecstasy she speaks of having felt in the ideas which it
inspired her with ; that she lent to Agnes the poetry of
her own aspirations.   But here again this is the poetry
which comes from the daily prose of mortals ; the prose
of social conflicts, and even of meetings in Trafalgar
Square ;   the facing of the mob ;   the struggle with
authority ;   the battle with convention and the minions
of the law.

In *Romeo and Juliet* she was face to face with the poetry
of the greatest of all poets : the flame of first love ; the
secret of summer night ; the divine dawn of youthful
passion ;   the summer lightning of love at first sight ;
the separation of two hearts by the sharp sword of circumstance, and the desperate courage of thwarted ecstasy,
ready to dare and face anything in Life, or in the Valley
of the Shadow of Death.   How did she deal with all
this ?   Opinion was divided ; but the majority agreed
that if the performance was not a great one, it was un-
deniably a thing of beauty, a living, breathing creation.

There are some plays which do not seem to exist until
they are acted.   There are others which seem to reveal
new and unguessed-of sides in the light of good acting ;
but Shakespeare's great parts are only partially lit,
sometimes they are even obscured, by acting that is good
and more than good, for only the greatest acting lights
them up completely.   Such power as Mrs. Campbell
revealed in the potion scene in *Romeo and Juliet* was like
the note of a reed compared with the roar of the tempest
she had called up in *Mrs. Ebbsmith*.   This was because
the part of Juliet was greater than her art ; that of Agnes
Ebbsmith on a level with it, or according to some people
beneath it.   Do what she would, she could not be as

powerful as Shakespeare's Juliet. She could not supply the gentle pressure and the large mastery that are necessary to sound all the whispering stops of that soft but tremendous organ.

In other words, few people said or would say that her Juliet was a great piece of acting—such a piece of acting as goes down to history and becomes legendary, like Salvini's Othello, Sarah Bernhardt's Phèdre, Irving's Becket, Chaliapine's Mephistopheles, or her own Paula Tanqueray.

But if it was not great, it was more than well worth doing. It was, as Mr. Walkley wrote at the time, " an exquisitely truthful and moving performance." It was, above all things, young ; and in the balcony scene Mrs. Campbell's star revealed a new and wonderful silvery phase. The words were not " recited," nor mouthed, nor dislocated, nor rendered artificial. They gave their natural fragrance like night-flowering stocks in the twilight, and were allowed, owing to her exquisite modulation and touch, to exercise their own beautiful spell. Mrs. Campbell not only showed that she was at home in the realms of gold, but she led us to guess at a fairyland we had not yet seen ; her own province of fairyland, which she, and she only, was queen of. She took us into it later when she played Mélisande.

When the run of *Romeo and Juliet* was over " the next production at the Lyceum," we are told, " was *Michael and His Lost Angel.* Mr. Robertson begged me to come and hear Mr. Henry Arthur Jones read this play. . . . I felt my part in this play was vulgar and it did not interest me, but I said I would play it if some of the lines were cut." She resigned her part. " The play was not a success," she adds, " and I was very severely criticised for having resigned my part in it. I did not like forsaking my manager, or offending Mr. Jones, or forgoing my salary ; but there was something in that play I could not stomach."

I believe I am not alone in thinking that *Michael and His Lost Angel* is the best play that Mr. Jones ever wrote, and that had Mrs. Campbell played in it, the effect might have been prodigious. However, there it was. Here again was one of those factors that are inseparable from theatrical life, or rather from life. An author writes a masterpiece which demands the qualities of a particular artist for its interpretation. The artist " cannot stomach it." Michael loses his angel, but the public loses Michael, and possibly a new and interesting phase of the angel as well. And when one thinks of some of the plays that received the privilege later of being produced by Mrs. Campbell, and over which she squandered mints of talent in vain, without captivating the large public or the suffrages of the critical few, one cannot forbear giving a slight gasp of wonder. If ever this play is revived in more favourable circumstances, and by an actress who could do it justice, I should not be surprised to see it triumph.

The next important part Mrs. Campbell appeared in, after an exquisite interlude in the shape of her Militza in *For the Crown*, translated from François Coppée's *Pour la Couronne*, was Magda in a play called *Magda*, translated from Sudermann's *Heimat*. Here again circumstance in the most freakish manner interfered with Mrs. Campbell's career. The play was produced on Derby Day, 2nd June 1896. I was present at the first night. I thought Mrs. Campbell played superbly. I had seen Sarah Bernhardt and Duse in the part, and I thought Mrs. Campbell's Magda was the most real, lifelike, and complete of the three renderings. I thought the audience

were sharing my enthusiasm. The people who were
with me certainly did. The next morning, to my intense
surprise, I woke up and read in the newspapers that
Mrs. Campbell had proved a complete failure in the
part. The play was shortly afterwards withdrawn. Mr.
Shaw, writing in the *Saturday Review*, said that Mrs.
Campbell had missed the most obvious points of the
part. The curiously ironical feature of this episode is
that when the play was revived by Mrs. Campbell in
1900, it was a triumphant success and ran for many
months. People raved about her acting in it, and I
heard many critics say she was the best of all the Magdas
we had seen.

Why the play succeeded then and not before is an
instance of one of those freaks of the public mood that
nobody can explain, but I am certain that Mrs. Campbell
played the part just as well in 1896 as she did in 1900,
and in exactly the same way. After this Mrs. Campbell
played Lady Teazle in *The School for Scandal*, the Rat-
wife and Rita in *Little Eyolf*, Lady Hamilton in an unsuccessful play called *Nelson's Enchantress*, and Lady
Macbeth. The chronology in this part of her book
is difficult to follow, and she makes no mention of the
production of *Macbeth* in London, although she tells
of its success in Berlin. I saw her play Lady Macbeth
at the Lyceum, but I have but a dim recollection of
her performance. (Her appearance was unforgettable.)
But I remember thinking once more, and far more than
after seeing her Juliet, how gigantic Shakespeare's tragic
parts were. Beauty, grace, and intelligence were there
in the interpretation, but where was the electric thrill ?
Where was the touch, the gesture, the look that makes
you shiver and tremble ? Later, I saw Mrs. Campbell
play Lady Macbeth with Mr. Hackett, and the play

was marred by inappropriate incidental music and a want
of cohesion between the members of the company, but
Mrs. Campbell gave one glimpses and hints of what
might have been if . . . if everything had been different.

Her third and last Shakespearean part was Ophelia
to Mr. Forbes-Robertson's most memorable Hamlet.
Mr. Bernard Shaw in his notice in the *Saturday Review*
pointed out that Mrs. Campbell lit up a tragic facet of
the tragedy which was generally obscured by playing
Ophelia as if she were really mad and not distraught.
This came as a shock to the audience, accustomed always
to have the part toned down and turned entirely to favour
and prettiness. There was no doubt about the madness
of Mrs. Campbell's Ophelia. I can see her haunting
glassy stare at this moment, a stare behind which there
was nothing. I thought it was a remarkable performance, but in her book she seems unconscious of having
done anything out of the way. Irving, she tells us,
after a performance came round and said to her :
" Beautiful, my child, beautiful." " But," she adds,
" the real truth was that Miss Terry had given such a
lovely Ophelia to the world still fresh in every one's
memory—there was no room for mine." The next turn
in fortune's wheel was a tour to Germany.

" I had a great treasure in my pocket," she writes,
" Maeterlinck's play. I accepted the offer to accompany Mr. Roberston if on our return he would produce
Pelléas and Mélisande ; this he agreed to do." It was
produced at the Prince of Wales' Theatre on 21st June
1898, for nine matinées, by Mr. Forbes-Robertson.
Gabriel Fauré wrote incidental music to it. Mr.
Martin Harvey played Pelléas, and Mr. Forbes-Robertson played Golaud. " The play," Mrs. Campbell tells
us, " had an overwhelming success."

Another and perhaps the most beautiful phase of the star was revealed. She took us to the fairyland which we suspected she knew of when she played Juliet. " This archaic poem of beauty, passion, and loveliness," she says, " un-thumb-marked and un-dog-eared by ' tradition,' gave me peace and certainty—I had come into my own."

In playing Mélisande she entered the capital of her kingdom. In that kingdom of poetic algebra, in that land of shadows and abstract landscape, of grey cardboard towers, " wizard twilight," and perilous seas, she was at home, and more than a citizen, a queen ! She wore a robe of Maeterlinck as if it had been made for her. Later on she played Mélisande in French to the Pelléas of Sarah Bernhardt, and the effect was just as beautiful. Indeed, she might have played it in Chinese, the effect would have been the same. It was not only that she was poetical, but she held the secret of glamour, and spoke with the accents and looked at us with the glance that belong to that mysterious world where Christabel slumbers and Sister Helen burns her waxen man, and fire-spirits shine in the Beryl, and the Knight-at-Arms loiters on the cold hillside, and where the cups of red wine turn pale, and the hound falls dead at the sight of a woman with the West in her eyes.

After this brief triumph came more vicissitudes, an unsuccessful Japanese play, a season at the Royalty, which was successful without being sufficiently lucrative to wipe off the debts of recent failure ; the South African War ; the death of Queen Victoria ; all of which various factors made a tour in the United States necessary. Before starting, Mrs. Campbell produced Björnstjerne Björnson's *Beyond Human Power* for a series of matinées.

As we turn over the pages of the record of Mrs. Campbell's career the same events seem to repeat themselves in a circle ; there is the same blend of success and failure ; the same interruptions of chance ; now a taxi-accident followed by long and serious illness ; now a broken knee-cap ; at one time a daring experiment, a production of a play by José Echegaray, or Hoffmannsthal; and at another time a leading part in a Drury Lane melodrama ; a failure in a fine play that had succeeded in America and everywhere else such as Sudermann's *Es Lebe das Leben*, or a success in a " straight " St. James's Theatre drama such as *Bella Donna* ; a disagreement with the management, as when *Hedda Gabler* was produced at the Court Theatre, or a quarrel over rehearsals, as when Frohman produced *The Joy of Living*. Sometimes the right play comes at the wrong moment (*Magda* was a case in point), sometimes the play is wrong altogether ; she plays in tragedy, comedy, melodrama ; Shakespeare, Bernard Shaw, Barrie, Ibsen, Robert Hichens, Hall Caine, world-famous dramatists and personal friends who had never written a play before. . . . It is a varied, restless kaleidoscope of many colours and shifting facets, rarely falling serenely together in a pattern of satisfaction and harmony. Rarely the time and the place and the loved play altogether ! " Such," Mrs. Campbell explains, commenting on the failure of *Magda* when she first played the part, and on her subsequent success in the same part, " is the battle of the theatre." Such, she might have added, is the battle of life.

When we think of the rarity of great talent, of her gifts, of the skill she displayed in certain parts, of the interest she almost invariably lent to everything she touched, of the heights she reached at times, of the spell of poetic glamour that she knew how to weave, and then of the comparative rarity of her appearances, of the failure that attended some of her most notable efforts and most satisfying impersonations, it is with a feeling of melancholy that one casts about for an explanation.

" I have never known," she writes towards the end of her book, " the art of acting really cared for in this country. It is first the player, then the play—and always, ' Who is your favourite actor or actress ? '

" I do not find people discussing exquisite gesture— variety of tone—and above all, that most difficult of technical difficulties, the subtle tones, temper and manner, which indicate the difference of feeling towards each character in the play—or broad human effects— atmosphere, breeding, and style. Now and then a critic points out these things, but an English audience does not look for them—or recognise them."

Is this the explanation ? To a certain extent perhaps, but perhaps not entirely. It is not the whole truth. It is true that the *corporate* intelligence and appreciation of an English audience as a rule are less and lower in kind than those of a French or a German audience. It is true that if the equivalent of plays that are welcomed in Paris and enjoyed almost entirely because of the beauty of the actual words, and of the way the words are spoken, were produced in London, they would probably have no success at all. It is true that it is a heart-breaking experience to note and certify, when a play such as Dryden's *All for Love* is produced in London, how the audience, although a picked one, and supposed to be intelligent, and although it seems to enjoy the play *as a play*, remains totally unresponsive, outwardly at any rate, to this or that beautiful line in the poetry. For instance :

> " For I have far to go, if Death be far,
> And never must return."

I remember this line being admirably spoken, but it did not pierce the crust of the audience. There was not a tremor or a flicker of *corporate* appreciation.

As I noted this lack of appreciation I remembered the peculiar subdued murmur, tremor and ripple, and sometimes the explosive thrill which seemed to go right through the whole of a French audience as some beautiful line was well spoken in a French classic or in the work of a modern poet. For instance, Bartet saying in *Bérénice* :

" Je vous croirai, Seigneur, sur un simple soupir,"

or Coquelin saying in *Cyrano* :

" Grâce à vous une robe a passé dans ma vie."

It is true that you don't find many people in England discussing the points Mrs. Campbell mentions, whereas only this summer I heard a masseur at a French wateringplace wax eloquent over the difference between the art of Lucien Guitry and his son Sacha. But all the same, I believe it is not the public that is entirely to blame. They may not notice these things. They do notice the absence of them. Take plays in which Mrs. Campbell frankly admits that she was not playing sympathetically : they were less successful than those in which she felt she was giving of her best.

Was it the public's fault or her fault that her Hedda Gabler at the Court Theatre was less successful than her Hedda Gabler as she plays it now ?

Mrs Campbell talks of Ellen Terry's " happy haste," and says that in playing Imogen she seemed to come from the moon. She talks of her " magical step." Yes, indeed ; but what an amount of solid, hard, continuous work and unremitting effort went to the making of that elusive pace and that careless magic ! The same with Sarah Bernhardt. What a prolonged wrestle with the angel of art went to the making of the infinitesimal gradations of nervous irritation and suppressed passion in, for instance, such a scene as that where Frou-Frou quarrels with her sister. Mrs. Campbell's art seems to be entirely instinctive ; if she does not get there at once she throws up the sponge.

It is not, heaven forfend ! that one does not realise, after reading her book, that her work was arduous. It was often much too arduous. When one reads of the rehearsals of *Fédora* going on simultaneously with the eight performances a week of *Mrs. Ebbsmith*, of the *School for Scandal* being produced at seventeen days' notice, at her assumption of the part of Rita in Ibsen's *Little Eyolf* literally at a moment's notice, of climaxes of fatigue, " I could not work any more," of loss of voice and broken limbs, and taxi accidents, the net amount of fatigue involved would be enough for an army retreating by forced marches. But what one feels the absence of is a foundation of solid hard work before all this began. There is, it is true, a tour with Ben Greet's pastoral company and an engagement at the Adelphi, but that is all. Compare this with the apprenticeship of artists such as Sarah Bernhardt, Duse, Mrs. Kendal, and Ellen Terry.

Mrs. Campbell leaps into fame at the outset of her career, and she never reaches a higher summit of success and popularity than in her first great success, Mrs. Tanqueray.

Sarah Bernhardt goes to the Conservatoire, then to the Français, then to the Odéon, and after an interval of ten years she returns to the Français, and it is six years after that even, sixteen years after her first almost un-noticed appearance, that she makes her first real success. In following Mrs. Campbell's career one has the impression of spasmodic spurts, of tremendous efforts followed by haphazard makeshifts.

Of course, one answer to this is, that the theatrical profession more than any other is the child of compromise and the creature of circumstance. So was Sarah Bernhardt's career *afterwards* ; but behind it all, behind the world-tours and the breathless trips across Europe, the toleration of indifferent plays, and the exploitation of melodrama that was unworthy of her, there remained, besides the time spent at the Conservatoire, the sixteen years of unremitting work in the best repertory, at the best possible school of acting and artistic experience, which nothing could take away or efface.

In England the theatre is not organised. There is no Conservatoire and no State Theatre, and a far less critical public. " Organise the theatre," said Matthew Arnold, " the theatre is irresistible " ; but that has not yet been done in England. Yet in spite of this English actors managed to find in the past, at any rate, a school of training and experience as arduous, if not as artistic, as that which France provides. Ellen Terry and Mrs. Kendal seemed to have learned to act ever since they were born.

The lack, then, one is chiefly conscious of in reading this record, is that of a solid foundation and of continuity of study. Mrs. Campbell is impatient of tradition. Even Shakespearean parts seem to her " thumbmarked " and " dog-eared " with it. But nobody—and Mrs. Campbell less than any one—would say that Ellen Terry's Imogen, her Beatrice, her Portia, or her Ophelia were marred by the dust of theatrical convention such as tradition engenders in the efforts of the mediocre ; or that Sarah Bernhardt's Phèdre suffered from the

6

memories of what Rachel or others had done with the part. These artists treated tradition as gymnastics ; when they had got the most out of what tradition could give them, and by using it had learnt to use their theatrical muscles freely, they discarded it, and by expressing themselves created a new link in it by their own individual creations. Mrs. Campbell seemed to have no use and no need for such gymnastics. She says somewhere that she was praised for her dancing when she played Juliet and for her singing when she played Ophelia, but that she could neither dance nor sing. The secret of this is perhaps that she was a born and a trained musician. She had gained in her youth a musical scholarship at the Guildhall. I think the most characteristic and significant episode in her book is her account of how she dealt with a stage direction in *The Second Mrs. Tanqueray*. There is a stage direction in the third act which reads : " She sits at the piano and strums a valse." " Now my mother," she says, " had never allowed any of her children to strum. . . . I played rather well, with a passionate love of touch and tone which gained me a scholarship at the Guildhall ; but I am not a musician in the true sense of the word. [A semi-musical person, we may notice, would never have made that avowal.] I sat down at the piano hesitatingly, asking twice to be excused, until I had prepared something suitable. A voice from the stalls : ' We would like to hear whether you can play ? ' This offended me. Holding my book in my right hand, with my left I played beautifully —and with impertinence—a piece written by a girl friend of mine. . . . Those who listened knew that my playing must be the outcome of serious study and some understanding of art." In this little story I think we have the key to the whole of Mrs. Campbell's peculiar

genius. Her inability to *strum*. It was never possible
for her to do anything ugly or ungraceful ; the teasing
malice of playing *impertinently*, the consummate effect
she got from her left hand alone, which those who saw
her play Paula Tanqueray will remember, became one
of the permanent and most effective features of her
performance.

It might therefore well be argued that tradition and
study having had such a happy effect on her music
would have done no harm to her acting, and that it is
the want of them which accounts for any disappointments
that her career may have given rise to. But now that
I have put the case for tradition, I wonder and doubt
whether in her case years of study and tradition would
have made any difference at all. I am inclined to think
the contrary : that she was one of those who can only
learn what they know already ; who never improve ;
who reach the goal and hit the bull's-eye at the first
attempt or not at all. But then, if this is so, if tradition
or want of tradition had nothing to do with the matter,
and if the state of the English stage and the want of
interest or education on the part of the public are neither
of them vitally to blame, how is it that Mrs. Campbell,
with her beauty, her grace, her poetry, her humour, her
personal magnetism, her power and her pathos, did not
achieve far greater things ? Why do we see her so
comparatively seldom ? Why did so many of the hopes
and dreams she inspired at the moment of her first
triumphs remain unfulfilled ? Every reader of her book
can make his own answer to this question. I am inclined
to think that she, like most great artists, was the victim
of her gifts, and especially of her audacious humour, her
Puckish mischief, her irrepressible desire to laugh and
to tease ; if she had been without these elements, which

are a vital part of her personality and her charm, she
would have taken everything more seriously.

One cannot imagine Sarah Bernhardt playing Fédora
after only having had time to study the death-scene, nor
undertaking such a part as Rita in *Little Eyolf* at a
moment's notice, whatever the circumstances ; nor
Eleonora Duse changing the colour of her wig during
the course of one and the same performance. But here
again, had an artist like Sarah Bernhardt wanted to
do such a thing, or to play a trick of that kind on the
public, the theatrical conditions in France, and the
critical temper of the public, would have made it
impossible.

I believe the real secret of Mrs. Campbell's career,
with its spasmodic triumphs and seemingly unfulfilled
possibilities and comparatively wasted opportunities,
is, after all, that which governs all of us : necessity.

I believe that Nature never repeats her effects—that
what applies to one temperament, to a Duse, a Sarah
Bernhardt, an Ellen Terry, may not apply to a Stella
Campbell ; and that the way Mrs. Campbell worked
out her artistic salvation was the only possible way it
could have been worked out at all, with everything it
left done or undone, hoped for, indicated or achieved.

However that may be, here, in her book of recollec-
tions, is the record of that career, and those who read her
book and who have the good fortune to remember Mrs.
Campbell in her triumphs will be grateful for it. To
these it will recall many imperishable moments, and they
will live through some wonderful experiences over again.
Paula Tanqueray's insinuating grace and the deadly
rapier-thrusts of her insolence, and the haunting expression of her great eyes, when she faces final disaster.
Agnes Ebbsmith defying and battling with the serene,

polished Duke of St. Olpherts (so inimitably played by
Sir John Hare), " Trafalgar-Squaring him " with an
overwhelming concentrated vehemence suggestive of
infinite reserve, and hurling her defiance, later, at the
champions of respectability and convention. Juliet
tripping on to the stage, calling up visions of " dance and
Provençal song and sunburnt mirth," and fluting her
ecstasy to the moon on the balcony ; Ophelia wandering
in another world, behind a thin, impenetrable veil
through which she looks out on the world of men, now
alien to her, with a frooning otaro ; tho Ratwifo with her
wonderful voice coming, as it were, from distant hills ;
Lady Teazle enchantingly mischievous ; and Militza, a
poem of Lermontov or Pushkin in the flesh ; and above
all, Mélisande, bewildered in the wood and at the
well, or lying still with so ineffably piteous and lovely a
majesty, as she slowly drifts to death. Those who have
not yet seen Mrs. Campbell can get a hint of the nature
of her art and her beauty by looking at two photographs
in this book ; one is that of Mrs. Campbell as Magda,
with its expression of defiant triumph and hard success,
making an uphill fight, and the other of Fédora lying
dead—lovely in death, defeated and happy. " How
well she photographs," it will be said, and indeed I have
already heard it said. But only a very great artist can
charge a photograph with so much character and so
much expression, and can produce and differentiate
between such sure effects by means of so impersonal a
medium.

1923.

CHALIAPINE

CHALIAPINE has come and gone. He has been gone several weeks, and it is too late no doubt to talk of him. But he may come back. His farewell concert at the Queen's Hall was unheralded by any announcement or advertisement in the newspapers. Even the singer himself seems to have been kept in doubt as to the actual hour of the concert, and he arrived late, almost as it were by accident. There were not many empty places in the Queen's Hall ; but, considering the nature of the performance and the degree of enthusiasm which it excited in the audience, it is strange that there should have been any. The merest slip of advertisement in a daily paper should surely have made an empty seat an impossibility. As it was, a great many people thought the concert was to happen in the evening.

The singer was late ; the audience expressed impatience ; some one told us from the platform that Chaliapine had not arrived ; there was another wait, and then at last some one opened the large pianoforte—and Chaliapine strolled on to the platform, easy, tall, large and smiling, as much at home as Louis XIV. at Versailles. He indicated the rhythm of his song to the accompanist with his pince-nez, with which he beat a little time, and then he began to sing.

I forget what he sang first ; I forget a great many of the songs he sang ; but that is of no consequence. From the first note he uttered one became aware of one over-

whelming fact : it did not matter a pin what he sang ;
whatever he sang was better—better by so infinite a
gulf—than the best that any one else could give us. I
thought of Du Maurier's Trilby and the German professor who, when he was asked what she sang, said he
would rather hear Trilby sing a bar of the silliest tune
in the world than the greatest prima donna interpret
the greatest music.

The world is full of singers who have voice without
training ; sometimes—and then the world goes mad
about them—you get voice and training combined ;
sometimes you get a slender voice and perfect interpretation, and the smaller public which is privileged to
enjoy this combination goes mad about that. But how
often do you get splendour of voice, perfection of training,
of *méthode*, and inspired interpretation combined in one
singer ? The answer, for our generation, is in Chaliapine
and in Chaliapine alone. I saw that some one writing
about him in the Press said it was possible that if
we were Russians we should appreciate him less.
Possibly, if *we* were Russians ; but Russians being what
they are they could not appreciate him more than they
did and do. Before the Russian revolution Chaliapine
was better known than any public man in Russia. That
statement gives no idea of the case. Chaliapine was
as well known as Trafalgar Square is to a Londoner ;
and other Russian public men were about as well known
as members of the Athenæum Club are known to the
general public. Chaliapine was the uncrowned King of
Russia; armies might perish, the throne fall, the Emperor
be assassinated, the population starve, but Chaliapine
remained, Lord of Music and autocrat of song.

A musical critic in a discriminating article rashly said
that he distorted Schumann's " Two Grenadiers." The

critic knew what he meant and what he was talking
about ; but the semi-intelligent and the totally unmusical,
delighted to have a ready-made counter of criticism to
produce, went about glibly saying : " Of course, he
can't sing German music." It perhaps did not occur
to them that the songs of Schumann and Schubert
which Chaliapine sings are translated into Russian ; this
involves a certain amount of distortion ; and the Russian
singer can only sing the Russian words that are given
him ; does he sing these well ? Could anybody else
sing them as he does ?

No other words in any other language can give the
effect of

" Mein Kaiser, mein Kaiser gefangen " ;

but when Chaliapine sings the equivalent :

" I sam Imperator v plenou,"

could an archangel interpret the *Russian* words better ?
As I heard him sing the song, I saw, as never before, the
épopée of Napoleon, with its catastrophic climax unrolled
before my eyes ; I heard the very accents of army
comradeship, and listened to the heartbeats of the *Grande
Armée*, to the death-rattle of all the hopes, desires, and
dreams of the young republic, and the undying loyalty
of the fighting men to the defeated eagles and the van-
quished Emperor.

But when he sang the *Doppelgänger*, the impression was
greater far ; one forgot there were German words behind
the Russian words, ghosts which in the " Two Grenadiers "
not even the genius of Chaliapine could exorcise—there,
in this song, there was nothing left but an immense
sadness, an infinite sorrow which widened and increased
in strength and depth and majesty until it overwhelmed
the world ; all the sorrow of all the poets : Dante's

bitterness and Shakespeare's pity and Dostoyevski's agony and reconciliation seemed to have been distilled and melted into the notes of this song ; and all Russia's history and all Russia's undying sorrow and unhealed pain, and everybody's sorrow and everybody's pain. One thought the singer could not survive such a recital, and when the song came to an end, I wished to hear nothing else. The stillness of the audience, the utter, complete stillness which fell on the large hall was more than all applause. You felt that the policemen at the top of the gallery were spellbound.

I never wished to hear another singer sing another song. To those who do not know Russian, Chaliapine's art gives an idea of what Russian literature—Pushkin's poetry and Turgenev's prose—is at its highest and best : it has the same ease, the same limpidity, the same natural, untaught grace of gesture, the same unpremeditated sureness of touch. " God-gifted organ-voice of Russia," I said to myself as I left the Queen's Hall. " Chaliapine, a name to resound for a comparatively short time, and with the help of the gramophone, for ' so very little longer.' "

1922.

A PLACE OF PEACE

" DOUBTLESS there is a place of peace," wrote
the poet Shelley. As a matter of fact, there
is no doubt about it at all. The place exists. It is
to be found in London. You will find it east of the
sun and west of the moon. To be more precise : north
of Waterloo Station ; south of Marylebone Road ; west
of Ludgate Hill, and east of the Albert Memorial.

The entrance to it is a door like any other door. You
approach it ; say the words " Open Sesame "—that is
to say, two words to that effect—and you enter into
another world : a world of peace and complete security.
" Here, where the world is quiet," might be written
over the door. No telephone can reach you ; you fear
no more the heat o' the sun nor the furious winter's
rages. Whatever the time of year, the climate in this
secluded world is so arranged that it is bound to meet
your momentary needs. In winter you go there to get
warm ; in summer you will go there to get cool ; on a
wet day you will go there to get dry, and on a dusty day
you will go there to get wet.

The secret which admits you to this earthly Paradise
is no secret : it is well known to many. But they rarely
mention it. They never discuss it nor argue about it
with the uninitiated. They are like the inhabitants of
the island of Tahiti, who never argue with strangers
about the climate of the South Seas or the advantages
of their island life ; because they don't think : they

know. Discussion, when you know for certain, and the other people don't, is a vexatious waste of time.

This little Eden has been known—and still is known—to all sorts and conditions of men. The poet Swinburne went there to write what was perhaps his finest poem. There you will meet representatives of all the leading professions : " The Army, the Navy, the Church, and the Stage," the Bar, Art, Music, Sculpture, Letters, Journalism, Finance, the Turf, and the Ring. There you might meet Lord Lonsdale, Father Bernard Vaughan, Steve Donoghue, Chaliapine, Charles Hawtrey, Novelists, Speakers, Chancellors, Yachtsmen, Millionaires from America, Elder Statesmen from Japan, Bolshevists from Bond Street, Conservatives from Ireland, poets from Fleet Street, Yogi from India, Dons from Oxford, but never a dun.

There you will not only meet men of all nations, but you will see them as they are, and not as they appear to be.

So that to enter this place is, in some ways, like attending an undress rehearsal of the Day of Judgment. For the denizens of the place are stripped of all artificial disguise. There you can eat, smoke, read, and sleep. There you may drink water at any time, and, at licensed hours, wine.

Conversation is not obligatory. On the other hand, it is not forbidden, and nobody would think it rude if you dropped to sleep while you were being spoken to. You can enter this kingdom at any time during the day or night. You can, if you like, be as lonely there and silent as a ghost, or as sociable as a magpie.

You are within reach of everything and out of reach of everybody. You can communicate with the world, but the world cannot molest or disturb you.

There you are energetic without making any effort, and

the more passive you are at rest there the more efficacious is your unconscious activity.

It is the only secular place in England in which, if they were alive, King Solomon, Cicero, Peter the Great, Napoleon, Mahomet, and St. Andrew the Apostle, and Tolstoy would feel completely at home and enter without a quiver of surprise.

This place—as you well might think it to be, from the hints I have already thrown out—is not a club. Clubs are conducted on rules. There are no rules in this place. At least, all the rules are unwritten ones, and are taken for granted. It possesses no committee. The English passion for framing laws which shall at one time or another be inconvenient to themselves is here allowed no free play. No member or visitor can suddenly suggest that another member shall not be allowed to smoke a pipe, or a cigar, or a cigarette, or a gasper at any particular time. Where people want to smoke, there they are allowed to smoke. Smoking is forbidden in such places where smoking is impossible, or where it would be no pleasure to smoke.

In this place man is allowed full play to his natural egoism. He can eat a grape fruit or a mango, or even an orange, without fear of criticism. The world forgetting, by the world forgot. The place possesses a library of books. Such a library as only chance can compile and only habit can consecrate. There you will find the original narratives of Sherlock Holmes' adventures; stray volumes of Turf reminiscences; an anthology of jokes from *Punch*; a treatise on how to be cured from morphine poisoning; a few novels; a little verse; in fact, such a library, and such literature as appeals, and only just that kind of literature that appeals, to the listless mind—the mind which wishes its attention to

be engaged without being riveted or in any way perplexed
or worried.

Physical appetites are provided for (unconsciously, I
think) on the same principle. You can obtain grape fruit
there, and different kinds of water—pure, impure, and
medicinal ; but if you definitely and decidedly want a
glass of beer, you must send out for it—out into the
world.

The books that are there are read over and over again
by the same people : which proves the wisdom of those
who unconsciously chose them. The food and liquid
that are available are ordered over and over again by
the same kind of hungry and thirsty people, which proves
the same thing, on a different plane.

No music comes near this quiet place. There is in it
no band ; no jazz, no organ, neither pipe nor barrel,
no chorus, no solo, no orchestra.

This place was invented, devised, and founded, I
believe, by an eminent scholar. His statue, made of pure
gold, should be placed in Trafalgar Square. But, like
many of the world's greatest benefactors—like Mr.
Macadam and Mr. Umbrella, and Mr. Martini, and
Monsieur Soubise—he is known by his work alone. His
name is synonymous with what he has created : by
itself, and of itself, and in itself it is unknown. " Oh,
East is East, and West is West, and never the twain shall
meet." That is the rule. The place I have written
about, that proves it, is the exception.

1922.

AUTHORS AND BOOKS

GOETHE AND VICTOR HUGO

(To Cecil Baring)

I

TWENTY-FIVE years ago, when I was working at a crammer's for the competitive examination which it was necessary to pass to enter either the Foreign Office or the Diplomatic Service, one of the subjects given in one of the examinations on which the candidates had to write an English essay was a comparison between Goethe and Victor Hugo. This did not occur when I went up for the examination myself, but it was given to us later at the crammer's, and I wrote an essay on the subject which was published in the *National Review*. I think the time given for writing the essay was two hours and a half, which seems a short space of time in which to tackle so tremendous a subject. Again, at first sight there is something perhaps incongruous and absurd in the comparison. Why should one compare Goethe with Victor Hugo? Is there any possible profit or sense in such a comparison? Is it not like comparing the Matterhorn with the Thames? On second thoughts, I do not think that it is on the whole so impossible or so absurd a subject for discussion—or rather, for a brief conversation, for, after all, what is an essay but a conversation between the writer and the reader?—as it seems at first sight. The comparison might possibly be fruitful in a few suggestive side-lights.

7

There are not only points for contrast between these two great writers, but there are also points of kinship. Goethe, nobody would dispute, was the greatest German writer of the nineteenth century, and Victor Hugo, I think most Frenchmen would agree, was the greatest French writer of the nineteenth century. The nineteenth century produced, perhaps, more perfect writers and more profound writers in France. There were, for instance, among the poets, Alfred de Vigny, Lamartine, Musset, Leconte de Lisle, and Baudelaire (not to mention the novelists : Balzac, Stendhal, and Flaubert) : each of them in his way either in one case more lofty, in another more harmonious, in another more passionate, in another more perfect, in another more original, considered as poets and nothing else. But Victor Hugo was more than a poet ; he was a novelist with a world-wide appeal, and he was a successful dramatist, and even a kind of politician. He initiated a new epoch both in the drama and in prose, and in the writing of romances ; and he wrote, on the one hand, verse which, while it pleased the multitude, charmed the elect, and, on the other hand, prose which touched the heart of the people all over the world. He made an appeal as popular as that of Dickens—he was a best-seller—and at the same time his work was as artistic as that of the most consummate artists. Other French poets may have done better in verse than he did, and a still greater number may never have done so badly as he did at moments— that is to say, never have been guilty of such grave faults of taste, or such wild absurdities or extravagances as those in which he sometimes indulged ; but if you take the mass of his work and judge it, not only by its extent and variety, but by its depth, breadth, and height, it represents a greater and more massive, a more striking

achievement than that of any other French poet of the
nineteenth century.   Towards the end of Victor Hugo's
life, a young Frenchman of the new school was once
asked who was the best living poet ; his answer was :
" Malheureusement, Victor Hugo."   I believe the
answer would still be the same if the question were
made now, and made to include the poets of the nineteenth century, living and dead, and those of our present
century, living and dead.

There are other points of kinship between Goethe
and Victor Hugo : they both of them began writing
young and lived to an extreme old age.   Goethe was still
alive when Victor Hugo's first poems appeared, and in
1827 he discussed them with Eckermann.   " He is,"
he said, talking of Victor Hugo, " a man of outstanding
talent " (the German word *Talent* is stronger than the
English word " talent ") " on whom German literature
has had an influence."   When he says in German, " Er
ist ein entschiedenes Talent," as he does, he means a
great deal more than a clever versifier.   He uses the
word *Talent* in the same way about Byron, and he considered Byron the greatest English writer of the nineteenth century.   He goes on to say that he regards
Victor Hugo as quite as important as Lamartine—that he
proceeds from Chateaubriand—that his poems are full of
excellent images and are distinguished by freedom of
treatment.   " What I praise in the French," said
Eckermann on this occasion, " is that their poetry never
abandons the firm ground of reality.   You can translate
their poetry into prose."   Goethe agreed with this, and
said the reason was that French poets had *knowledge*.
This criticism, in view of the whole of Goethe's production and the whole of Victor Hugo's, strikes one now
as curious.   To us now it would seem as if the main

characteristic of Goethe's poetry was that he never left the firm ground of reality, whereas Victor Hugo was tempted frequently in his long career to soar on the wings of extravagance into the intense inane. But perhaps the reason is that Goethe in some respects was not characteristically German, and that in some respects Victor Hugo was not characteristically French.

II

When I wrote my essay years ago on Goethe and Victor Hugo, I began by making this very point—the very point that Eckermann makes and that which Goethe agrees with, namely, that as a rule the Frenchman is rooted in reality, and that he looks at the world and tells us what he sees—often, perhaps, with less reserve than one might wish—whereas the Germans were sometimes inclined, in their account of the universe and its contents, either to see too much or not enough. The German critics, especially when they wrote about Shakespeare, were inclined to discover far-fetched meanings and hidden allegories in the simplest flights of fancy, and they were apt to censure any works in which they were unable to detect a lurking symbolism. Certainly in the case of Goethe, the first thing that strikes one about his genius is, perhaps, the clearness with which he saw things. " Nature," wrote Heine, " wishing to gaze on her reflection, created Goethe." Perspicuity, lucidity, limpidity, logic, a sense of proportion—these are the qualities which we generally get from French writers : and yet we get them in a far higher degree from Goethe than we do from Victor Hugo. " *And although Victor Hugo is, in a sense*," says my dead self of twenty-five years ago, " *an elemental poet, and renders admirably some of the larger as well as some of the more exquisite aspects of Nature, yet his whole genius is not one that reflects life with faithful accuracy. Victor Hugo was a romanticist, and he initiated a movement against classicism which affected even the realistic writers who succeeded it and set out to destroy it. For Balzac, Zola, and Taine, although they were christened realists and preached realism, in reality were just as much romantics as Victor Hugo : they belonged to the class of artists who begin in glory with Michael Angelo and end in disgrace with Gustave Doré, and whose distinguishing sign is that they see things not as they are, but in the glass of their portentous imagination. No woman quite resembles Michael Angelo's ' Night,' no man his ' David,' although, as an Italian poet has said, if the present race of men were exterminated, that statue would remain,*

> ' *Modello a Dio per un' altra stirpe umana.*'

These writers were poets—even Zola was a poet and wrote the epic *of the mine, the train, the market, and the Stock Exchange. Balzac saw the world through a strange distorting glass, and he was called a realist because the record of his vision is so terribly convincing.*

" *Others, such as Zola and Taine, were called realists partly because they said they were, and people don't take the trouble to think things out ; and partly for the same reason : they described what they saw with such vigour and in such detail.*

" *Zola saw the world through a glass that magnified and distorted in a higher degree than that of Balzac, and here again he convinced us of the truth of his vision by the power of his brush, but it is a magnifying-glass and not a looking-glass that he holds up to Nature.*

" *Victor Hugo sees the universe through an enchanted mist. But he does not break down in the recording of his visions. For distinctness of effect and for sureness of touch, he might be compared to an etcher. His work might be put with Blake's illustrations to the Book of Job, often sublime, sometimes ridiculous, sometimes sublime and ridiculous, above all things imaginative.*"

However that may be, nobody ever dreamed of calling Victor Hugo a realist. Although he abounds in detail, he is always more fantastic than realistic, and romantic in actual record as well as in vision, even when he is describing the drains of Paris. To seize the difference between the romantic and realistic conceptions of art, you must compare Victor Hugo, not with Balzac, nor with Zola, nor with Flaubert, but with Mérimée or Stendhal, better still with Goethe. And herein perhaps lies the sense and point of comparing Goethe and Victor Hugo. It is in reality a comparison between the romantic and the realistic attitude towards life, between the realistic and the romantic conception of art.

III

It is a curious thing to read what one wrote about poets (or anything else) after a lapse of twenty-five years, and one question presents itself. Are we more likely to be right when we are young or when we are older, when we are talking of poetry ? Which is the point of view most worth having when verse is concerned, that of a boy of twenty-five or that of a man of fifty ? Which is the most valuable judge of verse, the fresh or the experienced palate ?

In judging poetry, or rather in tasting poetry, such as

Shelley's and Victor Hugo's, I should say that the palate of the young man is that which should be considered as the more authoritative. The old man finds the metaphors of a poem such as *Epipsychidion* too bright, and too thickly-sown, and the melodies of such a poem a little overpowering, and so he says that the poem is bad and extravagant, wanting in sanity and in measure ; and he may be tempted to say that the poem has aged and not worn ; but he forgets that it is *he*, and not the poem, that has grown old and stale. To the young the colours probably seem just as bright as ever. But in judging a poet such as La Fontaine, or work such as Goethe's *Wahlverwandtschaften*, you have probably to be forty years old before you can read with any enjoyment at all.

When I was at school I remember telling the French master I thought the La Fontaine fables were insufferably tedious. He said it was impossible that I should think otherwise, but he was none the less certain that when I reached the age of forty I should think La Fontaine perhaps the most delightful of all poets : a prophecy which was literally fulfilled.

Victor Hugo is essentially a poet of youth and for youth. He is one of the first poets to appeal to childhood. Goethe has certain sides to his genius which appeal to the very young, and others which can only be appreciated by the middle-aged.

In looking at the essay which I wrote as quite a young man on Goethe and Victor Hugo, I find that it is a plea for considering Victor Hugo the greater poet of the two, if the first qualities of poetry are imagination and music. If that be the case, I maintained that the poet of *La Légende des Siècles*, *Les Châtiments* and *Les Contemplations* must rank above the creator of *Faust*. On the

other hand, I admitted that if criticism of life, philosophy, and suggestiveness were the more important
factors, then Goethe was immeasurably the greater
poet. The question, as I put it then, was whether it
was a greater thing for a *poet* to have soared high into
the heavens of music and passion, or to have dived deep
into the grey seas of reason. "*Into those seas,*" I said,
"*Victor Hugo never dived, and into those Heavens Goethe
certainly never soared.*"

Whether a young man is more or less likely to be
right or wrong about a poet one thing is certain, and
that is, that the young man is rarely able to state his
case properly. He may have quite a good case, but he
can't put it. Not being able to say exactly what he
wants to say, he says a great deal too much, he overshoots the mark and says a great deal more than he
means.

So, if I now wished to make the same case in the
matter of Goethe and Victor Hugo, as I tried to
make twenty-five years ago, I should make it quite
differently.

But, alas!—or perhaps I should say, thank Heaven!—
I no longer wish to make it, because I no longer agree
with it; and I repeat Alas!—for whether I was right
then and wrong now, or right now and wrong then, one
thing is certain, then I was young and perhaps foolish,
now I am perhaps a little wiser but I am certainly no
longer young. All I can do now is to hold a kind of
dialogue with my Dead Self, who, I cannot help thinking,
would, in this case, be the spokesman of many a young
virgo or *puer* who has not yet passed the enchanting age
of twenty-five, and who, in reading Goethe and Victor
Hugo, may perhaps be passionately certain that the
Olympian of Weimar is a less inspired bard than the

Olympio of Guernsey. He may, on the other hand, think precisely the opposite, such changes do the whirligig of Time bring about. In this case he will be enchanted with the opinions of my present self, and have a tolerant smile for the opinions which my Dead Self aired with such light-hearted vehemence so many years ago.

The two selves can now meet face to face in the arena.

IV

I begin now, as I began then, by raising the following point : If a plebiscite were to be taken in Europe as to who is the greatest poet, Goethe or Victor Hugo, I thought then, and I think now, that Goethe would be elected by an overwhelming majority. I am not sure that if the other rival candidates for election were not confined to the poets of France, but included all the poets of all the countries of Europe during the nineteenth century, Goethe would not still come out at the top of the list, even supposing England were represented by Byron, Wordsworth, Shelley, and Browning ; Italy by Leopardi, Carducci, and D'Annunzio ; Russia by Pushkin and Lermontov ; and Germany itself by Schiller and Heine. Take Russia, for instance : the Russian cult for Pushkin is universal, deep, and fervent ; no great poet has been better appreciated in his own country. The Russians praise not only his versatility, his humanity, his spontaneity, but his incomparable natural ease and grace of style, and yet if you ask a cultivated Russian whether Pushkin were a greater poet than Goethe, he nearly always says no. Of all the other poets I have mentioned, the one who has enjoyed the greatest fame and the

widest circulation in cultivated Europe is undoubtedly
Byron, and next to him I should say Heine and
D'Annunzio (who has been admirably translated into
French).   Shelley is known to a certain extent in Europe,
but not widely.   Byron, of course, was, and is still,
known all the world over and has appealed to all classes,
but the intoxication of his universal appeal subsided long
ago, although there is probably in England a reaction in
his favour.   But leaving out Byron's unique popularity, the
acute stage of which passed away with the romantic movement, the works of all the poets I have mentioned so far,
which are the most read, are certainly those of Victor
Hugo.   I am counting the prose as well as the poetry ;
not only is the prose considered to be entertaining and
read everywhere by every one, from universities down
to the convict prisons, but the poetry is enjoyed by
lovers of poetry and is thought to be extraordinarily
good, even by new poets.

The Dead Self of twenty-five years ago and the present-
day self both agree that of the two poets Goethe's name
stands in the higher repute, but that the works of
Victor Hugo are the more widely read.

The Self of twenty-five years ago then asks how much
of the bulk of Goethe's poetical work is known outside
Germany at all, and cheerfully answers, Gounod's *Faust*.
He then admits, for the sake of argument, that *Faust* is
as much read as it should be, and inquires what
other poetical works of Goethe are read outside
Germany ?

There are first of all the plays (besides the prose works,
such as *Werther*, which was a best-seller, and *Wilhelm
Meister*)—*Iphigenie auf Tauris*, *Tasso*, *Egmont*, *Götz von
Berlichingen*, *Clavigo*.   If Goethe's reputation rested
solely on these, and on the idyll of *Hermann und Dorothea*,

the Dead Self maintains that Goethe would not rank
much higher than the German poets of the second
rank :   Lenau, Uhland, Korner, and Platen, certainly
not higher than Schiller and Heine.

There remain, he goes on, *Faust* and the lyrical poems.
Are these sufficiently important title-deeds to put Goethe
with the greatest poets : with Homer, Virgil, Dante, and
Shakespeare, at an immeasurable distance from Victor
Hugo, Byron, Shelley, Leopardi or Keats ?   The Dead
Self says, No.   *Faust*, great poem as it is, docs not quite
achieve this : the German genius, he submits, corre-
sponding to Shakespeare and Dante, is not Goethe, is
not a writer at all ; he is Bach, or Beethoven, or Wagner.
(I should now have to substitute Mozart for Wagner.)

The criticism against Goethe's lesser known works,
especially the plays, might have been made stronger, to
my present mind, without appreciably affecting the
main argument.   It is easy to point out, for instance,
that as stage-plays—and Goethe's plays were written
for the stage (he took infinite trouble about their production) — they were and are comparative failures,
although they are still given in Germany.

His *Iphigenie* is not nearly so dramatically interesting
as any play of Racine's ; his *Egmont*, his *Tasso*, pale,
dramatically, beside the plays of Schiller and those of
Victor Hugo.   Goethe had not the sense of the stage,
and he admitted it ; but nevertheless there is a quality
in all these works, and not only in certain episodes,
passages, and lines, but throughout the whole of them, an
underlying luminous wisdom and serenity, a calm in the
substance that is the result and the aftermath of violent
struggles and tumultuous conflict, a majesty in the
accent and the gesture, and a mastery that belongs to the
great ones of the world.   They may not be great stage

dramas, but they are great works of art. Take, for
instance, the following lines from *Tasso* :

> " Nein, alles ist dahin !—Nur Eines bleibt :
> Die Thräne hat uns die Natur verliehen,
> Den Schrei des Schmerzens, wenn der Mann zuletzt
> Es nicht mehr trägt.—Und mir noch über alles—
> Sie liess im Schmerz mir Melodie und Rede
> Die tiefste Fülle meiner Noth zu klagen :
> Und wenn der Mensch in seiner Qual verstummt
> Gab mir ein Gott, zu sagen, wie ich leide."

Or the following from *Iphigenie auf Tauris* :

> " Der rasche Kampf verewigt einen Mann :
> Er falle gleich, so preiset ihn das Lied.
> Allein die Thränen, die unendlichen,
> Der überbliebnen, der verlassnen Frau
> Zählt keine Nachwelt, und der Dichter schweigt
> Von tausend durchgeweinten Tag- und Nächten,
> Wo eine stille Seele den verlornen,
> Rasch abgeschiednen Freund vergebens sich
> Zurückzurufen bangt und sich verzehrt."

Only a great poet could have written them, and if
Goethe's reputation rested on such lines and on such
lines only, he would—so does the Present-Day Self
speak, in flat contradiction to the Dead Self—be considered a great deal more than one of the German poets
of the second rank. If he had only written *Hermann und
Dorothea*, that would still be the case, for only Goethe
could have written that limpid, beautiful, realistic idyll
which has the ease and truth of a story of Georges Sand,
or of Turgenev. It was the one work of Goethe's
which he said he could read in his later life with complete
satisfaction. Its only drawback to our ears is that it is
written in hexameters, which, although more satisfactory than the best English hexameters, have to us

[1]. For philosophy and psychology they rank with *Le Misanthrope*
and *Bérénice*.

still something monotonous, and lacking in variety; they are not, however good, the " strong-wing'd music of Homer," and one of the reasons of this is, perhaps, that they are based on accent and not on quantity.

V

We now approach the main argument : Are *Faust* and the lyrics enough to give Goethe the right to the high place he occupies, in the rough and ready judgment of the world at large ?   In approaching *Faust*, the Dead Self—whom I will now call the *Advocatus Juventutis*, expresses what many have probably felt when they read *Faust* for the first time, a curious sense of disappointment.   There is so much glamour about the very name of *Faust* ; it suggests romance, magic, and mystery, and raises the highest expectations.   "*The expectations of admiration are realised*," says the *Advocatus Juventutis*, whom I will call A. J. for short, "*but probably in an unexpected fashion.*"   Here are his own words :

"*We probably expect, especially if we have read Marlowe's 'Faustus,' the tale of an immortal soul bartered away for a life of ecstasy, and the tragedy of the thirst for all knowledge, and the desire for all pleasure satisfied, and yet insatiable. What we do get is merely a hint of this, the foundation of such a story, the premisses of the question.*"

The young read it and may be disappointed at first. They expect Helen of Troy, they get Gretchen (and they don't at first realise this may be better) ; they expect Marlowe's Mephistophelis or Milton's Satan, and at first sight they do not realise the icy deadliness of Goethe's " affable familiar Ghost " ; they perhaps realise the pathos of the Gretchen episode, they feel to a certain extent the suggestiveness of the ideas ; but they say : " Is this all ? "   " Is it on account of this that Goethe is ranked with Dante and the creator of *Hamlet* and *Lear* ? ”

Yet they realise, perhaps, that the more they read *Faust*, the more they are impressed, the more there seems left to read in it ; they have an uneasy feeling they have not quite got to the bottom of it—at least, so the following sentence written by the A. J. seems to testify :

" *The more one reads ' Faust ' the more striking it appears, the more it grows upon one, till at last we regard and judge it, not as a fabric of art, but as one of Nature's secluded haunts in forest, valley, mountain or bay : barren and somewhat desolate, unimpressive at first sight, devoid of obvious attractions, and yet a spot which, after a time, inspires the traveller who revisits it with a certain awe, and with a sense of harmony in its very incompleteness and ruggedness, which, in spite of its manifestations of restlessness, in tree, wave or wind, is nevertheless a PLACE OF PEACE.*"

But, in spite of this, in spite of the magnetic atmosphere, in spite of the beautiful passages, surely it cannot be said that " Faust " is an achievement as great as the plays of Shakespeare or Sophocles ? Nobody ever dreamt of saying any such thing about Goethe's remaining works, then why (asks the A. J.) *is Goethe placed with Shakespeare and Dante ?*

How are we to account for Goethe's towering reputation, and for the unanimity of praise that is conceded to him ?

The answer to the Present-Day Self seems a simple one : it is that Goethe, in the first part of *Faust*, in the whole of the Gretchen episode, and in about a dozen of his lyrics, wrote some of the very best poetry in the world. The quantity doesn't matter. Nearly all Sappho's work is lost ; that does not prevent us from giving her, on the merits of what we have, the very highest place among lyrists. We judge poets and dramatists, as some one has said (Mr. Shaw ?) by their strongest links, and the strongest links of Goethe are as strong as the strongest links of any of the greatest poets in the world. At least, that is the contention of the middle-aged enthusiast.

In the love story of Gretchen, and in these dozen lyrics, Goethe wrote poetry which is *as good as the very best*. There is none better. In these poems he reached the Homeric-Shakespearean high-water mark : the line of divine simplicity, where there is nature, and nothing else ; no style, no ornament, no effort ; just the ordinary simple thing said in the simplest possible way, with the result that it is sublime, inimitable, and unapproachable. He did what Homer does nearly all the time, what Shakespeare and Dante do very often, namely, to say what should be quite ordinary things in such a way—it looks so simple and yet is so inexpressibly out of reach of the ordinary writer—that when you read the actual phrases you can hardly believe your eyes. For instance, when he says :

> " Denkt Ihr an mich ein Augenblickchen nur,
> Ich werde Zeit genug an Euch zu denken haben."

Or again :

> " Sie hören nicht die folgenden Gesänge,
> Die Seelen, denen Ich die ersten sang."

You get the same effect, or rather, you find the same thing in the greatest masterpieces of architecture, sculpture, painting, and music, in the Parthenon frieze and the Temple of Pæstum, in the portraits of Velasquez, in the chorales of Bach, and in certain phrases of Beethoven, Mozart, and Schubert.

Goethe was a man of science, say some, and therefore not a poet. He came as near being a poet as a man of science can, they argue ; but is not the truth rather that whether a man of science or not, he was not only a man of profound intellect, with a scientific bent and a scientific habit of mind, but a great man ? " Voilà un homme ! " Napoleon said when he saw him. Inspiration descended upon that intellect, and upon that greatness, like the rod of Moses on the rock ; and out of that towering fastness, that mountain of mind, that cliff of wisdom, the waters flowed ; and one drop of that water is perhaps more precious than all the fountains of Victor Hugo, Pushkin, and all the modern poets you choose to mention, although the rainbow plays in them and they reflect the sun. Goethe's came from a greater mind, and the world, like a vulgar merchant or a simple child, whichever you will, knows that the brand of Goethe denotes a still more precious and more valuable merchandise than the gorgeous jewels of Victor Hugo, the many-coloured beads of Pushkin, and all the various gems of the other modern poets. The world is right in the long-run ; for although it may stop its ears or listen to false gods, in the end it will re-echo the voice of God.

VI

It is, of course, true that outside the first part of *Faust*, and about a dozen lyrics, Goethe wrote a mass of work which, although sometimes extremely beautiful, and nearly always interesting, is not up to that high, rare level. He went on writing until he was over eighty, and the Heaven-sent moments, when inspiration came to him, grew rarer as his life went on.

Victor Hugo went on writing throughout his long life as well, but time seemed to have no effect on him. He seemed to be like an Æolian harp which remained absolutely stationary. It continued to respond, whenever it was swept by the wind, in exactly the same way, and to produce exactly the same kind of music. The lyrics in his posthumous volumes are just as beautiful in kind and degree as those he wrote when he was quite a young man.

But in examining the poetry of Victor Hugo, it is as well to let the Advocate of Youth take the stage and speak. He is better fitted for the task, and I quite agree with a great deal of what he says, although I am no longer capable of such vehement expression.

" *It is tempting to define Victor Hugo as the typical bard, and it is probably in this character that he appears to most of us ; but the prophetic mantle of Victor Hugo is to his real genius as stage accessories are to a play of Shakespeare's. Divest him of the illusions he had as to his importance as a man of action and a politician—illusions which were magnified and intensified by his prodigious imagination—and you have left an artist as conscious and deliberate as Giotto drawing his circle. Not only was he gifted with the most frenzied inspiration, he had also the faculty of controlling it ; he rode Pegasus when that animal was in its most undisciplined mood with the most unrelenting of curbs, and with the surest of hands.*

" *Here is an example of this quality of imagination under direction. They are perhaps the finest verse he ever wrote— his high-water mark—and they were certainly not excelled by any French poet of his century :*

> " ' L'ombre était nuptiale, auguste et solennelle ;
> Les anges y volaient sans doute obscurément,
> Car on voyait passer dans la nuit, par moment,
> Quelque chose de bleu qui paraissait une aile.
>
> La respiration de Booz qui dormait,
> Se mêlait au bruit sourd des ruisseaux sur la mousse.
> On était dans le mois où la nature est douce,
> Les collines ayant des lys sur leur sommet.

8

Ruth songeait et Booz dormait ; l'herbe était noire ;
Les grelots des troupeaux palpitaient vaguement ;
Une immense bonté tombait du firmament ;
C'était l'heure tranquille où les lions vont boire.

Tout reposait dans Ur et dans Jérimadeth ;
Les astres émaillaient le ciel profond et sombre ;
Le croissant fin et clair parmi ces fleurs de l'ombre
Brillait à l'occident, et Ruth se demandait,

Immobile, ouvrant l'œil à moitié sous ses voiles,
Quel dieu, quel moissonneur de l'éternel été
Avait, en s'en allant, négligemment jeté
Cette faucille d'or dans le champ des étoiles.'

" *Victor Hugo's poetic qualities are, first and foremost, poetical imagination. No other poet of this century, except perhaps Coleridge, saw such visions, and presented them in so definite a form. His vision is equally penetrating whether he saw, or whether he imagined ; and, as a carved crystal, his genius reflected every ray and colour of nature in the rainbows of its facets : again, as an echoing dome it vibrated and re-echoed to the sounds and voices of the universe. Nature plays on him and he interprets nature ; so that he is less like a passive Æolian harp on which the wind plays, than the bow, to which Nature, as he says in one of his poems, is the harp :*

" ' La nature est la grande lyre,
Et le poète est l'archet divin.'

He is the Wagner of poetry, in whose soul the mysterious voices of nature reverberate, and he expresses the elemental secrets of sky and sea, of forest and fire, of dawn and the sunrise, of dusk and the stars in a multitudinous orchestration in which each individual evolution is subordinated to and dominated by one ruling mind. Compared with this army of instruments, the poems of Goethe resemble the rare deliberate melodies of an accomplished but unequal violinist,

*who at times achieves the utmost perfection in the richness
and purity of his tone."*

Isn't the comparison of a violinist with an orchestra
somewhat equivalent to comparing quality with quantity,
and does it not seem as if the art of the performer were
being compared with the genius of a composer? However, one sees what the author was trying to say, although
he didn't say it; and letting that be, accepting the
metaphor and the challenge, cannot a passage by a great
composer, played by a great interpreter on a violin, be
as beautiful as any orchestral Wagnerian catastrophe or
climax? And as for interpreting nature: what about
the following lines?

> " Ueber allen Gipfeln
> Ist Ruh,
> In allen Wipfeln
> Spürest Du
> Kaum einen Hauch ;
> Die Vöglein schweigen im Walde.
> Warte nur, balde
> Ruhest Du auch."

There is no orchestration here, but the effect is as awe-
inspiring as that of a solemn sunset.

Victor Hugo in his old age wrote a most beautiful
poem on this same theme. It has all his old magic and
all the glamour of his sonorous imagery and poignant
utterance. I will quote it in full :

> " Un hymne harmonieux sort des feuilles du tremble ;
> Les voyageurs craintifs, qui vont la nuit ensemble,
> Haussent la voix dans l'ombre où l'on doit se hâter.
> Laissez tout ce qui tremble
> Chanter !
>
> Les marins fatigués sommeillent sur le gouffre.
> La mer bleue où Vésuve épand ses flôts de soufre
> Se tait dès qu'il s'éteint et cesse de gémir.
> Laissez tout ce qui souffre
> Dormir !

Quand la vie est mauvaise on la rêve meilleure.
Les yeux en pleurs au ciel se lèvent à toute heure ;
L'espoir vers Dieu se tourne et Dieu l'entend crier.
Laissez tout ce qui pleure
Prier !

C'est pour renaître ailleurs qu'ici-bas on succombe.
Tout ce qui tourbillonne appartient à la tombe.
Il faut dans le grand tout tôt ou tard s'absorber.
Laissez tout ce qui tombe
Tomber ! "

Victor Hugo says a great deal more than Goethe ; but he says, surely, much less. He writes a beautiful poem, but Goethe writes a great poem, one of the greatest. I will let the Youthful Advocate proceed :

" *In addition to his imaginative power, Victor Hugo's two principal qualities are, perhaps, his unsurpassed lyrical gift and his sense of pathos. He seldom thought, but he felt, and more generously than Goethe ; he experienced not only sadness and melancholy, but a profound and all-embracing pity for human beings: the rich pity of Virgil for mortal things. Goethe's lyric lyre had but practically one string : the reflective ; Victor Hugo's has a thousand ; he ' wakes to ecstasy the living lyre ' ; he strikes a note of passion which Goethe never knew. If Goethe has the ' thoughts that breathe,' then Victor Hugo has the ' words that burn,' in such lyrics as ' Gastibelza,' ' Le Chasseur Noir,' and ' Puisqu' ici bas toute âme.' *"

It is here that I join issue most vehemently with the Youthful Author. It seems to me, now, that Victor Hugo's love lyrics, beautiful and delicate and fanciful as they are, are always a little cold ; they have not the passion of Musset or Verlaine, and there is, I think, more real passion in Gretchen's song :

" Meine Ruh ist hin,"

than in all Victor Hugo's love lyrics put together. There

is in it the passion of a broken heart ; there is no such utter abandonment of desperate passion in Victor Hugo. Read the poem through :

" Meine Ruh ist hin,
Mein Herz ist schwer;
Ich finde sie nimmer
Und nimmermehr.

Wo ich ihn nicht hab',
Ist mir das Grab,
Die ganze Welt
Ist mir vergällt,

Mein armer Kopf
Ist mir verrückt,
Mein armer Sinn
Ist mir zerstückt.

Meine Ruh ist hin,
Mein Herz ist schwer;
Ich finde sie nimmer
Und nimmermehr.

Nach ihm nur schau' ich
Zum Fenster hinaus,
Nach ihm nur geh' ich
Aus dem Haus.

Sein hoher Gang,
Sein' edle Gestalt,
Seines Mundes Lächeln,
Seiner Augen Gewalt,

Und seiner Rede
Zauberfluss,
Sein Händedruck,
Und ach sein Kuss !

Meine Ruh ist hin,
Mein Herz ist schwer;
Ich finde sie nimmer
Und nimmermehr.

> Mein Busen drängt
> Sich nach ihm hin.
> Ach, dürft' ich fassen,
> Und halten ihn,
>
> Und Küssen ihn
> So wie ich wollt',
> An seinen Küssen
> Vergehen sollt'!"

Again, in such a lyric as the famous

> "Wer nie sein Brod mit Thränen ass,
> Wer nie die kummervollen Nächte
> Auf seinem Bette weinend sass,
> Er kennt Euch nicht, Ihr himmlischen Mächte!
>
> Ihr führt ins Leben uns hinein,
> Ihr lasst den Armen schuldig werden,
> Dann überlasst ihr ihn der Pein:
> Denn alle Schuld rächt sich auf Erden,"

Goethe may be said to express a depth and quality of grief and passion in words that scald like "tears of molten lead," and such as only happen when a great man is inspired to speak his soul in supreme verse. If this poem were all that remained of Goethe's work, it would be enough, so I now venture to think, to put him with Shakespeare and Dante.

VII

"*But*," the *Advocatus Juventutis* will say: "*what if Victor Hugo had less depth of passion than the German, what if he could never have touched Goethe's grave note that sets in motion endless vibrations of thought, what if he could never attain to his supreme moments of Homeric simplicity, we must not forget that Victor Hugo had his own unique and incomparable gifts. Goethe, it may just*

*as well be argued, could never have attained to the winged
passion, the grace, the freshness, the delicacy of a song such
as the ' Chanson d'Eviradnus ' in ' La Légende des Siècles.'
Victor Hugo's verse in lyrics such as this has the prismatic
splendour, the iridescent texture as of a dragon-fly or a
nautilus shell, or of some fugitive being made of ' spirit,
fire and dew.'*

*" Again, in many of his lyrics—and these, I think, are
greater than his love lyrics—there is a childlike simplicity
and a tenderness of the kind we find in the poems of Catullus :
here, as in the case of Michael Angelo, ' out of the strong
comes forth sweetness.'   His short lyrics have the intangible
charm of a spray of surf or of a thread of dewdrops, and
yet they are as distinct and delicate in outline as a crocus.
Here are some examples of what I mean."*

The following two stanzas, the beginning of a longer
poem, are examples of his soap-bubble-like lightness and
beauty :

> " Toute est lumière, toute est joie.
>   L'araignée au pied diligent
>   Attache aux tulipes de soie
>   Ses rondes dentelles d'argent.
>
>   La frissonnante libellule
>   Mire les globes de ses yeux
>   Dans l'étang splendide où pullule
>   Tout un monde mystérieux."

The following two poems are examples of his pathos
and simplicity, also of his unique characteristics.   They
are the essence of Victor Hugo.

" L'ENFANCE

> " L'enfant chantait ; la mère au lit exténuée,
>   Agonisait, beau front dans l'ombre se penchant
>   La mort au-dessus d'elle errait dans la nuée,
>   Et j'écoutais ce râle, et j'entendais ce chant.

L'enfant avait cinq ans, et près de la fenêtre
Ses rires et ses jeux faisaient un charmant bruit ;
Et la mère, à côté de ce pauvre doux être
Qui chantait tout le jour, toussait toute la nuit.

La mère alla dormir sous les dalles du cloître ;
Et le petit enfant se remit à chanter.
La douleur est un fruit ; Dieu ne le fait pas croître
Sur la branche trop faible encor pour le porter."

"L'enfant, voyant l'aïeule à filer occupée,
Veut faire une quenouille à sa grande poupée.
L'aïeule s'assoupit un peu ; c'est le moment.
L'enfant vient par derrière, et tire doucement
Un brin de la quenouille où le fuseau tournoie,
Puis s'enfuit triomphante, emportant avec joie
La belle laine d'or que le safran jaunit,
Autant qu'en pourrait prendre un oiseau pour son nid."

" *Again, there is Victor Hugo's sense of pity, his pathos ; it is here, perhaps, that his true greatness lies ; in his poems on children, on the poor, the suffering and sorrowful, the captive and the conquered, and all those who are desolate and oppressed. His poem on the death of his daughter, entitled ' A Villequier,' is, as in the English language, Gray's ' Elegy,' the natural language of grief ; and the ' Tristesse d'Olympio,' which is generally admitted by French critics to be one of the four greatest love poems in the French language, is the most perfect expression of the sadness that hangs about the memory of happy times, the melancholy fragrance of the past ; and it contains lines which are magical in their power of evocation, such as :*

" ' Les grands chars gémissants qui reviennent le soir.' "

Here I interrupt once more to remark that if it is pity you want, there is as much pity in Goethe's little poem, "Vor Gericht," than in the whole of *Les Misérables*, and that is, as I know, saying a great deal, for it is not for nothing that *Les Misérables* was the favourite book in Dartmoor

prison, and called by the convicts " Less Miserable."
I will quote the whole of Goethe's poem :

"VOR GERICHT

" Von wem ich es habe, das sag' ich euch nicht,
   Das Kind in meinem Leib.—
Pfui ! speit ihr aus : die Hure da !—
   Bin doch ein ehrlich Weib.

Mit wem ich mich traute, das sag' ich euch nicht.
   Mein Schatz ist lieb und gut,
Trägt er eine goldene Kett' am Hals,
   Trägt er einen strohernen Hut.

Soll Spott und Hohn getragen sein,
   Trag' ich allein den Hohn.
Ich kenn' ihn wohl, er kennt mich wohl,
   Und Gott weiss auch davon.

Herr Pfarrer und Herr Amtmann ihr,
   Ich bitte, lasst mich in Ruh !
Es ist mein Kind, es bleibt mein Kind,
   Ihr gebt mir ja nichts dazu."

(Note the last line of stanza 3.)
And for expressing the melancholy of the past, has it
ever been done with more poignant majesty and with
more moving dignity than in the dedication to *Faust* ?

" *Yes*," the *Advocatus Juventutis* says, " *I know that
Goethe was a great thinker, that he always thought and
sometimes felt ; that to the moments when he felt we owe
the power and pathos of ' Faust ' and the few lyrical masterpieces ; I know that his verse reaches at times to the level
of perfect beauty ; but don't you see that Victor Hugo
had gifts just as unique ? that he was a wizard who not
only saw visions and heard voices denied to other mortals,
but was endowed with the craft and cunning of a Merlin,
and was able to make his infinite dreams visible in concrete*

jewels or in shapes and textures as impalpable as fairy soap-bubbles? And just as Wagner can shatter our nerves with the tragedy of the fall of Valhalla, with the love and death of Tristan and Isolde, or entrance us with the rustic notes of a shepherd's pipe or the call of a horn in the wood, so can Victor Hugo distil his rapture or his sorrow into a dewdrop of song as simple as a tear, or weave for us, as in La Légende des Siècles, *out of the harmonies of wind and wave, out of the ' gloom of earthquake and eclipse,' phantasmagorias of light and sound, of cloud and flame. Like Shelley's ' Pan' :*

> " ' He sang of the dancing stars,
> He sang of the dædal earth.'

" *Consequently, it might be argued that if the first qualities of poetry are imagination and music, as many critics and poets have contended—Swinburne, for instance— passion, emotion, and vision expressed in song, the poet of ' La Légende des Siècles,' ' Les Châtiments,' and ' Les Contemplations,' must rank above the creator of Faust. On the other hand, if criticism of life, philosophy, and suggestiveness are the more important factors, then Goethe is immeasurably the greater poet.*"

And so we get back to the beginning of the argument, as I stated it at the outset. My answer is that it is not a question, on the one hand, of thought and philosophy *versus* imagination and fire on the other hand ; that both poets had a combination of both, that Victor Hugo at moments had more fantasy and that Goethe at moments had more passion, but there were times when each of them reached his high-water mark of thought and expression, when the fusion of all that was in them, the whole of their nature and the whole of their heart, their whole soul and their highest powers, were exerted in delivering their message. I maintain now that at such moments Goethe's supreme utterance reaches a higher level than that of Victor Hugo, and I refer the *Advocatus Juventutis* to Gretchen's speeches and songs, Mignon's songs, the Roman Elegies, " Prometheus," the " Trilogie der Leidenschaft," and, above all, to the " Dedication " to *Faust*.

All these things seem to me more momentous as utterances, while being just as perfect artistically, than the most important poems of Victor Hugo—say, for instance, " Booz," " Tristesse d'Olympio," " A Ville-quier," and the " Chanson d'Eviradnus."

But, in any case, we can enjoy both. And after all it is only examiners who seek to make such comparisons.

VIII

" *As artists, both Goethe and Victor Hugo suffered,*" says the *Advocatus Juventutis*, " *from the same fault, although it is manifested in different ways, namely, a want of the sense of proportion. With Victor Hugo it took the shape of confusing the great with the grandiose, and the grandiose with the puerile, and this led him often from the sublime to the ridiculous. His genius was like that Djinn in the ' Arabian Nights,' found in a chest by a fisherman. It towers to the sky in an instant of time. It is a colossal, chaotic want of proportion, which sometimes leads him to sheer absurdity. With a few alterations and some com-pression,* Les Misérables *would make an excellent harlequinade. People are constantly coming through the window, the fireplace, the ceiling, or the drains, anyhow but by the front door. You could not make the ' Elective Affinities,' do what you would, into a Christmas pantomime, and this is, perhaps, a merit on the negative side. With Goethe,"* the A. J. proceeds, *" the fault took the form of a want of concentration, a diffuseness, an incurable incompleteness. Goethe's work often resembles his own famous comparison about Hamlet. It is a tree planted in a flower-pot ; the tree grows and the flower-pot is shattered."*

I should say now that although this criticism is untrue about the lack of proportion, it is true about the lack of completeness in Goethe's work. Goethe says, in his conversations with Eckermann, that all poetry should be *occasional* ; he deprecates the undertaking of a large whole ; and even his greatest works were written at odd moments, and from time to time (some parts of them at one moment of his life, others when he was far older). But, like many other great poets, he wrote his best things in rare moments of inspiration ; but in addition to this, he wrote whenever he felt inclined ; he always wrote well, because he could not write badly, nor could he write in an uninteresting way ; but the moments when he reached the high-water mark of his inspiration, although they are not entirely confined to his youth, were, given the length of his life, comparatively rare. Victor Hugo, on the other hand, reached his high-water mark, and his low-water mark, constantly and sometimes simultaneously, throughout his lifetime ; there are no drab epochs in his life. His work has the same gorgeous qualities, the same crying defects throughout, and his artistic competency and craftsmanship never fail him.

Only the difference between Goethe and Victor Hugo is, I think, when all is said and done, what I have already said—namely this : that Goethe's high-water mark is that of the very greatest poets of all time ; Victor Hugo's high-water mark is that of the greatest poets in the second class. Goethe, although his title-deeds for a place may be slender, is nevertheless with Homer, Shakespeare, and Dante, whereas Victor Hugo is with Byron, Shelley, Leopardi, Pushkin ; and the reason is perhaps that Goethe was a great man and poet as well ; Victor Hugo, although he was more than a mere poet, was not a great man.

In saying this, I am merely repeating the verdict of the world at large, of the European man in the street. I have tried to give a few sidelights on the grounds and possible causes for such a verdict.

1807-1923.

LA FONTAINE'S *FABLES*

I

WHEN I was a child I was given the *Fables* of
La Fontaine to learn by heart in the schoolroom. These *Fables* played the same part to other
poetry as the meat at luncheon did to the pudding.
I was not allowed to learn a poem by Victor Hugo, say,
or Casimir Delavigne, which I thought so much more
exciting, till I had learnt my Fable. I used to think the
Fables tedious and incomprehensible, and I realise now
that the reason was that I understood very little of the
words. I thought " Va-t'en, chétif insecte," was all one
word : Vatenchétivinsecte, a formula of exorcism. It
never occurred to me that *Le rat de ville* was a rat. I
thought *Rat-de-Ville* was a proper name, and that *ortolans*
was a place like Orléans.

Later on, at school, I had to read La Fontaine for an
examination, and I used to annoy our excellent French
master by saying the *Fables* were not poetry. " What
about the English poets ? " he used to retort. " You
cannot say that what they write is *verse*."

His favourite modern poet was Ponsard, a dramatist
whose plays I also had to read for the same examination,
and whom the French master praised for the smoothness
of his lines. They were terribly smooth, as smooth as
they were flat. It was a modern play in verse that we
had to read, called *L'honneur et l'argent*. It reminded me,

later, a little of Lord Lytton's *Money* as to its substance, and the less inspired portions of Tennyson as to its style.

But our French master's favourite poet was, nevertheless, La Fontaine, and he sympathised to a certain extent with my want of appreciation. " They are not meant for boys, nor for the young," he said, speaking of the *Fables*. " You will appreciate them when you are forty ; but not before."

It was true.

One of the compensations for what some one called " Le néant d'avoir quarante ans," is to be able to appreciate the *Fables* of La Fontaine. At least that has been my experience. At the present moment, I should put him at the head of all the French poets. I think he is the most unique. The other great French poets enter into competition with the great poets of other nations, and meet with formidable rivals, equals, at any rate, if not superiors. Shakespeare is as good a comic dramatist as Molière, and he wrote *Lear* and *Romeo and Juliet* and the Sonnets, into the bargain. Victor Hugo sang as one inspired on many themes, and evoked a host of gorgeous visions, but he saw nothing more marvellous than the visions of Coleridge, and his music is less celestial than that of Shelley, and no more sumptuous than that of Swinburne. Musset struck a wonderful chord of passion, but Byron did the same thing, and wrote *Don Juan* and the *Vision of Judgment* into the bargain.

Shakespeare equalled Racine's passion and knowledge of the female heart in *Antony and Cleopatra* and in all his tragedies, and he far excels him as a comic dramatist.

But La Fontaine has no rival and no equal in the literature of Europe. Nobody can approach him nor touch him in his sphere. In Russia there is, it is true, an admirable writer of fables, namely, Krilov ; but while he rivals La Fontaine when he is serious, and when he is describing nature, in raciness and in charm, La Fontaine leaves him far behind in the deftness and sharpness of satire, and in the general level of elegance, grace, wit, and distinction.

Krilov, weighed with him, seems heavy and coarse, and his style compared with that of the French poet seems at times wantonly careless and even slovenly.

La Fontaine was called by his contemporaries the " inimitable," and nothing has occurred in the kingdom of literature since his death, in France, or indeed anywhere else, to make us wish to qualify or to reverse this verdict.

One other point, he is the most French of all the French authors. He has developed to the full the gifts and qualities that are most peculiarly and exclusively French ; a lightness as of the bubbles of Vouvray wine, a texture of style as delicate as the finest lace, a wit as unobtrusive and as radiant as a thread of gossamer on a September morning, a brush that deals with colour as delicately and as economically as Corot, as poetically, sometimes, as Watteau, as realistically as Millet, a pencil as firm in outline as that of Ingres, a lucid, solid fund of good sense, a savour of the Gallic soil ; and something homely, familiar, racy, " tasting of Flora and the country green," the farmhouse and the vivid talk of country folk ; something proverbial, like Mrs. Poyser's conversation ; in fact, *Der Volkston*.

II

It is a curious thing that La Fontaine's *Fables* should have become one of the principal assets and weapons of the children's schoolroom and the schoolboy's classroom. One cannot help thinking that it is the last thing that La Fontaine would have wished himself. Children often learn the fables without understanding (as I have already pointed out) what they are about, and they may, moreover, be pleased at the mention of some of the animals. But a more grown-up work in substance than La Fontaine's *Fables* does not exist.

La Fontaine in these little pictures gives the abstract and chronicle of the whole of his time and period—the whole of the *Grand Siècle*. The life he observes is highly centralised, centralised around the Court. The King is the centre of the solar system—a gorgeous, irresponsible sun ; his favour means life, his disfavour means death : eclipse is death. Around him swarm a host of courtiers, each of them not only striving for his place in the sunlight, but, at the same time, doing his best to oust his neighbour and to thrust him into the shade. Then come the Powerful, the men who count, the major courtiers, and beneath these their lesser fleas, their satellites and parasites ; the minor courtiers, who have still smaller fry—still lesser fleas—dependent upon them.

La Fontaine does not confine his observation to Court life ; beneath the courtiers and the *noblesse* and the squires, come the clergy, the monks, the *bourgeoisie*, the men of business, the law and all the learned professions, magistrates, doctors, professors, pedants, schoolmasters, schoolboys even—merchants, tradesmen, and, finally, the people, the workers, the artisans, the peasants, the labourers.

La Fontaine describes them all. He looks life straight in the face and sees all round his characters just as Homer did. He is, indeed, a miniature Homer ; he

9

describes life as it is, without making things either
better or worse. His is the true *comédie humaine*. His
slender books of fable deserve that title more than the
monumental work of Balzac, because he looks at life
without the aid of any distorting glass. He is, perhaps,
the first and last realist in the whole of French literature.
He looks at life without illusions. It is a sorry spectacle,
a sad world; but he makes the best of it; a little common
sense will carry one a long way. Common sense, charity
(but it depends to whom, he tells us), and tolerance are
the only lubricants that enable one, he thinks, to cope
with the creaking machinery, the clumsy, ramshackle
vehicle of life, and he not only uses them freely himself,
but is for ever advocating their need and their use.

But it is a cruel world, this brilliant epoch of Louis
XIV., although we know he feels it is no worse than what
has been, nor than what will be. It is a world where
there is no mercy, no pity, no hope, and no escape for
the downtrodden ; it is a world sharply divided into two
categories : the powerful and the helpless ; capital
and labour ; the master and the slave, and the slave
goes to the wall. There is one law for the powerful and
one for the weak ; one for the rich and one for the poor :

"La raison du plus fort est toujours la meilleure."

"Selon que vous serez puissant ou misérable
   Les jugements de cour vous rendront blanc ou noir."

First of all there is the King, symbolised by the lion,
who addresses his minor subjects as " miserable insect "
or " miserable creature " as the case may be. The lion
can do no wrong. If, as he is sometimes generous enough
to admit, he has chanced to eat a few sheep and perhaps
the shepherd as well, his creatures tell him that he confers
on them, by so doing, a great favour, and an honour.

The fox, who in the fables is the symbol of all the courtiers, says to him :

> " Vous leur fîtes, Seigneur,
> En les croquant, beaucoup d'honneur ;
> Et quant au berger, l'on peut dire
> Qu'il était digne de tous maux."

The Court is pictured as a world that is glittering without, but hollow, false, and pitiless within.   Here is La Fontaine's own definition :

> " Je définis la cour un pays où les gens,
> Tristes, gais, prêts à tout, à tout indifférents,
> Sont ce qu'il plaît au Prince, ou, s'ils ne peuvent l'être,
> Tâchent au moins de le paraître ;
> Peuple caméléon, peuple singe du maître ;
> On dirait qu'un esprit anime mille corps ;
> C'est bien là que les gens sont de simples ressorts."

He says to the courtiers :

> " Vous êtes dans une carrière,
> Où l'on ne se pardonne rien."

And he sums up their life in a brief phrase :

> " Bref, se trouvant à tout, et n'arrivant à rien."

Put not your trust in the mighty, he seems to repeat on every page, and least of all in Princes.   And he adds a little piece of advice at the end of the fable from which my longer quotation is taken, which, perhaps, throws a more sinister light and is more penetrating in its intuition than anything he has said so far.   It is this :

> " Amusez les rois par des songes,
> Flattez-les, payez-les d'agréables mensonges :
> Quelque indignation dont leur cœur soit rempli,
> Ils goberont l'appât ; vous serez leur ami."

Beguile the mighty of the earth with fables and vain

imaginings ; however indignant they may have been to start with, they will swallow the bait.

When one reflects not only how true this is, but how disastrous the results of such worldly wisdom may be, say in the case of the unfortunate Emperor Nicholas II. and Rasputin, La Fontaine's intuition appears positively terrifying.

The courtier in the fables is symbolised throughout by the fox, who is, with his fine coat and magnificent brush, his infinite resource, his cunning, his agility, the perfect incarnation of the courtier who is greedy, impudent, pitiless, but, at the same time, witty, full of resource and presence of mind. Sometimes he overshoots the mark and is too clever, and suffers for it ; but, as a rule, he gets so much the best of it that even his enemies and his victims are forced to admire and applaud his ingenuity. La Fontaine sums up the complete deadliness of his perfidy in the fable of the sick Lion.

The Lion is sick and old, and sends for the doctors. They arrive from every quarter with their remedies and advice, only the fox remains absent ; and the wolf arrives and calumniates his absent comrade. The Lion, greatly incensed, gives orders for the fox to be smoked out of his lair and brought into his presence. The fox arrives and understands what the wolf has been about. He has not been able to come before, he says, because he had been making a pilgrimage and praying for the King's health. He had even during his travels met with some wise and clever men who told him that His Majesty, the Lion, was simply suffering from cold, and that the sole remedy was the coat of a wolf who has *just* been flayed alive. Nothing can exceed the terseness and the vigour of expression with which the fox on this occasion is made to express himself by La Fontaine :

> " D'un loup écorché vif appliquez-vous la peau
> Toute chaude et toute fumante ;
> Le secret sans doute en est beau
> Pour la nature défaillante.
> Messire loup vous servira,
> S'il vous plaît, de robe de chambre."

If the fox is the consummate knave, the wolf is the more foolish evil-doer, the clumsy, squalid, and miserable dupe. He thieves, but without profit. He does evil, but he is unhappy and derives no profit ; he is the type of the poor, miserable criminal in all times and in all countries ; exploited by knaves, punished by the just, despised by the successful, frowned on by the respectable, and overlooked by the virtuous.

Then we have the cat : the religious hypocrite, soft in mien and gait :

" une humble contenance, un modeste regard, et pourtant l'œil luisant."

He is the type of the Pharisee, the hypocrite of the Church—the clergy and the religious orders, just as the fox is the hypocrite of the Court.

Then we have the smaller fry : the clumsy bear ; the stupid, honest dog ; the patient, long-suffering jackass ; and, last of all, the sheep and the lamb who are destined to be eaten.

Yes, it is a cruel world that La Fontaine unrolls before us, more cruel than the jungle which Mowgli found so unkind. The icy flippancy of La Fontaine's thrifty *fourmi*, with her unflinching economy and her scathing wit, is more pitiless and cruel than the coils of Kipling's Python Kaa.

III

But if it is a cruel world, if Nature and all her inhabitants and inmates and dependants are pitiless, " red in tooth and claw," if man is envious, shallow, and ungrateful, if the mighty crush the weak, if there does not appear to be " une trace de justice pour les moutons " ; if the whole of life seems to consist in futile hopes and prematurely interrupted dreams that are never realised, such as the day-dream of Perrette and the *Pot-au-lait*, and the Curé Chouart's speculation of what the burial of the corpse will bring him in, which is so rudely and fatally interrupted by the leaden coffin falling on him and crushing his skull ; if life be but

" un vain bruit,"

there are, nevertheless, two attributes in it which La Fontaine notices, prizes, and praises with as much charm and eloquence as any writer—ancient or modern— and these are love, and the beauty of nature ; besides the *vain bruit*, there is *l'amour*.

The world is very beautiful, and nobody appreciated this fact more clearly and nobody painted the aspects of nature more faithfully, with surer mastery and greater gusto, than La Fontaine. It is on this aspect of his genius, and on this aspect alone, that I want to dwell and end. Ample justice has been done to the various and numerous sides of his genius by more capable pens and by many exalted writers ; but in England, in any case, it has not perhaps been sufficiently pointed out—it cannot be too often pointed out—that La Fontaine is a supreme, a unique interpreter of nature. To say that he rivals Virgil and Horace, Crabbe and Tennyson, as a lover and a painter of landscape, would astonish many, and yet it is, none the less, no exaggeration. The country and the landscape he paints is the beautiful country of northern France, and no other French writer, with the exception of Guy de Maupassant, has left us more vivid and more unforgettable pictures of French landscape than he.

In 1914, when the war broke out, I took part in the retreat from Mons to Coulommiers, and passed almost every day and almost every night of that exciting period in a different village. The country we passed through, the little villages, the farmhouses, the gardens we stayed in or fed in or slept in, seemed, during those uncannily beautiful August days and nights, like the landscapes in La Fontaine's fables which had suddenly come to life, and sometimes the human incidents which took place seemed to be the rough material out of which La Fontaine would have made an exquisite fable. For instance, I remember having luncheon in a farmhouse at a place called Sérès, with a prosperous family. It was just such a host and just such a family as La Fontaine would have described in two or three words. Near the house was a beautiful, well-stocked garden, and the fruit trees were literally weighed down with fruit—pears, apples, plums. There was a smell of cider in the air ; we were given excellent food. And while the old lady of the house was courteously doing the honours, a great discussion was taking place between her and the different members of the family. A fat, bearded, middle-aged man, his bourgeois wife and his cousin, were trying to persuade his mother-in-law, the lady of the house, to go away. She said she had been through the war in 1870, and that she considered one ought to stay in one's house till the end : householders and priests should never desert their posts. The son-in-law said this was ridiculous, and everything was packed up in a great hurry and a cart was harnessed. In the end they persuaded the old lady that she must go ; the Germans, they said, were not five miles off. The old lady gave in ; but when everything was ready and the cart was harnessed, she went out by herself in her little black bonnet and sat in the garden—the beautiful prosperous garden—and she laughed bitterly.

Here were all the actors, I thought, and here the stage was set for one of La Fontaine's fables.

I will illustrate his variety and power of description by a series of quotations. In the case of La Fontaine one can never have too many quotations, and when one lover of the poet's works presents his favourites to another lover, the latter will retort with an entirely new series which had escaped the notice of the first admirer.

I will begin by an invocation to solitude :

> " Solitude, où je trouve une douceur secrète,
> Lieux que j'aimai toujours, ne pourrai-je jamais,
> Loin du monde et du bruit, goûter l'ombre et le frais ?
> Oh ! qui m'arrêtera sous vos sombres asiles ?
> Quand pourront les neuf Sœurs, loin des cours et des villes,
> M'occuper tout entier, et m'apprendre des cieux
> Les divers mouvements inconnus à nos yeux,
> Les noms et les vertus de ces clartés errantes
> Par qui sont nos destins et nos mœurs différentes !
> Que si je ne suis né pour de si grands projets,
> Du moins que les ruisseaux m'offrent de doux objets !
> Que je peigne en mes vers quelque rive fleurie !
> La Parque à filets d'or n'ourdira point ma vie,
> Je ne dormirai point sous de riches lambris :
> Mais voit-on que le somme en perde de son prix ?
> En est-il moins profond, et moins plein de délices ?
> Je lui voue au désert de nouveaux sacrifices.
> Quand le moment viendra d'aller trouver les morts,
> J'aurai vécu sans soins, et mourrai sans remords."

Are not these lines worthy to stand beside any of the numerous invocations in which Virgil and Horace expressed their weariness of the bustle and strife of towns and town life, and their desire for and delight in the solitary retreats of the country ?

> " Rura mihi et rigui placeant in vallibus amnes ;
> Flumina amem silvasque inglorius. O ubi campi,
> Spercheusque, et virginibus bacchata Lacænis
> Taygeta ! O qui me gelidis convallibus Hæmi
> Sistat et ingenti ramorum protegat umbra ! "

Or :

> " Dulce pellitis ovibus Galaesi
> Flumen, et regnata petam Laconi
> Rura Phalantho."

And now for a little private gallery of pictures and vignettes :

> " Il arriva qu'au temps que la chanvre se sème,
> Elle vit un manant en couvrir maint sillon."

(A suggestion of Millet here.)

> " Un Agneau se désaltérait
> Dans le courant d'une onde pure."

(What divine economy ! What an illustration of his favourite maxim, *Rien de trop* !)

> " Le long d'un clair ruisseau buvait une Colombe,
> Quand sur l'eau se penchant une Fourmis y tombe."

(Note the exactness of the observation, the *reserve* in the expression.)

> " Dans le cristal d'une fontaine
> .Un Cerf se mirant autrefois . . .
>
> C'est un parterre où Flore épand ses biens ·
> Sur différentes fleurs l'abeille s'y repose,
> Et fait du miel de toute chose."

(What ease there is in his touch !)

> " Progné me vient enlever les morceaux:
> Caracolant, frisant l'air et les eaux,"

(What life and what accuracy of vision !)

" Il s'en alla passer sur le bord d'un étang.
Grenouilles aussitôt de sauter dans les ondes ;
Grenouilles de rentrer en leurs grottes profondes."

(A divine snapshot.)

" Ils arrivèrent dans un pré
Tout bordé de ruisseaux, de fleurs tout diapré,
Où maint mouton cherchait sa vie :
Séjour du frais, véritable patrie
Des Zéphirs.

L'onde était transparente ainsi qu'aux plus beaux jours ;
Ma commère la Carpe y faisait mille tours
Avec le Brochet son compère."

These hang on the walls of the first room of my little picture-gallery : they are all of them fresh and gleaming landscapes, exquisitely painted.

In the next room there is a chosen collection of Watteau-like pictures :

" Eh ! ne voyez-vous pas, dit-elle,
Que la fin de cette querelle
Sera l'exil de l'un ; que l'autre, le chassant,
Le fera renoncer aux campagnes fleuries ?
Il ne régnera plus sur l'herbe des prairies."

(Just a touch of wistfulness—a prophecy of Verlaine's note.)

" Tircis, qui pour la seule Annette
Faisait résonner les accords
D'une voix et d'une musette
Capables de toucher les morts,
Chantait un jour le long des bords
D'une onde arrosant des prairies
Dont Zéphyre habitait les campagnes fleuries."

And here, another Watteau :

" Guillot, le vrai Guillot, étendu sur l'herbette,
Dormait alors profondément ;
Son chien dormait aussi, comme aussi sa musette
La plupart des brebis dormaient pareillement."

My next room is filled with examples of the painter's more realistic, more " modern " manner :

> " La sœur de Philomèle, attentive à sa proie,
> Malgré le bestion happait mouches dans l'air,
> Pour ses petits, pour elle, impitoyable joie,
> Que ses enfants gloutons, d'un bec toujours ouvert,
> D'un ton demi-formé, bégayante couvée,
> Demandaient par des cris encor mal entendus.
>
>   L'Escarbot indigné
> Vole au nid de l'oiseau, fracasse, en son absence,
> Ses œufs, ses tendres œufs, sa plus douce espérance :
>
> Les Alouettes font leur nid
> Dans les blés quand ils sont en herbe,
> C'est-à-dire environ le temps
> Que tout aime et que tout pullule dans le monde.
>
>   Du palais d'un jeune Lapin
>   Dame Belette, un beau matin,
>   S'empara : c'est une rusée.
>   Le maître étant absent, ce lui fut chose aisée.
>   Elle porta chez lui ses pénates, un jour
>   Qu'il était allé faire à l'Aurore sa cour
>   Parmi le thym et la rosée."

This picture of the rabbit and the dew and the thyme is as delicate and silvery as a Corot ; and here there is a touch of Monet :

> " Un jour, dans son jardin il vit notre Ecolier
> Qui, grimpant sans égard sur un arbre fruitier,
> Gâtait jusqu'aux boutons, douce et frêle espérance."

Come to another room, devoted to pictures which are completely realistic. These are, as far as detail and reality are concerned, as true, as familiar, and as direct as a picture by Teniers. Here you have the description first of a little garden, just such a garden as the one I described as having seen during the Retreat ; and it was fated to be destroyed by a *grand seigneur*

whom the owner of the house had unfortunately called in
to hunt a hare, just as, who knows, the house that I saw
was subsequently ravaged by the circumstances of war.

> " Un amateur du jardinage,
>   Demi-bourgeois, demi-manant,
>   Possédait en certain village
> Un jardin assez propre, et le clos attenant.
> Il avait de plant vif fermé cette étendue.
> Là croissait à plaisir l'oseille et la laitue,
> De quoi faire à Margot pour sa fête un bouquet,
> Peu de jasmin d'Espagne, et force serpolet."

Next, the unforgettable picture of the stage-coach climb-
ing the hill :

> " Dans un chemin montant, sablonneux, malaisé,
>   Et de tous les côtés au soleil exposé,
>   Six forts chevaux tiraient un coche.
>   Femmes, moine, vieillards, tout était descendu ;
>   L'attelage suait, soufflait, était rendu."

Another picture, Dutch in its realism and its frank-
ness :

> " Dès que l'Aurore, dis-je, en son char remontait,
>   Un misérable Coq à point nommé chantait ;
>   Aussitôt notre Vieille, encor plus misérable,
>   S'affublait d'un jupon crasseux et détestable,
>   Allumait une lampe, et courait droit au lit
>   Où, de tout leur pouvoir, de tout leur appétit,
>   Dormaient les deux pauvres Servantes.
>   L'une entr'ouvrait un œil, l'autre étendait un bras ;
>   Et toutes deux, très mal contentes,
> Disaient entre leurs dents : Maudit Coq ! tu mourras !"

And, finally, the grimmest, saddest picture of all—the
poor woodcutter—typical of the whole working population of France in La Fontaine's day—almost an Albrecht
Dürer :

" Un pauvre Bûcheron, tout couvert de ramée,
  Sous le faix du fagot aussi bien que des ans
  Gémissant et courbé, marchait à pas pesants,
  Et tâchait de gagner sa chaumine enfumée.
  Enfin, n'en pouvant plus d'effort et de douleur,
  Il met bas son fagot, il songe à son malheur.
  Quel plaisir a-t-il eu depuis qu'il est au monde ?
  En est-il un plus pauvre en la machine ronde ?
  Point de pain quelquefois, et jamais de repos :
  Sa femme, ses enfants, les soldats, les impôts,
        Le créancier, et la corvée,
  Lui font d'un malheureux la peinture achevée.
        Il appelle la Mort."

In a little gallery connecting the rooms, there is a little
picture which hangs by itself, for it is unlike the others.
It glows like an enamel :

" Est-ce à toi d'envier la voix du Rossignol,
  Toi que l'on voit porter à l'entour de ton col
  Un arc-en-ciel nué de cent sortes de soies ? "

In another room, there is one large picture which hangs
by itself—without a rival. It is the most " important "
picture in the collection and is generally considered to be
the painter's " masterpiece." Only a Frenchman and
only La Fontaine could have painted it :

" A l'heure de l'affût, soit lorsque la lumière
  Précipite ses traits dans l'humide séjour,
  Soit lorsque le soleil rentre dans sa carrière,
  Et que, n'étant plus nuit, il n'est pas encor jour,
  Au bord de quelque bois sur un arbre je grimpe,
  Et, nouveau Jupiter, du haut de cet Olympe,
        Je foudroie, à discrétion,
        Un lapin qui n'y pensait guère.
  Je vois fuir aussitôt toute la nation
        Des lapins, qui, sur la bruyère,
        L'œil éveillé, l'oreille au guet,

S'égayaient, et de thym parfumaient leur banquet.
Le bruit du coup fait que la bande
S'en va chercher sa sûreté
Dans la souterraine cité.
Mais le danger s'oublie, et cette peur si grande
S'évanouit bientôt ; je revois les lapins,
Plus gais qu'auparavant, revenir sous mes mains."

I think I have quoted enough to show that La Fontaine is one of the most accurate, faithful, and skilful observers of nature and painters of landscape. He is as minute as Tennyson in his observation, as true as Crabbe, and as poetical as Keats, and withal what grace, what charm, what a bewitching accent, what an inimitable gesture !

IV

Before taking leave of La Fontaine, although it is outside the framework of what I intended, I cannot help paying, as it were, three special little tributes to three of his masterpieces ; and if you wish to place garlands on La Fontaine's shrine, you must weave them of his own verse ; for there is nothing else in this world delicate and rare enough for the purpose.

The first is to one of the best known of all his fables. Just for the pleasure of seeing the lines in print, I cannot resist quoting the opening of the *Deux Pigeons*, and of adding, that those who had the good fortune of hearing Sarah Bernhardt recite the opening of this fable, which she used to do in *Adrienne Lecouvreur*, heard what I cannot help thinking must have been the high-water mark of human utterance : the most perfect words, recited in the most perfect and poetical manner :

" Deux Pigeons s'aimaient d'amour tendre :
L'un d'eux, s'ennuyant au logis,
Fut assez fou pour entreprendre
Un voyage en lointain pays.
L'autre lui dit : ' Qu'allez-vous faire ?
Voulez-vous quitter votre frère ?
L'absence est le plus grand des maux.' "

My second tribute is to the graver, more robust side of La Fontaine, which one is apt to overlook, so captivated is one by his charm and his grace. Nevertheless, just as Horace showed in his stanzas on Regulus what a fine, manly note as of bronze he could blow through his delicate instrument, so La Fontaine from time to time as, for instance, in his fable of *Le Paysan du Danube* and in that of *Le Mort et le Mourant*, struck a note of incomparable majesty and dignity. The few lines I will quote from the latter fable will prove it ; they are well known, but they cannot be quoted too often :

" La Mort avait raison. Je voudrais qu'à cet âge
On sortît de la vie ainsi que d'un banquet,
Remerciant son hôte, et qu'on fît son paquet ;
Car de combien peut-on retarder le voyage ?
Tu murmures, vieillard ! Vois ces jeunes mourir ;
    Vois-les marcher, vois-les courir
A des morts, il est vrai, glorieuses et belles,
Mais sûres cependant, et quelquefois cruelles."

(Note the familiarity, the *Volkston*, in the third line.)

Finally, I wish to pay tribute to the fable which is my special favourite, and which is less well known. It is the story of *Le Berger et le Roi*. The King, seeing that the shepherd was a capable shepherd, promoted him to be a judge. He left his flock : " Il avait du bon sens ; le reste vient ensuite," says La Fontaine. But presently, the very sincerity and merits of the judge raised suspicion. People began to intrigue ; those whom he had condemned accused him of peculation ; he had, it was said, built himself a palace out of his ill-gotten gains. Some went so far as to say that he had a chest with ten locks, full of precious stones. The chest was opened, and inside all his detractors found were his peasant's clothes ; and we will let La Fontaine tell the rest of this story, for never was a story more exquisitely told and more beautifully ended :

> " Le coffre étant ouvert, on y vit des lambeaux,
>   L'habit d'un gardeur de troupeaux,
> Petit chapeau, jupon, panetière, houlette,
>   Et, je pense, aussi sa musette.
> ' Doux trésors, ce dit-il, chers gages, qui jamais
> N'attirâtes sur vous l'envie et le mensonge,
> Je vous reprends : sortons de ces riches palais
>   Comme l'on sortirait d'un songe !
> Sire, pardonnez-moi cette exclamation :
> J'avais prévu ma chute en montant sur le faîte.
> Je m'y suis trop complu ; mais qui n'a dans la tête
>   Un petit grain d'ambition ? ' "

1923.

RACINE

I

WHAT I am going to write immediately would be unintelligible to an educated Englishman in the eighteenth century or even at the beginning of the nineteenth century. I wish merely to state a simple fact : that Racine is a great poet and a great dramatist. It is, of course, taken for granted in France. In the eighteenth century and at the beginning of the nineteenth century it was also taken for granted in England, not only by the literary world, not only by the elect and the élite, but also by the ordinary educated man. It is a sad fact that culture decreases as education spreads. The truth of the matter is that the spread of education does not mean that people are better educated, but that more people are semi-educated : the spread of education means the extension of half-baked education. To say now that you admire Racine is equivalent to being considered an exclusive superior person. In the eighteenth century or at the beginning of the nineteenth century, such a taste, I repeat once more, would have been taken as a matter of course, not only in the literary but in the educated world. I can furnish a good example : Harriet Wilson, the famous courtesan, mentions in her memoirs one of her admirers—I forget which—Mr. Brougham, I think, who (certainly not a superior person) was passionately devoted to French tragedy. This

was in the year 1815 ; compare that with the situation
nowadays. Nowadays, even in the literary world,
although the young are now said to approve of him, it is
considered slightly supercilious to admire Racine. Two
or three generations ago, when Matthew Arnold was the
high priest of culture, he told literary England that they
need not admire French poetry, least of all the French
poetry of the seventeenth century. This set the intellectuals who did not know French at rest for generations
to come ; but it simply meant that he did not know
French well enough to understand, to appreciate, and to
feel what did or did not constitute the excellence or the
difference of French verse. Mr. Edmund Gosse, from
time to time, would say a word which showed that he
was of the true faith ; Mr. Arthur Symons did the same
thing more explicitly and more elaborately ; and later on,
Mr. Lytton Strachey, in his *Outline of French Literature*
and in a subsequent collection of literary essays, pointed
out the subtle beauties of Racine as a dramatist and as a
poet. But it was all useless ; they all of them preached
to deaf ears ; they are only considered—not by the general
public, but by the literary public—to parade their
superiority. Soon after Mr. Lytton Strachey's latest
book came out, the late Mr. Maurice Hewlett wrote an
article in *The Times* in which he said that there was no
difference between Voltaire's plays and those of Racine,
and he added that he felt certain, in saying such a thing,
that when Mr. Lytton Strachey became aware of the
statement, he would turn up his intellectual nose or
beard in scorn. My point is, that at the bottom of all
this, there is a great misunderstanding based on a very
simple fact. Those intellectual English people who
when certain other people—intellectual or otherwise—
say that they admire or enjoy Racine, put down the

admirers as the perpetrators of a given pose, are quite sincere ; but they do not happen to know French well enough to see the values which differentiate one kind of verse written in the seventeenth century from another kind. " Who are you," the reader will say, " to arrogate to yourself the right of appreciating values which, you say, escaped the notice of such gifted people ? " The answer is—through no merit of my own, but merely by accident, I happened to learn French as a child and, therefore, the difference between such values is to me to a certain extent—I say to a certain extent only, I do not pretend that these matters affect me in the same way as they affect a Frenchman—these things, I repeat, are to me *to a certain extent* plain. I think, too, I can explain how the misunderstanding arises.

An Englishman is confronted with certain verses from Racine ; for instance, take any two typical lines from *Andromaque* or *Phèdre* :

> " Captive, toujours triste, importune à moi-même,
> Pouvez-vous souhaiter qu' Andromaque vous aime ? "

> " J'ai voulu, devant vous exposant mes remords,
> Par un chemin plus lent descendre chez les morts,"

and he is told that such lines are exquisite. In form and manner, as well as in substance, they seem to him almost indistinguishable from certain other lines of, say, Voltaire, which, he is told by the same authorities, although they may be possibly clever and competent, are different in kind. Take, for instance, any two lines from Voltaire's *Zaïre* : I open the book at random :

> " Mon frère, ayez pitié d'une sœur egarée,
> Qui brûle, qui gémit, qui meurt désesperée."

He says " bosh," for the two things are exactly alike : in

a way they are very much alike ; but there is just the difference. " The little more and how much it is ; the little less and what worlds away." To any English literary man it is extremely easy to give an instance which will explain the whole matter. Take English poetry. Tell a Frenchman who can speak English, say, quite fluently enough to teach boys at a school ; tell such a Frenchman, I repeat, that the English poets write very good verse. He will receive the remark with scepticism, but he may make an effort to believe you ; he will ask for an instance. If you give him certain examples, lines in which there is, say, a gorgeous image or a flash of imagination or a profound thought which translation can neither conceal, nor dim, nor spoil, he may concede that there is something in it, something there which, although he cannot entirely apprehend, he will grant may be evident in the original and to the barbarous ears of the English. But give him a line of poetry from one of our great poets, from one of our greatest poets, in which the greatness of the writing depends not necessarily on a profound thought, not necessarily on a gorgeous image, not necessarily on a combination of music and imagination ; but simply and solely on the *style* : take a passage just written by a great English poet and which any trained and educated Englishman would agree is great *verse* : or take any passage from Milton's *Paradise Lost* or *Paradise Regained*—show it to a foreigner who knows English, or rather to a Frenchman who knows English (because some foreigners are too sympathetic, too catholic, too receptive)—and the Frenchman in question will not see any difference between what you have shown him and the lines of a fiftieth-rate poet, say Robert Montgomery. I will now open *Paradise Regained* at random and quote a few lines :

> " Here thou behold'st
> Assyria, and her empire's ancient bounds,
> Araxes and the Caspian lake ; thence on
> As far as Indus east, Euphrates west,
> And oft beyond ; to south the Persian bay,
> And, inaccessible, the Arabian drouth."

Equally at random I will quote lines from a poet who has been pilloried by Lord Macaulay as being one of the worst poets who ever achieved popularity. Here are the lines :

> " O Death ! thou dreadless vanquisher of earth,
> The Elements shrank blasted at thy birth !
> Careering round the world like tempest wind,
> Martyrs before, and victims strew'd behind ;
> Ages on ages cannot grapple thee,
> Dragging the world into eternity ! "

Now give the educated Englishman, who knows French well enough to read and to converse, the following lines from Racine : I open *Britannicus* at random :

> " Excité d'un désir curieux,
> Cette nuit je l'ai vue arriver en ces lieux,
> Triste, levant au ciel ses yeux mouillés de larmes,
> Qui brillaient au travers des flambeaux et des armes ;
> Belle, sans ornement, dans le simple appareil
> D'une beauté qu'on vient d'arracher au sommeil."
>
> *Britannicus*, Act II. Scene 2.

I will now take five lines at random from a volume of Casimir Delavigne's plays, from *Les Enfants d'Édouard* :

> " Je ne les ôte pas, ces anges bien-aimés.
> Qu'un ami généreux protège leur enfance,
> Qu'ils restent sur la terre, et que je les devance,
> Quand ils prendront leur vol vers l'asile de paix,
> Où la mère et les fils ne se quittent jamais.
> Adieu."
>
> *Les Enfants d'Édouard*, Act III. Scene 10.

I maintain that it will be as rare for the Englishman to see the difference between the verse of Racine and the

verse of Casimir Delavigne, as it would be for the Frenchman to see the difference between the verse of Milton
and the verse of Robert Montgomery. Or if this example
be thought too violent in its extremes, take two lines
from *Lycidas* :

> " Ay me ! whilst thee the shores and sounding seas
>   Wash far away, where'er thy bones are hurl'd " ;

what difference would a foreigner see between the
calibre of such verse and a line, say, of a well-
known poet of the second order, say Southey, for
instance :

> " And when she pours her angel voice in song,
>   Entranced he listens to the thrilling notes,"

and I feel confident that a foreigner would not see any
greater difference between the two samples than an
Englishman sees between the verse of Racine and
Voltaire.

That is all I have got to say on the subject of modern
depreciation of Racine by English intellectuals. I will
now proceed as if they all took for granted that Racine
was a great poet and a great dramatist, which is what
all educated Frenchmen do.

II

Is Racine the greatest of French poets ? I will not be
so bold as to answer. There is Molière, and there is La
Fontaine. Molière as a dramatist is more universal,
and La Fontaine as a poet is more peculiar—by more
peculiar I mean more exceptional. He is a product of
France and of France only, and is *hors concours* in his
line, whereas Racine competes with all the poets of the

world. It is unnecessary to draw up a list, to place him here or there, above this one or below that one. It is enough to say that he is a great poet, and I think one could safely add that his work constitutes the purest gem of French dramatic literature. There is no drama in French literature which is at the same time so passionate, so strong (as far as the matter is concerned), so disciplined as to the form, so truthful, and so poetical. Let us take him first as a dramatist. As a playwright, he is a writer of human plays—of plays which, although they are about kings and queens, ancient Greeks, Roman emperors, Jews, Turks, and Sultanas—are in reality French men and French women of the epoch of Louis XIV. That is to say, they are men and women, and that is enough. The style in which they talk matters no more than their wigs, or their broad brocaded hoops. All that is a question of externals ; it is the frame, the vehicle, the cup ; if the cup is exquisite, the wine is none the less exhilarating. Mozart's music is none the less divine because it is written for an eighteenth-century harpsichord.

Under the trappings of the eighteenth century, Racine discerned and portrayed the eternal passions of the human heart, and although his verse has the accent of his epoch it has also, since it is sincere, noble, and beautiful, an underlying note which belongs to all time. There is nothing tedious about his drama in itself ; actors can make it tedious by acting it badly ; but when it is well acted, it is not considered tedious by the crowd, by the holiday-makers in Paris : it fills a large theatre ; it is popular ; it pays. Badly acted it disgusts—to see *Phèdre* badly acted is an excruciating experience—that is another question. It is not of any age, but for all time ; the theme, and the manner in which the theme is dealt with, appeals just as much to an audience of the present day as it did to audiences in the days of Louis XIV. Take, for instance, the play of *Bérénice*. It is built out of a sentence of Suetonius. *Titus reginam Beronicen, cui etiam nuptias pollicitus ferebatur . . . statim ab urbe dimisit invitus invitam* ; or, as Racine translates it, " Titus qui aimoit passionnément Bérénice, et qui même, à ce qu'on croyait, lui avait promis de l'épouser, la renvoya de Rome, malgré lui, et malgré elle, dès les premiers jours de son empire." That is the whole subject of the play. There are no incidents and no action. Racine, in his preface to the play, comments on this lack of incident in the following manner :

" Il n'y a que le vraisemblable qui touche dans la tragédie. Et quelle vraisemblance y a-t-il qu'il arrive en un jour une multitude de choses qui pourraient à peine arriver en plusieurs semaines ? Il y en a qui pensent que cette simplicité d'action est une marque de peu d'invention. Ils ne songent pas qu'au contraire toute l'invention consiste à faire quelque chose de rien, et que tout ce grand nombre d'incidents a toujours été le refuge des poètes qui ne sentaient dans leur génie ni assez d'abondance, ni assez de force pour attacher durant cinq actes leurs spectateurs par une action simple, soûtenue de *la violence des passions, de la beauté des sentiments, et de l'élégance de l'expression.*"

There is no action, but out of this *rien* Racine has made a perfect work of art, which rivets our attention and touches our feelings by the passion, the beauty of what is felt and how it is said.

I wish to analyse this play ; but I wish to translate it from the particular terms in which it is written into more general terms. The subject of the play, as it is written, concerns the marriage of Titus, emperor of

Rome, and Bérénice, queen of Palestine : an unsuitable match. The marriage has been arranged ; it is to happen—such is the latest gossip—immediately. Titus, the emperor of Rome, is desperately in love with Bérénice, queen of Palestine, and is determined to marry her whatever the drawbacks may be ; but there is another person who is in love with Bérénice, and you can call him Antiochus, king of Commagene, or you can call him Mr. Jones. In the first act we learn through a conversation between Mr. Jones and a friend of his that Mr. Jones has loved Bérénice for five years, but that she has never loved him. At last he presents an ultimatum ; he tells her that he has made up his mind to leave Rome for ever ; and when she asks him why, he says to her : I have loved you all this time although I have said nothing about it, and I can no longer bear your " friendship," which means that you tell me every day, in detail, how and how much you love some one else. He says good-bye ; and his way of expressing what he feels affords a fine example of Racine's talent ; of his knowledge of the human heart, and of his power of expressing what he knows. The words might have been spoken in Rome in the days of the Cæsars, or at Versailles at the Court of Louis XIV., or in Paris or in London to-day, or anywhere. So long as unrequited passion exists, and so long as a man loves a woman who in her turn needs him merely as a friend—so long as this situation exists, the following speech will always seem poignant and new :

> " J'évite, mais trop tard,
> Ces cruels entretiens où je n'ai point de part.
> Je fuis Titus ; je fuis ce nom qui m'inquiète,
> Ce nom qu'à tous moments votre bouche répète :
> Que vous dirai-je enfin ? Je fuis des yeux distraits,
> Qui, me voyant toujours, ne me voyaient jamais.

Adieu. Je vais, le cœur trop plein de votre image,
Attendre, en vous aimant, la mort pour mon partage.
Surtout ne craignez point qu'une aveugle douleur
Remplisse l'univers du bruit de mon malheur ;
Madame, le seul bruit d'une mort que j'implore
Vous fera souvenir que je vivais encore.
Adieu."

So much for the first act.

In the second act we see Titus, emperor of Rome, the statesman, the public man, the man of duty, talking over the question of his marriage with his private secretary. He asks his secretary what impression his marriage would make on public opinion, on the man in the street ; he tells him he wishes to know the truth. The secretary tells him the truth ; and the truth, as usual, is unpleasant ; it is to the effect that the Emperor's marriage with the Queen of Palestine would be looked upon by the man in the street as a disgrace, an insult, a national calamity. The Emperor repeats the story of his love—it has never been stronger than it is now—he confides the hope he has entertained that his love might one day be fulfilled with the crowning end of marriage ; but at the same time he confesses that he has no delusions about the effect of his marriage. He knows quite well what his subjects would think about it. He only says this so as to hear his own feelings confirmed by another. He knows quite well that he must sacrifice his own private happiness to the public welfare, and he realises what it will mean both to her whom he loves and to himself. His friend—the man we have called his private secretary—whom Racine calls Paulin—applauds his patriotism and his sense of duty, and the Emperor speaks as follows :

" Ah ! que sous de beaux nôms cette gloire est cruelle !
Combien mes tristes yeux la trouveraient plus belle,
S'il ne falloit encor qu'affronter le trépas ! "

Bérénice, he says, was the cause of his regeneration and his victories, those which he won over himself and those which he won over his enemies :

> " Je lui dois tout, Paulin. Récompense cruelle !
> Tout ce que je lui dois va retomber sur elle :
> Pour prix de tant de gloire et de tant de vertus,
> Je lui dirai : Partez, et ne me voyez plus."

Nothing could be more true to life, nor more subtly expressed, than the speech which I am about to quote, and in which he tells his friend the truth about his relations with Bérénice. It is what we call *modern* ; when in a Greek play, or in Cicero's *Letters*, or an Icelandic Saga, we feel that something hits the bull's-eye because it expresses what we ourselves have felt, we call it *modern* ; it would be more correct to call it *human*, because it is neither ancient nor modern, but eternal. The following passage is human :

> " PAULIN.
>
> Sur cent peuples nouveaux Bérénice commande.
>
>
> TITUS.
>
> Faibles amusements d'une douleur si grande !
> Je connais Bérénice, et ne sais que trop bien
> Que son cœur n'a jamais demandé que le mien.
> Je l'aimai ; je lui plus. Depuis cette journée,
> (Dois je dire funeste, hélas, ou fortunée ?)
> Sans avoir, en aimant, d'objet que son amour,
> Etrangère dans Rome, inconnue à la cour,
> Elle passe ses jours, Paulin, sans rien prétendre
> Que quelque heure à me voir, et le reste à m'attendre.
> Encor, si quelquefois un peu moins assidu
> Je passe le moment où je suis attendu,
> Je la revois bientôt de pleurs toute trempée :
> Ma main à les sécher est longtemps occupée.

> Enfin, tout ce qu'amour a de nœuds plus puissants,
> Doux reproches, transports sans cesse renaissants,
> Soin de plaire sans art, crainte toujours nouvelle,
> Beauté, gloire, vertu, je trouve tout en elle.
> Depuis cinq ans entiers chaque jour je la vois.
> Et crois toujours la voir pour la première fois."

After this Titus tried to tell Bérénice the truth, but he breaks down ; he cannot bring the words across his lips. He leaves her in bewilderment, but with a faint suspicion of the truth ; she suspects it, but dismisses it from her mind.

In the third act the Emperor commands his friend to tell the whole truth to Bérénice, and, further, he commits her to his charge ; he bids them both leave Rome together. But the friend in question is almost convinced that if he should break the news to Bérénice, her love for the Emperor would turn to hate. He breaks the news to her as gently as he can ; at first she disbelieves it, but when, at last, she is convinced, stunned and overcome by the news, she bids the Emperor's friend, namely, Antiochus, king of Commagene, or Mr. Jones, leave her sight, and never come back no more.

In the fourth act we come to the climax. Titus and Bérénice meet when she is fully aware of the truth. Titus tells her that life to him without her will be as death ; his life can but end with their separation :

> "Scheiden ist der Tod!"

after that, he will go on reigning, but not living. She answers him in what are, perhaps, the most beautiful lines of the play :

> "Hé bien, régnez, cruel, contentez votre gloire :
> Je ne dispute plus. J'attendais, pour vous croire,
> Que cette même bouche, après mille serments
> D'un amour qui devait unir tous nos moments,

Cette bouche, à mes yeux s'avouant infidèle,
M'ordonnât elle-même une absence éternelle,
Moi-même j'ai voulu vous entendre en ce lieu.
Je n'écoute plus rien : et, pour jamais, adieu, . . .
Pour jamais ! Ah, seigneur ! songez-vous en vous-même
Combien ce mot cruel est affreux quand on aime ?
Dans un mois, dans un an, comment souffrirons-nous,
Seigneur, que tant de mers me séparent de vous ;
Que le jour recommence et que le jour finisse
Sans que jamais Titus puisse voir Bérénice,
Sans que de tout le jour je puisse voir Titus ? "

Here we reach the high-water mark of Racine's verse :
the words are those of everyday conversation, the sentiments exactly what a woman in the situation of Bérénice
would say at any time in any country, and the effect that
of great poetry. Never has the immense despair of
separation been contracted into so close an utterance.
For the moment Titus hesitates, but, finally, he regains
his self-control, and he recalls the countless examples
of self-sacrifice on the part of his ancestors. Bérénice
leaves him saying she means to kill herself, and the
Emperor is summoned to the Senate House.

In the last act Bérénice has decided to take her life ;
she means to leave Rome, leaving a letter behind for the
Emperor, telling him what she has done. The Emperor,
being informed that she means to go, insists on seeing
her once more : they meet. He tells her that his love is
stronger than ever, and she upbraids him with toying
with her despair. He reads the letter which she had
written to him when she meant to kill herself, and he
says his cup of sorrow is full, that since she is determined to die, he can no longer battle with life ; but—
and this is what gives nobility and dignity to his character
and to his speech—he is resolved more than ever now,
not to disobey the dictates of his conscience, nor to
thwart the wishes of his people :

> " L'Empire incompatible avec votre hyménée
> Me dit qu'après l'éclat et les pas que j'ai faits
> Je dois vous épouser encor moins que jamais."

He will not leave all and follow her, for, he says, she would merely be ashamed of him for having chosen thus. This is what he says :

> " Il est, vous le savez, une plus noble voie ;
> Je me suis vu, Madame, enseigner ce chemin
> Et par plus d'un héros et par plus d'un Romain ;
> Lorsque trop de malheurs ont lassé leur constance,
> Ils ont tous expliqué cette persévérance
> Dont le sort s'attachait à les persécuter
> Comme un ordre secret de n'y plus résister."

The end is brought about by Antiochus (Mr. Jones), who reveals to the Emperor that he has loved Bérénice for so long. Now that I have brought you together, I hope that you both will live happily for ever after ; as for me, I shall not live at all ; I shall kill myself. Bérénice, self-disgusted, blames herself for being the cause of all this trouble, and, with serene resignation, bids a last farewell to Titus. She explains to him what she has passed through. She had feared at first that he had ceased to love her ; but now that she has realised her mistake, she is willing to leave him, and ready to live. She bids Antiochus learn submission from her example, and from that of Titus :

> " Je l'aime, je le fuis ; Titus m'aime, il me quitte :
> Portez loin de mes yeux vos soupirs et vos fers.
> Adieu. Servons tous trois d'exemple à l'univers
> De l'amour la plus tendre et la plus malheureuse
> Dont il puisse garder l'histoire douloureuse.
> Tout est prêt. On m'attend. Ne suivez point mes pas.

> (*à Titus*.)
> Pour la dernière fois, adieu, Seigneur.

> ANTIOCHUS.
> Hélas ! "

Racine shows his instinct in ending the drama softly
with a sigh : the " Hélas " of Antiochus.   Thus, at the
end, *dimisit invitus invitam*.   Coventry Patmore's " Ode "
applies to the final situation :

> " With all my will, but much against my heart,
>   We two now part.
>   My Very Dear,
>   Our solace is, the sad road lies so clear.
>
>   .   .   .   .   .   .
>
>   .   .   .   .   .   .
>
>   Go thou to East, I West."

This play would be just as interesting if transposed in
terms of 'Arry and 'Arriet, and if it all took place in
Green Park, or on Hampstead Heath, on a Bank holiday.

I have analysed the play thus, in detail, in order to
show the framework of Racine's architecture—to show
how out of nothing he produces a play more rich in
human interest, more poignant and passionate, than
dramas crowded with incident and noisy with action ;
arousing our pity and our interest, simply, as he says,
by the nobility of the sentiments, the conflict of the
passions, and the beauty of the language : and thus
attaining high ends by simple means.   *Bérénice* remains,
and probably will remain, the final utterance of the
tragedy of lovers separated by the conventions of the
world.   Just as, in *Macbeth*, Shakespeare said the last
word on the subject of murder, and touched every fibre
of the psychological situation, so does Racine in *Bérénice*
exhaust the possibilities of the subject of the seemingly
causeless but inevitable separation of lovers ; the conflict
between love and duty which it brings with it ; the various
phases of hope, fear, doubt, altercation, despair, reconciliation, and submission which this twofold conflict
passes through.

Even in a bald analysis such as I have made, the harmonious proportions of the construction will be apparent. But the play must be read, and still better, seen played (fortunate are those who have seen Madame Bartet—the ideal Bérénice—in the part!), for the delicate gradations to be appreciated by which the scale of passion rises, swells, and subsides, and dies away on a note of melancholy resignation. The architectural beauty of Racine's work, the reasonableness of proportion, the purity of outline, the absence of any jarring note, of anything forced, exaggerated, or unnecessary, are nowhere better displayed than in this play. The drama arises naturally and inevitably from the characters, and the circumstances in which the characters are placed— the one acting on the other—and proceeds, step by step, to its logical and inevitable close. We know from the first that, given the character of Titus, and the circumstances in which he is placed, he cannot possibly marry Bérénice, and that however deeply she may suffer, no misunderstanding can be finally possible between the two lovers. The great merit of this kind of work is apparent when we compare it with that of lesser masters. In such plays the drama, instead of arising out of the characters of the persons, is brought about by an external and fortuitous *Deux ex machinâ*. Misunderstanding is caused in such plays not tragically, by the blundering of souls in the darkness, but in a concrete fashion, by the intercepting of letters, or the overhearing of conversation behind doors, or possibly the arras. Racine, on the other hand, knows and is able to show, that there is quite enough in the human soul to cause tragedy, without having recourse to the adventitious aid of any melodramatic trickery, accident, or coincidence. Here character is destiny and " passions spin the plot." To

find a parallel to this in modern drama, we have to turn
to Ibsen and Maeterlinck ; or to Turgenev's novels
and Tolstoy's and Tchekov's plays.

I said that in *Bérénice* Racine exhausted the subject of
separation. You will realise this if you see or read one
of the most successful plays of modern times : M.
Donnay's *Amants*, the play which made the author's
reputation. It is a modern *Bérénice*, or rather, as
M. Lemaître called it, a *Bérénicette* ; its fundamental
framework is built upon precisely the same lines as
Racine's work.

Bérénice illustrates in the subtlest manner the first
great fact about Racine's genius ; his power of psychological analysis and presentation. The psychology of
all his dramas is as true, as subtle, and as " modern "
as that of any modern French or even Russian psychologist. The " classical " drama arising from the incidents
of everyday life is just as strong as is the " realist "
drama of Ibsen. The passion from being expressed
with dignity and restraint is none the less vehement and
even violent. Racine's women are as wild in their
impulses, as uncontrolled in their passion, whether it be
ambition or love, fear or rage, as any of the heroines of
Bourget or Alexandre Dumas fils, or Bernstein. If you
wish to test the quality of Racine's dramatic power at its
youngest and at its freshest, you must turn to *Andromaque*. Here the quality of the passion is swifter and
more fiery, more youthful, perhaps, than in any of his
other plays. *Andromaque* is to Racine's work what
Swinburne's *Atalanta in Calydon* is to his other plays ;
it has the high, pure note as of silver cymbals and celestial
harps. The verses blossom like white lilies, and march
past in white and shining ranks. But in order to realise
Racine's full power as a dramatist and as a psycholo-

gist, his insight into the human heart, his sensibility ;—
his unique blend of sensitiveness and violence, it is
necessary to study *Phèdre* ; to read it and to re-read it,
and to see it played.

Phèdre is without doubt the most important play in the
French classical repertoire. It is the *Hamlet* of the
French stage, and the actress who triumphs in the part
must needs be a great personality. *Phèdre* is too well
known to need any analysis or description ; but there
is one point to which I should like to call attention.
It is this : the objection which is made to all Racine's
plays about the discord between the remoteness of his
subject-matter and the seventeenth-century accent and
tone of his characters, has been more vehemently urged
in the case of *Phèdre*, since, whereas the framework and
central idea of the play are Greek, its spirit is Christian.
But in making Phèdre herself a Christian, conscious
of her guilt, and horrified at herself, Racine has merely
heightened the tragedy of her plight. Again, what I
have already said about the eternal fundamental essence
of Racine's characters and the superficial and external
nature of their manner and accent, applies especially
to this case. For the important fact about *Phèdre*
is that, just as in *Bérénice*, Racine wrote the eternal
tragedy of separation, so in *Phèdre* he gives us the eternal
tragedy of the woman who is the prey of an involuntary
criminal passion ; and nowhere has this passion been
more faithfully portrayed, nor the gradation of the
martyrdom more subtly traced. Here are two instances
of Racine's delicacy of treatment. The first occurs in
the initial scene between Phèdre and Œnone, before
she has confessed her guilty secret ; she lets the first
hint of it be perceptible when suddenly, in a moment
of distraction—and unconsciously giving way to her

dominating preoccupation ; the thought of Hippolyte—
she says :

> " Dieux, que ne suis je assise à l'ombre des forêts ?
> Quand pourrai-je, au travers d'une noble poussière,
> Suivre de l'œil un char fuyant dans la carrière ? "

Could any indication be more subtly introduced ?

The second passage occurs when Phèdre, after having
confessed her passion to Hippolyte, learns that her
husband Theseus is still alive.

> " Mourons. De tant d'horreurs qu'un trépas me délivre ;
> Est-ce un malheur si grand que de cesser de vivre ?
> La mort aux malheureux ne cause point d'effroi.
> Je ne crains que le nom que je laisse après moi.
> Pour mes tristes enfants quel affreux héritage !
> Le sang de Jupiter doit enfler leur courage :
> Mais quelque juste orgueil qu'inspire un sang si beau,
> Le crime d'une mère est un pesant fardeau,
> Je tremble qu'un discours, hélas ! trop véritable
> Un jour ne leur reproche une mère coupable !
> Je tremble qu'opprimés de ce poids odieux
> L'un ni l'autre jamais n'osent lever les yeux."

Nothing could be more exquisitely delicate and
tender ; nothing more true : no utterance more dignified.
It is especially in his women that Racine is psychologically most successful. Women in his work play a more
important part than men, although the studies of
Mithridates, and of Nero in *Britannicus* rival those of
Hermione and Phèdre in subtlety. Certainly among his
women-characters the most subtle and striking of all is
Phèdre.

One more word about *Phèdre.* It is sometimes said
that Racine's drama, fine as it is, is vastly inferior to the
Hippolytus of Euripides ; that in Racine's drama the
character of Hippolyte himself, with his trumpery love
affair for Aricie, is a poor creature compared with the

fatal victim and unblemished devotee of Artemis. But this simply means that Euripides was a Greek and Racine a Frenchman, and it would have been altogether wrong and untrue to nature for Racine to have portrayed an Hippolytus after the manner of Euripides in the setting and atmosphere and among the other personages he chose for his play. His play is a reflection of his period, just as Euripides' drama is a picture of his time ; but if you wish, from the purely technical point of view, to study how extraordinarily skilful a dramatist Racine is, you have only to read the opening dialogue in the Greek play between Phèdre and the nurse, and then turn to the French play and see what Racine has made of the same situation. From a few bare hints in the Greek he has written the most lovely and subtle piece of music and evocation. In the Greek the dialogue reads as follows—I quote from the translation of Leconte de Lisle :

" PHAIDRA.
O mère malheureuse, de quel amour tu as aimé !

LA NOURRICE.
Elle aima un taureau, ma fille ! Pourquoi parles-tu de cela ?

PHAIDRA.
Et toi, malheureuse sœur, épouse de Dionysos !

LA NOURRICE.
O fille, qu'est-ce donc ? Tu outrages tes parents !

PHAIDRA.
Et je meurs la troisième, et combien malheureuse ! "

Or in the translation of Edward Coleridge :

" PHÆDRA. Ah ! hapless mother, what a love was thine !
NURSE. Her love for the bull, daughter ? or what meanest thou ?
PHÆDRA. And woe to thee ! my sister, bride of Dionysus.
NURSE. What ails thee, child ? speaking ill of kith and kin.
PHÆDRA. Myself the third to suffer ! how I am undone ! '

This is what Racine makes of it :

" PHÈDRE.

O haine de Vénus ! O fatale colère !
Dans quels égarements l'amour jeta ma mère !

ŒNONE.

Oublions-les, Madame ; et qu'à tout l'avenir
Un silence éternel cache ce souvenir.

PHÈDRE.

Ariane, ma sœur, de quel amour blessée
Vous mourûtes aux bords où vous fûtes laissée

ŒNONE.

Que faites-vous, Madame ? et quel mortel ennui
Contre tout votre sang vous anime aujourd'hui ?

PHÈDRE.

Puisque Vénus le veut, de ce sang déplorable
Je péris la dernière et la plus misérable. "

And yet *Phèdre*, although it is the most subtle, the most theatrically effective, the most arresting, the most rich in human interest, is not generally reckoned Racine's masterpiece. Racine himself preferred it to all his plays. But I think it is universally recognised among French critics that his crowning masterpiece is *Athalie*. Other poets have written plays as fully charged with passion and subtlety as *Phèdre* ; no one has written just such a work as *Athalie* ; it is in its way unique, unique as *Lycidas* and *The Tempest* are unique. Nobody in the world could have written it save Racine. *Phèdre* may be said to suffer from the comparison with the *Hippolytus* of Euripides ; no such damaging comparison can be made in the case of *Athalie*, although the influence of Euripides is felt in *Athalie*, and contributes to its beauty. Voltaire, writing about *Athalie*, called it " l'ouvrage le plus approchant de la perfection qui soit jamais sorti de la main des hommes." Sainte-Beuve said the final word on the subject : " *Athalie*, comme art, égale tout." The work is the fruit of the maturity of the poet's genius ; the fruit of twelve silent years of meditation. It is as if Shakespeare had written a play after his six years of retirement at Stratford. All Racine's qualities are seen here in their highest development : his nobility, his religious fervour, his passion for the Scriptures, and for antiquity.

But what makes Racine's plays so great is not only that the human passions in them are dealt with by a master hand, and that the psychology is subtle, interesting, and true, but also that the background, the historical and mythological background, is poetical. There is no local colour in Racine's plays, and yet he suggests a mythological, legendary, or historical setting, as the case may be, by the subtlest means. He has atmosphere ; and here again he proves that he is a great poet. So much for Racine as a dramatist. To sum up : he is not only a dramatist, but a psychologist—the first Frenchman to introduce psychology into drama—and one of the greatest, most subtle analysts of woman's heart. Even in a translation, even in the baldest prose translation, any student of human nature would admit this to be true, should he read of the doings and follow the utterances and actions of Racine's heroines : Phèdre, Hermione, Roxane, Bérénice, and Athalie. There is another great fact about Racine : he is a truthful writer ; he does not shun the truth even although it may hurt and shock his principles or his beliefs. He depicts human nature as it is ; he faces facts as fearlessly as a surgeon.

Last of all, his diction, his verse is poetic, and he is, perhaps, the greatest of all French verse-writers. It

surprises and even shocks intellectual Englishmen if you
say that Racine is a greater poet than Victor Hugo, or
Musset, or Leconte de Lisle ; but there is nothing more
surprising or shocking in such a statement than there
is in saying that Milton is a greater poet than Byron,
Shelley, or Keats. You may maintain the contrary—I
do not say that one theory is more right than the other—
but I do say that, just as you can make out a case for
considering Milton a greater poet than any of the later
English poets, so, and in exactly the same way, you
can prove that Racine is a greater poet than Victor
Hugo or any of the French poets of the nineteenth
century.

To compare him with Victor Hugo may be said to be
unfair ; because Victor Hugo is a lyrical poet and Racine
is a dramatic poet. But Victor Hugo has also written
plays—plays in which he sought to shatter the tradition
established by the plays of Racine ; plays which are
still acted with triumphant success. Some critics
indeed, and among them one of the most scholarly and
delicate of judges (William Cory, for instance), say that
Victor Hugo's plays are the finest that have been written
since those of Shakespeare. But the French put the
qualities of Racine still higher. At first sight the range
of Victor Hugo's work, the elemental quality of the
passions with which it deals, the lyrical heights to which
it rises, the depths of feeling into which it dives, the
variety and multiplicity of the strings of his lyre, would
seem to form a more portentous achievement ; compared
with this multitudinous orchestration the work of Racine
seems like the thin utterance of four stringed instruments delicately played in an eighteenth-century drawing-
room. This, however, is exactly the point. Let us say
that in an eighteenth-century drawing-room four fiddles

or a fiddle and a clavier are interpreting the music of
Mozart or of Beethoven. What actually takes place ?
Bach or Beethoven or Purcell—let alone Mozart and
Schubert—can write a melody, perhaps one of three bars
only, or even of one single bar, and review it in all its
architectural possibilities ; and this review, which may
entail the marriage of the tune with another tune (thence
permutation and commutation), will need for its interpretation perhaps only four stringed instruments, perhaps
only a fiddle and clavier, harpsichord, or pianoforte ;
perhaps only a little portable clavichord—the instruments
were played possibly in an eighteenth-century drawing-
room by people in cities, or on a London concert platform by spectacled Teutons, and yet . . . from this
simple conception and with these limited means of
execution things are said and suggested, doors are
opened, temples and pyramids are built, unearthly
fabrics, whose building the educated and cultivated
musician will enjoy *consciously*, and the uneducated and
uncultivated listener will (if he hears it often enough)
enjoy *unconsciously*, and whose architecture and proportion will not escape him ; and these unassuming
methods, this seemingly modest and limited means and
vehicle of expression, may and do lead the listener up
to a catastrophe, when he feels as if he were standing on
the edge of his own planet, and enjoying the sense of
being caught up in the wheels of unchangeable harmonious laws, or of being borne on a stream that

> " Broadens for ever to infinity,
> And varies with unvariable law,"

and of being whirled into eternity.

This effect will seem greater to the musician than the
catastrophe achieved by terrific engines, by hypnotic

persuasion, complex machinery, and accessories in the music dramas of Wagner, in which the factor of literary inspiration is almost always present.

To some, Wagner's catastrophe will seem in comparison with that of Bach or Beethoven or Mozart like a railway accident.

Now, in the opinion of the French, Racine is to Victor Hugo much like what Beethoven or Bach is to Wagner in the opinion of the trained musician. Of course the comparison must not be pushed too far, but the principle of Racine's greatness, and the reason of his superiority over Victor Hugo (in the eyes of those who think he *is* superior), resembles the principle of the greatness of the music of Purcell ; say, for instance, " When I am laid in Earth " in *Dido and Æneas*, or any of Beethoven's or Mozart's great phrases and melodies that seem to open out their arms and embrace the universe ; and the *reason* of their superiority over Wagner (in the eyes, that is to say, of those who think they *are* superior).

This was written before any one had discovered that Beethoven had no sense of " musical form." Perhaps some one will discover that in Racine's verse there is no scansion, no order, no shape, and no sense.

One of the secrets of the greatness of Racine's verse is, as in the case of Milton, his nobility of purpose and design, and his loftiness of utterance. Since in Racine's poetry the form is inseparable from the subject-matter, by illustrating the one it is possible to indicate the other ; for his diction, at its finest, is accompanied generally by a majestic and magnificent gesture, which appertains alone to great souls.

The following passage from *Andromaque* represents his diction at its finest :

" Non, non, je te défends, Céphise, de me suivre ;
Je confie à tes soins mon unique trésor :
Si tu vivais pour moi, vis pour le fils d'Hector.
De l'espoir des Troyens seule dépositaire,
Songe à combien de Rois tu deviens nécessaire.
Veille auprès de Pyrrhus. Fais-lui garder sa foi :
S'il le faut, je consens qu'on lui parle de moi.
Fais-lui garder l'hymen où je me suis rangée ;
Dis-lui, qu'avant ma mort je lui fus engagée ;
Que ses ressentiments doivent être effacés ;
Qu'en lui laissant mon fils, c'est l'estimer assez.
Fais connaître à mon fils les héros de sa race ;
Autant que tu pourras, conduis-le sur leur trace.
Dis-lui par quels exploits leurs noms ont éclaté,
Plutôt ce qu'ils ont fait, que ce qu'ils ont été.
Parle-lui tous les jours des vertus de son père,
Et quelquefois aussi parle-lui de sa mère."

Still finer, perhaps, is Phèdre's vision of the infernal
regions :

" Misérable ! Et je vis ! et je soutiens la vue
De ce sacré soleil dont je suis descendue !
J'ai pour aïeul le père et le maître des Dieux ;
Le ciel, tout l'univers est plein de mes aïeux.
Où me cacher ? Fuyons dans la nuit infernale.
Mais que dis-je ? mon père y tient l'urne fatale ;
Le sort, dit-on, l'a mise en ses sévères mains :
Minos juge aux enfers tous les pâles humains.
Ah ! combien frémira son ombre épouvantée,
Lorsqu'il verra sa fille, à ses yeux presentée,
Contrainte d'avouer tant de forfaits divers,
Et des crimes peut-être inconnus aux enfers !
Que diras-tu, mon père, à ce spectacle horrible ?
Je crois voir de ta main tomber l'urne terrible ;
Je crois te voir, cherchant un supplice nouveau,
Toi-même de ton sang devenir le bourreau.
Pardonne. Un Dieu cruel a perdu ta famille ;
Reconnais sa vengeance aux fureurs de ta fille."

Sometimes by one word he evokes a picture, as in the
line which used to make Flaubert shiver :

" La fille de Minos et de Pasiphaé."

Sometimes he strikes a sonorous note as of beaten bronze, as in the famous and hackneyed passage of Athalie's dream, beginning :

" C'était pendant l'horreur d'une profonde nuit " ;

or he enchants us with honied sweetness of phrase :

" Dans l'orient désert, quel devint mon ennui !
Je demeurai longtemps errant dans Césarée ;
Lieux charmants, où mon cœur vous avait adorée."

The following is an example of the loveliness of the visions he can evoke, making such a transparent veil of melody with them :

" Prêts à vous recevoir mes vaisseaux vous attendent,
Et du pied des autels vous y pouvez monter,
Souveraine des mers qui vous doivent porter."

For beauty of cadence and mysterious melody the lines which I have already quoted from the first act of *Phèdre*, when Phèdre hints at her secret to the nurse, are unrivalled in French poetry.

The decadent poets wrote a whole treatise to prove that the vowel *u* had a colour of its own, and signified melancholy ; but Verlaine alone among the French poets has rivalled the melody of Racine's famous distich on Ariane, and even he has never surpassed their music.

Again, for honied sweetness what could be more captivating than this ?

" Soutiendrai-je les yeux dont la douce langueur
Sait si bien découvrir les chemins de mon cœur ? "

Here is an instance of his simplicity. The words are spoken by the child Joas in *Athalie* :

" Dieu laissa-t-il jamais ses enfants au besoin ?
Aux petits des oiseaux il donne leur pâture."

The passages which I have quoted, although few, are sufficient to illustrate the qualities of Racine as a poet ; in order to appreciate his merits as a playwright, you must see his plays well acted, and acted by the players of the Comédie française, who are trained in the ancient traditions of declamation. If an Englishman is able to perceive beauty in these quotations, he is able to appreciate the genius of Racine ; if not, he is tone-deaf to the language, and there is an end of the matter. He should admit it, and pass on ; as a rule, he is not content with such a course. Unable to apprehend these beauties, he denies their existence, just as one denies the likeness of a portrait which, perceived by others, does not strike one's own eye. Yet the beauties are there ; to the French they are an object of reverent adoration ; the richest jewel of their national inheritance. They are perceptible, too, to all continental artists and critics who know French well. It is only the proud and insular Briton who has the arrogance to deny their existence. Matthew Arnold maintained that French poetry was not poetry ; but Matthew Arnold's criticism of French poetry has the same value as would have had Dr. Johnson's criticism of German music. Charles XII. and Prince Eugene, Schiller and Dostoyevski, bore witness to the beauties of Racine. Napoleon said that Racine was *son favori*. I have tried to indicate the nature of his qualities, to illustrate his peculiar charm and excellence. But when all is said and done, when we have pointed out the harmony of proportion, the absence of effort and emphasis, the delicate tact and talent of selection, the suppleness, the grace, and the distinction which mark the works of Racine, there is still something left—an indefinable suavity, an intangible sense of perfect balance, an elusive play of light and shade, a delicacy and charm of texture, a tenderness, a sensitiveness, which cannot be defined by any stereotyped formula. All we can say is, that Racine is among the noble few of whom in reality it deserves to be said that they " built the lofty rhyme "—and he built it after the serene and noble fashion of Sophocles. He ranks with the radiant children of Apollo, whose notes of music are like fountains of pure water. He may not be with Homer, Shakespeare, and Dante ; but he is with Praxiteles, with Virgil, and Mozart :

Μουσάων θεράπων καὶ ἑκηβόλου Ἀπολλῶνος.

1908–1923.

HIPPOLYTE TAINE

ROBERT BROWNING gave us the poetry of the scholar's life in his lyric " The Grammarian's Funeral "; nobody as yet has given us the romance of the scholar's life. We have had satire in plenty, and figures such as George Eliot's Casaubon, or the Professor in Tchekov's play *Uncle Vanya*, have often been exposed to our laughter or blame by novelists and satirists ; but should some day some future Balzac or Henry James need a rewarding subject for a novel or romance on the subject of a learned man, a scholar, of the struggles, adventures, failures, and successes of the man who starts out not to live but kick, he will nowhere find more fruitful material for such a work than in the life of Hippolyte Taine.

The wind bloweth where it listeth, and Hippolyte Taine was born at Vouziers on the 21st of April 1828. He was the son of an attorney. He stayed at home until he was eleven, and received lessons from his father and, at the same time, attended a small school. His father died in 1840, leaving a widow, two daughters, and his son, Hippolyte, moderately well off. Taine was sent to Paris with his mother, and attended the classes of the *Collège Bourbon*. Taine immediately distinguished himself. The child was father of the man, and he was only fourteen when he drew up a scheme of study from which he never deviated. According to this rigid rule, he allowed himself twenty minutes' playtime in the after-

noon and an hour's music after dinner ; the rest of the
day was given up to work. His efforts were rewarded.
In 1847, he won all the first school prizes. At the *Collège
Bourbon*, too, he made friends with several of his school-
fellows who afterwards exercised a lasting influence upon
him.

Education was the career which seemed made for Taine
after his brilliant school successes. In 1848, he took
his degree in Science and Letters, and passed First into
the *École Normale* which, at that time, was going through
a brilliant phase. Many of Taine's fellow-students
afterwards became famous in education, literature,
journalism, the stage, and politics. Taine made himself
felt at once in a circle of exceptionally gifted young men,
which included Perraud, Ferry, Weiss, and Prévost-
Paradol. Taine amazed them all, not only by his knowledge but by his industry ; not only by his energy, which
was prodigious, but by his facility in French and Latin,
in verse and in prose. Taine enjoyed this period of
his life to the full. He revelled in the contact and
friction with other minds—minds which were opening
and open to all ideas, full of keenness, and in the
delight of a whole-hearted devotion to work, thought,
and endless discussion. His reading was immense—
he devoured Plato, Aristotle, the Fathers of the Church,
and he analysed and classified all that he read. He
already knew English, and he set about to master German
in order to read Hegel in the original. In the brief space
of the leisure he allowed himself, he made music. His
rare quality of intellect and his fabulous industry placed
him beyond the range of rivalry. His teachers were
unanimous in recognising the nobility of his character,
the power of his mind, and the distinction of his style ;
they were equally unanimous in blaming his unmeas-

ured taste for classification, abstraction, and formula. The director of studies, Monsieur Vacherot, gauged his capacity at the end of his second year with the insight of the prophet. He said that Taine would be a great savant, and added, that " he was not of this world," that Spinoza's motto, *Vivre pour penser*, would apply to him. In 1851, Taine tried for a fellowship in philosophy, but failed to pass—that is to say, he passed with five other candidates, but finally only two were admitted, and he was not one of them. The decision created almost a scandal. Taine's reputation had spread beyond the college ; his defeat was attributed to the tone and colour of his ideas. But, in reality, his examiners were quite sincere in thinking his ideas were absurd and his style tiresome.

The Minister of Public Instruction judged Taine less severely, and he was given an appointment at the College of Toulon in 1851. His educational career began smoothly, but in 1851 came the *coup d'état*, after which university professors were all of them looked upon with suspicion. Many were relieved of their duties, others resigned. Taine considered that after the plebiscite of 10th December it was the duty of every citizen to accept the new régime in silence, but the universities were asked not only for submission but for approbation. At Nevers (where Taine was teaching) they were asked to sign a declaration of gratitude to the President of the Republic for the measures he had taken. Taine was the only professor who refused to sign. He was at once marked down as a revolutionary, and now after several vicissitudes and transfers from post to post, and after being moved from one minor appointment to another, he went to Paris in 1852, where an appointment awaited him which was equivalent to a suspension. This meant

that his career as a professor was over, and he was obliged
to take up Letters as a profession.   He took his degree in
1853, and this was the last act of his university career.
He had written two essays—one called *De personis
platonicis* and the other on La Fontaine's *Fables*.   He
sent these in to the Sorbonne, and at once began an essay
on Livy for one of the Academy competitions : in this
work he revealed a new phase of his knowledge ; but the
tendency of his ideas again excited opposition, and after
considerable discussion the competition was postponed.
Taine toned down some of the passages which had been
censured, and the work was crowned by the Academy
in 1855 and published in 1856 with a preface in which he
marshalled his determined doctrines.   In the beginning
of 1854, Taine, after six years of uninterrupted work,
broke down and was compelled to rest.   He was ordered
for his health to the Pyrenees, and Mr. Hachette asked
him to write a guide-book on that subject.   Taine's book
is singularly unlike a guide-book—it contains glowing
descriptions of nature, sharp and satirical sketches of
watering-place society, and underlying the whole book
there is a vein of stern and bitter philosophy.   This
book was published in 1855.   Enforced leisure, the
necessity of mixing with his fellow-men and of travel,
tore the recluse from his cloistered existence and brought
him into contact with reality.   His method of philosophy
underwent a change during that momentous year of
1854.   Instead of starting from the abstract idea and
proceeding to the concrete reality, he henceforward
started from the concrete reality and arrived at the
central idea by a succession of facts.   His style, too,
changed and became vivid, and began to glow with
colour.   His life became less self-centred.   He lived
with his mother in the Isle St. Louis and associated

12

once more with his old friends. He made the acquaintance of Renan, and through Renan that of Sainte-Beuve, and renewed his friendship with Hanet. From 1853 to 1856 was the period of Taine's greatest activity and happiness in production. He published during these years many articles in serious reviews on the most diverse subjects—ranging from Menander to Macaulay. But he was seeking for a larger field, which would allow him to develop his theory on race, period, environment, and the master faculty. In 1856, his *History of English Literature* was announced, and, at the beginning of 1857, he published a volume of collected articles on French philosophers of the nineteenth century. In this book, he attacked the principles which were at the basis of this so-called " classic " spiritual philosophy, with energy and fierceness and irreverent irony. This book was instantaneously successful and made Taine famous. From this moment he took his place in the front rank of the new generation of men of letters. He was attacked in the Press by great people—he answered all attacks by publishing new books.

In 1858, he published his *Essais de Critique et d'Histoire*; in 1860, *La Fontaine et les Fables,* and a second edition of his *Philosophes Français.* All this time he was working at his *History of English Literature*, which appeared in three octavo volumes at the end of 1863. It was from this moment that Taine's influence began to be widely felt ; he was in constant intercourse with Renan, Sainte-Beuve, Scherer, Gautier, Flaubert, Saint-Victor, and the Goncourts, and he spared a few morsels of his time for his friends. In 1863 he was appointed examiner on the entrance examination board of St. Cyr, and in 1864 he was appointed Professor of Æsthetics at the Collège de France. His *History of English Literature* was published in 1863, preceded by an introduction in which Taine stated his determinist philosophy in the most uncompromising fashion. In 1864, Taine se .. in this work to the Academy to compete for the " Prix Bordin." The work excited discussion and opposition, but it was finally awarded the prize.

From 1864–1870 was perhaps the happiest period of Taine's life, and during these years he published two volumes on Italy, his Collected Essays on Dutch and Greek art,[1] and further essays in criticism and history, and between 1863 and 1865 the notes he had made during the last two years on Paris and on French society appeared in *La Vie Parisienne* under the title of " La Vie et les Opinions de Thomas Graindorge." These were published in a volume in 1868. This is the most personal of Taine's books, and an epitome of his ideas. In 1867, a supplementary volume of his *History of English Literature* appeared, and in 1870 his *Théorie de l'Intelligence*. In 1868 he married. His *Notes sur l'Angleterre*, the fruits of two prolonged stays in England, appeared in 1872. A visit to Germany was abruptly interrupted by the outbreak of the Franco-Prussian War, and the book on Germany which he had planned had to be abandoned. After 1870, Taine, who was deeply shaken by the war, felt that it was the duty of every Frenchman to work solely in the interests of France, and it was now that the more or less vague ideas which he had hitherto entertained of writing on the French Revolution began to crystallise and to take a new and definite shape. His purpose was to find in the Revolution of 1789 the causes of the political unrest from which modern France was suffering.

From the autumn of 1871 until the end of his life, his

[1] *La Philosophie de l'Art, l'Idéal dans l'Art Nouveau, Essais de Critique et d'Histoire.*

great work, *Les Origines de la France Contemporaine*, took up all his time, and in 1884 he gave up his Professorship so as to devote himself entirely to his historical task. But he succumbed before it was ended. He fell sick in the autumn of 1892 and died in March 1893. The portion of the work which he did not live to finish was to have consisted of a picture of French society and the French family, tracing the development of the scientific spirit in the nineteenth century. He had also planned a treatise on the Will (*Un Traité de la Volonté*). The *Origines de la France Contemporaine*, Taine's monumental achievement, stands apart from the rest of his work ; his object in writing it was to explain the existing constitution of modern France, by studying the immediate causes of the present, namely, the last years of what is called the *Ancien Régime*, the Revolution, and the beginning of the Nineteenth Century. He had another purpose as well, although he was perhaps scarcely aware of it, and that was to study man in a pathological crisis. Taine made searching investigation into human nature, and the historian checked and endorsed and confirmed the pessimism and misanthropy of the satirist, the author of *Thomas Graindorge*. The question which Taine attempted to answer in his historical works is why modern France is so highly centralised that all individual initiative is practically non-existent, and why the central power, whether it be in the hands of one man or of an Assembly, is the sole and only power. He wished also to point out the error underlying two prevalent ideas :

(1) That the Revolution destroyed Absolutism and set up Liberty. The Revolution, he maintains, merely caused Absolutism to change hands.

(2) That the Revolution destroyed Liberty instead of establishing it ; that France was less centralised before

1789 than after 1800. He maintains that the centralisation was as great before 1789 as after 1800. France was already a centralised country before 1789, and grew rapidly more and more so from the time of Louis XIV. onwards. The Revolution was the last step in the work of centralisation. It completed what had already been done, it neither destroyed nor created despotism, it merely gave it a new form. These were the ideas which Taine developed with an array of fresh matter and a fresh illumination of facts.

The *Origines* differs from the rest of Taine's work in this : although he applies the same method to his period of History which he had already applied to Literature and Art, he no longer approaches his subject in the same spirit ; he loses his philosophic serenity ; he cannot help writing as a man and a Frenchman, and he lets his feelings have play ; but what the work loses in impartiality it gains in life. The most important part of this great work is that in which Taine traces step by step the succession of facts and the succession of ideas, later on converted into facts, by which modern France grew out of ancient France.

Taine was the philosopher of the epoch which succeeded the Romantic period in France. The Romantic era lasted from 1820 to 1850. It was a reaction against the classical school, or rather against the conventionality and the lifeless rules of this school in its decadence.

The school preached individual liberty in matter and style ; it was a brilliant epoch, bright with men of genius and rich in beautiful work ; but towards 1850 it had turned towards its decline, and the young generation, tired in its turn of its conventions, its rhetoric, its pose of melancholy, arose armed with new principles and fresh ideas, and set up their banner in the citadel of literature. Their idea was truth; their watchword liberty; their purpose to get as near as possible to scientific truth. We can trace their ideal in all branches of art; in the pictures of Meissonier, Millet, and Bastien Lepage; in the poetry of Leconte de Lisle and of Sully-Prudhomme; in the historical works of Renan; in the fiction of Flaubert, Zola, and Maupassant. Taine was the mouthpiece of this period, or rather one of its greatest spokesmen. He did not create the movement, but he expressed its spirit in tones of imperative authority, the authority of a great mind and of a brilliant stylist. His influence was great because he arrived at the right moment, his ideas fell on favourable soil; but chiefly because he was a man of genius.

If, applying one of Taine's favourite theories to himself, we ask what was his master-faculty, the answer is it was the power of logic (and this answer, as we shall point out later, is incomplete)—a power which was the source of all his weakness and all his strength. He had a passion for abstraction. " Every man and every book," he said, " can be summed up in three pages, and those three pages can be summed up in three lines." He looked upon everything as a mathematical problem, whether it was the universe or a piece of china. " C'est beau comme un syllogisme," he said of a sonata of Beethoven's. Taine's theory of the universe, his message, his system of writing criticism and history, his philosophy, were all of them the fruit of this gift of logic, this passion for classification and abstraction. As a teacher, Taine's message consisted of an inexorable determinism, a negation of metaphysics; as a philosopher he was a positivist. He loved what was precise and definite, and the " spiritualist " philosophy in vogue in France in 1845, of Cousin, Tonkin, etc., maddened him. He went back to the

philosophy of the eighteenth century, especially to
Condillac and to the theory of transformed sensation,
that is to say, the theory which lays down that man knows
nothing save by the senses. Sensations are transformed
by man's faculty of abstraction into ideas, and everything
that exists is presented to the mind of man in the shape
of abstract ideas. Since all man can do is to make an
abstract and a generalisation, his whole knowledge must
be limited to phenomena and to the laws of phenomena.
He can never arrive at the knowledge of a cause. He
never can obtain to the *by whom*, the *by what*, or the
why ; they belong to the region of metaphysics, but
he can get to know more and more about, although he
can never attain to a complete knowledge of, the *how* ;
the *how* belongs to the province of science. Metaphysics
are non-existent ; but science exists ; so philosophy to
be a science must stop short on the threshold of metaphysics. This philosophy was not, and did not pretend
to be, original ; but Taine presented it vividly and
vigorously, and his solid, highly coloured, glowing style
made his works more accessible and consequently more
influential than those of Auguste Comte. To the men
of 1860 Taine was the true representative of positivism,
and, as such, his influence was great.

Taine's critical work was important, but all his
criticism is history. Hitherto, history had been to criticism what the frame is to the picture ; Taine reversed
the process and studied literary figures simply as speci-
ments of a given epoch. He laid down as an axiom that
the complete expression of a society was to be found in
its literature, and that the way to understand a society
was to study its literature. When Taine studies a great
writer he does not approach him as an isolated being,
but as the result of a thousand causes : firstly, of his

race ; secondly, of his environment ; and thirdly, of the circumstances which surrounded him in his period of development. Race, environment, period—these are the three things according to him which we must study before forming an opinion of a man. *Race, Milieu, Moment*, this is Taine's favourite theory, and he complemented it by another, that of the *master faculty*, the *faculté maîtresse*. According to this latter theory, every man, and more especially every great man, has one ruling faculty, which is so strong that all others are subordinate and subservient to it ; it is the centre of the man's activity, and it guides him into one particular groove. The theory is the secret of Taine's power and of his weakness. He always looked for the ruling quality, the particular groove, and when he had once made up his mind what it was, he piled up all the evidence (sometimes mere anecdote) which corroborated and underlined this one quality so that whatever might have tended to point to another side of the question was left out. He was thus naturally inclined to lay stress on one side of a character or a question to the exclusion of all others, and in his study of mankind and in his historical work, he did what he had blamed the classical authors in France for doing. They saw and portrayed the type exclusively, and neglected the individual. Taine, the philosopher, *generalised* in the same manner. He believed that in every average man there was one ruling passion, the mainspring of his life, and that in intellectual men there was one preponderant mental quality which was the centre of the brain. Hence the one-sided character of Taine's work. As a moralist, a philosopher, and a critic of life, Taine was a pessimist ; he disbelieved in mankind and in all religion. He did not even believe in science, or, rather, he expected nothing from it ; he served science un-

falteringly, without looking forward to any possible fruit
or result, and herein he differs from the English and
from some of the German positivists, philosophical
critics, and men of science of the same epoch, who
expected everything from science : they *believed*, that
is to say, in possible results. Taine did not. In
Taine's work there is neither enthusiasm nor bitterness,
neither hope nor despair ; not a hopeless resignation
so much as a resignation without hope. The proper
study of mankind in Taine's opinion, as in Pope's,
was man, and he studied man according to the system
which already has been described. He cross-examined
humanity ; he subjected humanity to the question,
ordinary and extraordinary, and his verdict was : guilty
without extenuating circumstances. In *Thomas Graindorge* he is staggered by the spectacle of man's bestiality
and woman's folly. Man is to him the primeval savage,
the gorilla, the carnivorous, bloodthirsty, vicious, las-
civious animal, or else the poor, piteous maniac with a
diseased body and disordered mind who is only healthy
either in mind or body by a fluke. Taine is appalled
by the possibilities of the *bête humaine* ; and in everything that he wrote we feel, as we do with Voltaire, the
terror with which the possibilities of human folly inspire
him.

It is doubtful whether Taine's system, which he
thought was so important, is really the lasting part of his
work, just as it may be permissible to doubt whether a
sonata of Beethoven bears any resemblance to a syllogism ;
but Taine was an artist as well as a musician, and not
only an artist but a poet. Here we come to the second
half of his " master faculty." The best and most
complete definition of it would be one which embraced
his two supreme and salient qualities : that of abstract

reasoning and that of poetic imagination. M. Lemaître defined Taine as a *poète-logicien*. The artist, the poet in Taine painted what he saw with a large brush and in bold, glowing colours. From Taine, the artist, we get the essay on La Fontaine, the articles on Balzac and Racine, and the passages on Voltaire and Rousseau in the *Ancien Régime*. And as an artist, Taine was not only not free from the influence of the romantic school, but by his very method and style he was a romantic.

His emotions were deep and almost violent ; his vision at times verges on the lurid. He sees everything in startling relief and sometimes in exaggerated outline, just like Balzac and Victor Hugo. He had a passion for exuberance, strength, and splendour, for the opulent, the gorgeous, the rich ; artists and writers such as Shakespeare, Titian, and Rubens ; he delighted in strong, high-coloured subjects. What a curious spectacle ! Here is a man who is fighting and attacking the classical spirit of generalisation with all his might, and who yet spends his whole life in generalising ; here is a man who comes to destroy and to supplant the romantic school and who yet is himself a complete and striking example of the style and method of thought which he seeks to destroy. Taine arrived too quickly at his conclusions and trusted too much to formulæ, and he was by so doing guilty of those very things which he blamed so severely in the French classical writers ; and by systematically suppressing (in his *Origines*) a whole series of facts, which would be necessary to make his picture intelligible as a whole, his historical work gives us the impression of being a vast trunk without limbs, exceedingly striking to the imagination. In this respect he is romantic, and belongs to the romantic period.

Nothing remains now of Taine's system which was not there before he began to apply it ; but whether it be false or whether it be true, the work which Taine did with it was work on a great scale, and his fabric of history—shapeless though it may be, and although half of it is in ruins—is imposing by its huge mass. In criticism he left the world richer for many lasting works of art, as well as for the impressions of a French scholar of the middle of the nineteenth century, who happened to be a man of genius, on English literature, and French literature of the seventeenth century. Taine's system did not prevent him from expressing the strong prejudices, predilections, and partialities he felt for the works he criticised.

Taine's influence was great, and twofold. He influenced his own generation ; during his lifetime a wave of pessimism swept over French literature, and Taine became the high priest of the cult of misanthropy, a cult in which even science was held to be but an idol worthy of respectful devotion, but not of faith. Taine's influence—or rather the great phase which he formed part of, which he influenced in that he expressed with the power and authority of genius the ideas which were floating in the air at the time—can be traced in current French literature from 1870 to 1880, in novels, and even in plays. This phase in its turn brought about another reaction ; a reaction against positivism and pessimism, and an attempt at a spiritual renascence—a moment which we were watching when this article was written in 1900, and which is still proceeding, twenty-three years later, at the present day in France ; and as the work of Taine was a powerful factor in the first movement, he must be credited with a measure of responsibility for the reaction. Around so remarkable a man as Taine a school is certain to grow up ; Taine's school, which inculcated positivist doctrines, rigid formulæ, and resigned pessimism, was certain to produce at some time or another a school of determined opponents to its ideas and to its system. So if the tone which underlies and pervades the works of Zola, the Goncourts, and Maupassant can be immediately attributed to the influence we call Taine's, then we must ultimately trace his influence to the so-called " reactionary " writing and ideas of the present day. Writing in 1900, we might have here cited Rostand as an example of the fruit of the reaction ; twenty-three years later we might cite Claudel.

FRENCH POETRY

SOME years ago a discussion arose in the columns of the *Saturday Review* about the merits of the French language as an instrument for verse, and the claims of French poetry in general. The discussion started with a criticism on a French prose translation of *Hamlet*, in which the critic (who was none other than Mr. Max Beerbohm) said : " The French language, limpid and exquisite though it is, affords no scope for phrases which are charged with a dim significance beyond their meaning and with reverberations beyond their sound. The French language, like the French genius, can give no hint of things beyond those which it definitely expresses . . . it is not, in the sense that our language is, suggestive. It lacks mystery. It casts none of those purple shadows which do follow and move with the moving phrases of our great poets."

The phrase set me thinking, and tempted me to answer it. I argued that to the critic who wrote the words I have just quoted, the French language was a vehicle and nothing more. In English, every word has its associations for us, and touches off a train. Some words are enough in themselves to redeem a page ; they are like men and women with identities ; while French words seem to many of us to be, like Noah's Ark men, merely symbols. But, I argued, to the French and to those who have imbibed the French language in their childhood,

French words possessed identity and association in the very same way. I quoted instances to illustrate my point. My letter set fire to a powder-mine of correspondence. A professor wrote to say that the French language was an emasculated language, in fact, a Pidgin Latin. Some one else replied that English then must be an emasculated Anglo-Saxon. But the majority of the correspondents agreed that the French language was not poetically suggestive. One correspondent admitted that for descriptive effect it could rival the English language, but that when we reached the plane of thought and philosophical reflection, of deep feeling and lofty musings, its inferiority became apparent. The same writer went on to say : " It is a commonplace among those competent to judge that, if French is a language of prose, English is a language of poetry." The discussion wandered away therefore from the point at issue, as discussions will (the point being whether the French language was as suggestive to a Frenchman as the English language is to an Englishman), into a general debate on the comparative merits of French and English poetry. But one fact was brought to light by this discussion : the majority of those who took part in it knew their own language well, but they had a less intimate knowledge (in the case if the professor it amounted almost to ignorance) of the French tongue.

Now it is precisely this question—the question of the comparative merits of the two poetries—which I wish to avoid. Latin is a fine language ; and it would be absurd to say that Latin is not a vehicle for poetry, because Greek is a finer language and a still finer vehicle for verse. Critics do not say this, because they know Latin and appreciate Latin verse. But our critics and our professors, as a rule, do not know French, and so

they say there is no such thing as French poetry ; because
it has not the qualities of English poetry. I wish to
consider the special qualities of French poetry, its
particular excellence. Every language has a native
quality which can neither be translated nor transmuted,
a quality which is special to it, and unique : a quality
which has no equivalent in any other language. English
critics say the unique qualities of the French language
are lucidity and idiom ; that French is the language of
prose and cannot, in poetry, be suggestive. In support
of their argument they usually quote a string of English
words for which they say there is no exact equivalent or
no poetical equivalent in French. Here are some words
actually quoted by a writer in support of this very argument : *fragments, sunny, ripple, shadow, motion, crag.*
This may be quite true, but it must be remembered
that there are also French words for which there is no
exact poetical equivalent in English, such as : *nénuphar,
nacelle, taillis, clairière, onde, frisson, clarté, étincelle,
lisière.* Now French poetry exists. We are confronted
with the works of Marot, Villon, Du Bellay, Ronsard,
Louise Labé, Malherbe, Corneille, Molière, Racine,
La Fontaine, André Chénier, Alfred de Vigny, Alfred de
Musset, Lamartine, Victor Hugo, Béranger, Baudelaire,
Gautier, Sully-Prudhomme, Théodore de Banville,
Paul Verlaine, Leconte de Lisle, Heredia, Henri de
Régnier, and Madame de Noailles. If the argument of
the English critic holds good, the works of these poets
should lose nothing by being translated into French
prose, and should positively gain by being translated into
English verse. They do not gain by the process ; there
are no English translations of French poetry which
convey more than a shadow of the original. Nobody has
even attempted a serious translation of the works of

Racine into English,[1] and you need only compare the most successful English versions of the best-known French lyrics with the originals in order to realise the difficulty, the impossibility of accomplishing the task. This, then, tends to prove that French poetry has certain qualities proper and special to itself alone. What, then, are they ? Let us consider them. French poetry has, among other qualities, an incomparable grace, a delicacy of texture, an exquisite freshness and lightness—" le coup d'aile, l'envolée," which makes other languages seem heavy, clumsy, and pedestrian beside it. Such a quality cannot be called prosaic. Let us take instances ; first of all Du Bellay's famous song of the winnower to the winds, which cannot be quoted too often :

> " À vous troupe légère
> Qui d'aile passagère
> Par le monde volez,
> Et d'un sifflant murmure
> L'ombrageuse verdure
> Doucement ébranlez :
>   J'offre ces violettes,
>   Ces lis et ces fleurettes,
>   Et ces roses ici,
> Ces vermeillettes roses,
> Tout freschement écloses,
> Et ces œillets aussi.
>   De votre douce haleine
> Éventez ceste plaine
> Éventez ce séjour,
> Cependant que j'ahanne
> À mon bled que je vanne
> À la chaleur du jour."

Here is another instance from a more modern poet, Alfred de Musset :

[1] Since this was written, Mr. Masefield has transported the bones of Racine into English, but not the peculiar beauty.

" Bonjour, Suzon, ma fleur des bois !
Est-tu toujours la plus jolie ?
Je reviens, tel que tu me vois,
D'un grand voyage en Italie.
Du paradis j'ai fait le tour ;
J'ai fait des vers, j'ai fait l'amour.
    Mais que t'importe ?
Je passe devant ta maison ;
    Ouvre ta porte.
    Bonjour, Suzon !

Je t'ai vue au temps des lilas.
Ton cœur joyeux venait d'éclore,
Et tu disais : Je ne veux pas,
Je ne veux pas qu'on m'aime encore.
Qu'as-tu fait depuis mon départ ?
Qui part trop tôt revient trop tard.
    Mais que m'importe ?
Je passe devant ta maison ;
    Ouvre ta porte.
    Bonjour, Suzon ! "

A song like this seems to have the freshness of the morning dew and the smile of the leaves in the sunlight. In other languages there are songs as beautiful, but there are none fledged with more airy and delicate wings ; none with a more fragrant gusto. There is yet another instance of the grace of the French language ; this time from a forgotten author called Roy, who wrote the following quatrain under a picture of some people skating :

" Sur un mince cristal l'hiver conduit leurs pas ;
    Le précipice est sous la glace.
Telle est de vos plaisir la légère surface ;
    Glissez, mortels, n'appuyez pas."

Finally, an instance from La Fontaine :

" Il était allé faire à l'Aurore sa cour
    Parmi le thym et la rosée."

So much for grace, freshness, and delicacy. The

13

qualities illustrated in these quotations can, I think, be said to be unrivalled in any other modern language. They are unqiue, and essentially French; as distinctly a product of the French temperament as a landscape by Corot or a bust by Clodion; as germane to the French soil as a delicate vintage of claret, or a bubbling wine of the Loire.

Let us take another quality, one which I will call wistfulness; a tremulous plaintiveness, which brings with it the breath of half-lit gardens, the tinkle of melancholy strings, and the thin and dainty echoes of a spinet. It is to be found both in ancient and modern French poetry. One instance of it is the celebrated sonnet of Ronsard to Helen, beginning, " Quand vous serez bien vieille." Four lines will indicate what I mean :

> " Je serai sous la terre, et fantôme sans os
> Par les ombres myrteux je prendrai mon repos.
> Vous serez au foyer une vieille accroupie,
> Regrettant mon amour et votre fier dédain ! "

Here is another instance from Verlaine's *Fêtes Galantes*. It is also well known; but as it is less known to the English public than the hackneyed arguments against French poetry, I will venture to quote it :

> " Votre âme est un paysage choisi
> Que vont charmant masques et bergamasques
> Jouant du luth et dansant et quasi
> Tristes sous leurs déguisements fantasques.
>
> Tout en chantant sur le mode mineur
> L'amour vainqueur et la vie opportune,
> Ils n'ont pas l'air de croire à leur bonheur,
> Et leur chanson se mêle au clair de lune,
>
> Au calme clair de lune triste et beau,
> Qui fait rêver les oiseaux dans les arbres,
> Et sangloter d'extase les jets d'eau,
> Les grand jets d'eau sveltes parmi les marbres."

In this poem, besides its delicacy and its matchless grace, the pathos and the yearning quaver of its music, there is another mysterious and elusive quality ; just that quality which so many critics deny to French poetry, namely, suggestiveness ; in it I maintain that the words are " charged with reverberations beyond their sound." And if the English critics say that they do not apprehend these remoter echoes, the fault, I think, must lie with them, because to French senses the suggestiveness is perceptible. M. Anatole France, in writing of this poem, says : " Soudain tel coup d'archet vous déchire le cœur. Le méchant ménétrier vous a pris l'âme. Il vous la prend en jouant, par exemple, le Clair de lune . . . l'accent était nouveau, singulier, profond." But my point is this, that this singular accent, this sighing plaintiveness, " avec je ne sais quoi de gauche et de grêle d'un charme inconcevable," is a quality not to be found in this tenuous degree, in this extreme exquisiteness, in any other language but the French. And here again the French have added a string to the harp of the poets of the world, or rather a stop to the immense organ.

But, it may be objected, all this is very pretty and graceful, but it is not the finest poetry ; the music of this tinkling guitar must not be spoken of in the same breath as the organ voice of Milton, Dante, Virgil, and Goethe.

Grace and wistfulness are by no means the only qualities of French poetry ; they are unique qualities of their kind ; that is all ;—they are not to be found elsewhere in such a degree ; nor can you find their equivalent in other languages. But French poetry has many other qualities. Consider it from the side of its supposed limitations. French, we are told by the English critics, is the language of prose ; by the French we are told that it is the language of common sense. M. Brunetière, in his work on the *Pléïade*, writes as follows : " On dira en vers des choses qu'il semblera qu'on pourrait dire en prose ; et à la vérité, ce ne sera souvent qu'une illusion . . . mais ce sera comme un hommage rendu aux qualités de clarté, de précision, de concision, de force et de rapidité, de mouvement et d'action qui vont devenir celles de notre poésie. On ne ' délirera ' pas en vers français. [The younger decadents have done so in spite of this authoritative mandate !] Ni l'enthousiasme de l'inspiration, ni la perfection de la forme—et en admettant qu'on puisse en notre langue la distinguer de la solidité du fond—n'autoriseront le poète à manquer de bon sens." Now this is exactly the point upon which the English critics insist when they argue that French is an unpoetical language. They say that just because it is the language of common sense, just because it is lucid, precise, concise, forcible, and swift, it must necessarily sacrifice poetic suggestiveness which is incompatible with these virtues. Well, I maintain that it is possible, or that it has been possible, for French poets, without sacrificing their lucidity, precision, and conciseness, and even by employing the language of everyday prose, to be poetical at the same time ; and the poet who has most signally succeeded in this achievement is Racine.

When Wordsworth writes lines like :

" The light that never was on sea or land,"

he is using the language of everyday prose ; he is being not an atom less precise, lucid, and concise than Racine ; and we say he is a great poet because in using this ordinary everyday language the style disappears altogether and only perfection remains : the perfection of poetical or

emotional utterance expressed with absolute simplicity
and directness.   If this is the result of art, it is the
supreme triumph of art ; the 'art in which all artifice is
concealed ; if it is merely the automatic expression of
unconscious nature, the result is the same, for we speak
of " ces traits de nature qu'on dit le comble de l'art quand
l'art a le bonheur de les trouver." It is precisely the
poets who do this whom we acclaim as the greatest poets—
Goethe at his best as in such lines as :

> " Allein ein Schwur drückt mir die Lippen zu,
> Und nur ein Gott vermag sie aufzuschliessen " ;

and Dante constantly in such lines as :

> " E se non piangi, di che pianger suoli ? "

So, if the performance of this feat constitutes great
poetry, it is absurd to say that Racine is not a great poet ;
for he not only accomplished it, but he did so con-
tinually.   The following two lines from *Britannicus* will
serve as an illustration :

> " D'où vient qu'en m'écoutant vos yeux, vos tristes yeux,
> Avec de longs regards se tournent vers les cieux ? "

These lines have the same simplicity, the same majesty
of utterance, which distinguishes and stamps the works
of the great poets of other countries.   And here the
conciseness and precision of the French language, so
far from being an obstacle, becomes a cause of further
effectiveness.   But there are other poets besides Racine
who, by their handling of the matter-of-fact French
language, strike poignant notes of wonderful beauty.
Take the following lines, for instance, from Victor
Hugo's *Hernani* :

> " Ils sont morts ! Ils sont tous tombés dans la montagne,
> Tous sur le dos couchés, en braves, devant Dieu,
> Et, si leurs yeux s'ouvraient, ils verraient le ciel bleu " ;

or the following lines from *Les Burgraves* :

> " Vite ! à tire-d'ailes !—
> —Oh! c'est triste de voir s'enfuir les hirondelles !—
> Elles s'en vont là-bas, vers le midi doré " ;

or Alfred de Vigny's beautiful line :

> " Dieu, que le son du cor est triste au fond des bois ! "

or Baudelaire's :

> " Comme un long sanglot tout chargé d'adieux,"

or his

> " L'Aurore grelottante en robe rose et verte."

So much for the effects to be drawn from the prosaic French instrument, or rather from one string of it.   There are other strings—those of imaginative vision and poetic meditation ; for these we must turn to the works of Lamartine ; we meet with the same quality, only in a more vehement degree, in the works of Victor Hugo. Again, there is the purely lyric note, the " lyrical cry " ; for this one has only to turn to Victor Hugo, to Musset, and to Verlaine.   And when the lyrical impetus is combined with the French grace, the result is something like the " unbodied joy " to which Shelley compares the singing skylark.   That these qualities exist, as illustrated in the song of Musset's I have already quoted, nobody who has read Victor Hugo and the French lyrical poets of the century would probably deny.   What I need lay stress on are the merits of a particular kind of verse, which appeals perhaps more strongly to the French than any other, and to which English people generally cannot see is poetry at all.   I mean the verse to which Brunetière alludes—the verse in which the common sense is luminous, the expression pellucid, and the idea concise.   The lines of

Racine quoted just now show that such writing is not
necessarily prosaic ; but it is worth going further into the
matter, for the whole ideals of French poetry can be
determined in considering this question. Before doing
so, I will strengthen my case by one more brief quotation, from Malherbe this time, one of the most precise
and solid of verse-writers :

> " La moisson de nos champs lassera la faucille,
> Et les fruits passeront la promesse des fleurs."

M. Brunetière, in the passage I quoted, makes the
significant statement " ni la perfection de la forme—
*et en admettant qu'on puisse en notre langue la distinguer
de la solidité du fond.*"
This is the main ideal of French poetical art ; the
form is all-important ; but the very perfection of form
presupposes some solidity of subject-matter. We often
argue about the comparative value of form and subject-
matter. The French view—not only preached but
practised with a few exceptions by the French poets
from Villon to Heredia—is that the form should be as
perfect as possible ; and that this perfection should be
the exact expression of an idea, a fancy, or an emotion
worth expressing. The expression is, as M. Brunetière
says, inseparable, in French, from the subject-matter.
Everything should serve to adorn, but nothing to ornament ; nothing should be dragged in solely for the sake
of ornament ; but the harmony between the idea and
the phrase in which it is clothed should be complete—
absolute. Such, says Maupassant, was the ideal of
Flaubert. " Il ne comprenait pas que le fond pût exister
sans la forme, ni la forme sans le fond." Listen to
Maupassant himself : " La profonde et délicieuse
jouissance qui vous monte au cœur devant certaines

pages, devant certaines phrases, ne vient pas seulement de ce qu'elles disent ; elle vient d'une accordance absolue de l'expression avec l'idée, d'une sensation d'harmonie, de beauté secrète échappant la plupart du temps au jugement des foules."

So when the French say that a poet writes good verse, they do not mean that he is a mere virtuoso who astonishes us by feats of vocalisation or of technique, but a man who has got something poetical to say and knows how to say it. Because, according to this standard, he must have something definite to say, and because the manner in which he says it must be clear and precise, English critics argue that verse in France merely adopts and fulfils the functions of prose. In French, prose and verse *are* ruled by the same standard ; but the verse written in submission to this standard is nevertheless poetry. The idea may be precise, but the idea may also be poetical ; it may be precise and luminous like a ray of light. The expression may be concise, and yet the phrase may be charged with music and suggestion. It may be like a solid casement which opens on to the infinite.

Even if we admit that the critics who contend that French is exclusively the language of prose are right. French prose is perfect, they say ; but in what does its perfection consist ? Surely not *only* in lucidity, precision, and idiom ?

The most beautiful passages of French prose are also suggestive—suggestive in the same way that poetry is ; Chateaubriand's phrase, " La cîme indéterminée des forêts," is a suggestive phrase. The following passage from Flaubert is poetically suggestive : " Quand tu parais il s' épand une quiétude sur la terre ; les fleurs se ferment, les flots s'apaisent, les hommes fatigués s'étendent la poitrine vers toi, et le monde, avec ses océans et ses montagnes, comme en un miroir se regarde dans ta figure. Tu es blanche, douce, lumineuse, immaculée, auxiliatrice, purifiante, sereine."

Likewise this from Renan :

" Je suis née, déesse aux yeux bleus, de parents barbares chez les Cimmériens bons et vertueux qui habitent au bord d'une mer sombre, hérissée de rochers, toujours battue par les orages. On y connaît à peine le soleil ; les fleurs sont les mousses marines, les algues et les coquillages coloriés qu'on trouve au fond des baies solitaires . . . des fontaines d'eau froide y sortent du rocher, et les yeux des jeunes filles y sont comme ces vertes fontaines où, sur des fonds d'herbes ondulées, se mire le ciel."

It is only the French who can tell us whether they feel their own language to be suggestive ; they are themselves the only judges on this question. Listen to what they say. Here is the opinion of Maupassant—and there is no more competent authority : " *Les mots ont une âme.* La plupart des lecteurs, et même des écrivains, ne leur demandent qu'un sens. Il faut trouver cette âme qui apparaît au contact d'autres mots. . . . Il y a dans les rapprochements et les combinaisons de la langue écrite par certains hommes *toute l'évocation d'un monde poétique* que le peuple des mondains ne sait plus apercevoir ni deviner. Quand on lui parle de cela, il se fâche, raisonne, argumente, nie, crie, et veut qu'on lui montre. Il serait inutile d'essayer ; ne sentant pas, il ne comprendra jamais."

Does not this mean that to French ears the French language, handled by certain writers, is charged with poetic suggestion ?

But to return to poetry, the so-called prosaic poetry. When Racine says :

"On ne voit pas deux fois le rivage des morts,"

he is making a bald statement of fact. There is no metaphor, no flight of fancy, no taking conceit, no display of imagination, no virtuosity ; and yet the result is a supremely beautiful line. Any one who has heard Sarah Bernhardt say this line will understand that it has the force and value of great poetry ; because they will have understood that it says more than it seems to say, and can be interpreted in a poetical manner ; because it touches a chord in the mind of the reader ; because, in fact, it is charged with a signification beyond its meaning and with reverberations beyond its sound. When Sarah Bernhardt speaks the line, a door seems to have been opened on to the dominions of the dead, and we feel the mysterious breeze of Lethe.

This is what French people call good verse. I maintain that it is good verse, judged by any standard whatsoever ; that it is good verse, in the same way as the lines in Gray's *Elegy*, the *Ode to the Nightingale*, or *Lycidas* are good verse.

A distinguished Orientalist and scholar once said to me that the French were the surest judges of poetry that any nation could show, because when they said, "good verse," it meant the whole thing ; not only nspired fancy, or agreeable modulations, but the fusion and harmony of both, and that in this they resembled the Persians, who judged poetry in the same way.

Here are—to end up with—three more quotations of verse of this kind ; one is from André Chénier :

"C'est le Dieu de Nysa, c'est le vainqueur du Gange
Au visage de vierge, au front ceint de vendange ;
Qui dompte et fait courber, sous son char gémissant,
Du lynx au cent couleurs le front obéissant."

The second is from Baudelaire :

> " Je te donne ces vers afin que si mon nom
> Aborde heureusement aux époques lointaines
> Et fait rêver un soir les cervelles humaines,
> Vaisseau favorisé par un grand aquilon,
> Ta mémoire, pareille aux fables incertaines,
> Fatigue le lecteur ainsi qu'un tympanon,
> Et par un fraternel et mystique chaînon
> Reste comme pendue à mes rimes hautaines."

The third is from La Fontaine :

> " Par de calmes vapeurs mollement soutenue,
> La tête sur le bras et son bras sur la nue,
> Laissant tomber les fleurs, et ne les semant pas."

These are also good verse, and here the perfection of the form is inseparable from the solidity of the subject-matter.

THE OXFORD BOOK OF FRENCH VERSE

THERE were once upon a time two schoolmasters. One was a Frenchman and the other an Englishman. Whenever they met they discussed literature and art. The Englishman admired French prose and the Frenchman admired English painting. There was one subject on which they disagreed—verse.

The Frenchman used to say that Shakespeare and Milton were doubtless men of mark, but he could not admit that their poetry was *verse*. To which the Briton would reply that the French were no doubt skilful metrical composers, but the idea of their metre being *poetry* was preposterous. The view of the British schoolmaster lies at the root of most English criticism of French poetry.

There was once upon a time a French critic who wrote an article concerning Tolstoy's criticisms of Shakespeare. Tolstoy, it will be remembered, maintained that Shakespeare had *aucune espèce de talent*. The French critic said the judgment was too sweeping : Count Tolstoy had attacked *King Lear*, which was a shame, since that work was obviously the pardonable freak of a generous if overtaxed intellect. Moreover, there were passages in the play which had positive merit ; not to mention that in this, and in all the works of Shakespeare, there were probably certain verbal felicities which perhaps escaped both him and the Count, *since they neither of them understood the English language*. English critics of French verse should lay this saying to heart. They should reflect, before they issue edicts from their professorial altitudes that Racine is no poet, that his works possibly contain verbal felicities which their ear is unable to catch. The French believe his work to be full of excellence. They think that Racine is a poet, just as we believe Milton to be a poet. And when the British critic fails to detect poetry in lines such as these :

> " Mais la mort fuit encor sa grande âme trompée,"

or :

> "Princesse, en qui le ciel mit un esprit si doux,"

he should remember that it is equally difficult for foreign critics who are not intimately familiar with the English tongue to detect a spark of beauty in lines such as :

> " Not that fair field
> Of Enna, where Proserpin gathering flowers,
> Herself a fairer flower, by gloomy Dis
> Was gathered—which cost Ceres all that pain
> To seek her through the world—"

I do not for a moment wish to imply that Mr. St. John Lucas, who has compiled this anthology, belongs to the band of invincibly tone-deaf professors who clothe their want of sympathy with condescension. Mr. Lucas is evidently a fine French scholar, and keenly sensitive to the shades and beauties of the French tongue ; he has not included a single bad poem in his anthology, and the criticisms in his preface display the nice judgment which comes only from " fundamental brainwork " and a discrimination kindled by sympathy. But there is nevertheless a faint reflection in his preface of the atmosphere of patronage—that patronage founded on ignorance of foreign literatures, whose very citadels are Oxford and

Cambridge—as though he were making a concession to the accepted views of his colleagues, which are unfortunately so limited and so wide of the mark with regard to all things French.

Mr. Lucas's preface is a small panorama of French poetry throughout the ages. He begins with the *Chansons de Geste*, which, he says, are " dreary and monotonous enough to our impatient modern sense, yet often redeemed by a sudden note of rugged pathos." If this is meant to apply to the *Chanson de Roland*, the criticism is inadequate—one might just as well say the Saga of Sigurd the Volsung contained stammering hints of grandeur, or that there were flashes of feeling in the *Iliad*. On the other hand, his characterisation of Villon's work is perfect, especially where he talks of Villon's sympathy " for the pathos of old age and weariness." Equally fine are his remarks on the *Pléïade*, whose ideal he sums up in a shining phrase : " style, and a language which should express noble and delicate emotions, uniting the wistful beauty of Theocritus and the *Georgics* with the resonant ardour of Pindar and the *Æneid*." Again, nothing could be better than Mr. Lucas's appreciation of André Chénier when he writes of the elegies that " have the soft yet clearly cut beauty of a Sicilian coin of the great period," or of the " little pictures in which the beauty of some incident of pastoral life, some golden moment of a long summer day, is made eternal."

With regard to the poetry of the " Grand Siècle," Mr. Lucas writes as follows : " With the beginning of the so-called classical epoch comes the decline and fall of lyric poetry." I presume that so fine a critic as Mr. Lucas admires Racine as a poet, if not as a lyric poet. I presume that he has omitted any passage from Racine's plays on the ground that no dramatic poetry is included.

But surely it would have been as well to say that the French regard the works of Corneille, Racine, and La Fontaine as the crowning achievement of the French genius, because whether you appreciate Racine or not he is regarded by the French as the supreme model of all versification, even by the Symbolists. For instance, M. Jean Moréas, after having made every possible experiment in revolt, anarchy, and innovation, came to the conclusion after many years of labour and experiment that there was only one right way of writing verse in French, and that was the way of Racine. To say " Poetry became domesticated and went to live at the Hôtel de Rambouillet, or, rather, it went there to die," is not a sufficient summary of that epoch.

The following sentence, too, is open to objection : " La Fontaine realised that the language of his time was not the absolute property of a muse on stilts " ; for the last half of the phrase might lead one to believe that Mr. Lucas considered that the muse of Racine did walk on stilts. It might arouse in one a misgiving that the critic's admiration of André Chénier, Alfred de Vigny, and Lamartine was subject to suspicion, since he failed to discern the qualities of their towering model. It is as if a critic were to say, " I admire sculpture ; I admire Rodin and Hildebrand " ; and to add, " Praxiteles is not a sculptor." I repeat that Mr. Lucas has said no such thing. But he has omitted to mention what is the purest and greatest manifestation of the French poetical genius.

About the choice of poems through the volume there is nothing but praise to be given. Mr. Lucas might have included some of the choruses from Racine's *Esther*, which are not only lyrical but singable, and have been set to beautiful music. But nothing is more foolish in judging an anthology than to complain of the omission of one's personal favourites. The question is, " Are the poems included good ? Are the chief poets included ? " They are. The selection from Victor Hugo's work is admirable. It might be objected that the presence of so many of Musset's longer poems makes the book slightly top-heavy, and prevents the inclusion of certain less famous poets who have written nevertheless poems exquisite enough for any anthology ; for instance, Gabriel Vicaire, Albert Samain, and Louis Bouilhet. The only vital omissions are Heredia, whose work was not available, and Sully-Prudhomme, whose absence is conspicuous and inexplicable. The Symbolists are omitted to a man. I mean the dead Symbolists.

But I presume that the object of the book was neither to give a complete panorama of French poetry nor a collection of ignored, if exquisite, flowers, but samples of what is best and most important. If so, the object has been achieved, but I repeat that space might have been found for a few poems by lesser-known modern writers, and in any case the following lines by Bouilhet ought to be included in any French anthology. A famous living French critic once told me he thought these four lines had never been surpassed as far as writing is concerned by any French poet. Here they are :

" Tun'as jamais été, dans tes jours les plus rares,
　　Qu'un banal instrument sous mon archet vainqueur,
　　Et, comme un air qui sonne aux bois creux des guitares,
　　J'ai fait chanter mon rêve au vide de ton cœur."

JULES LEMAÎTRE ON RACINE

THE insularity and the perhaps unconscious arrogance of a particular kind of British criticism which grows at Oxford and Cambridge are never more strikingly illustrated than when our scholars and professors deal with the literature, and more especially with the poetry, of France. Matthew Arnold spent his life in attacking this insularity and this arrogance, yet he himself made the sweeping statement that the poetry of France was not poetry at all. In saying this he did a deal of harm ; it caused a number of lesser men to imagine that their ignorance in matters of French literature had received a high sanction.

In France, and in most other countries, scholars and critics, when they deal with the famous poets of another country, before they pass a verdict of sweeping condemnation on them, generally add some qualifying statement hinting that there are possibly in the works of the writer condemned certain shades and felicities in the diction which they, being of another race, training, and education, are perhaps unable to apprehend. In criticising a poet such as Milton, for instance, it is not usual to find either a French or a German critic begin by saying that Milton could not write verse, or that his verse, though creditable, is not poetry. Such criticism,

especially if we subsequently discover that the critic
was entirely ignorant of the English language, would not
greatly affect us, but it is precisely this kind of criticism
that is made by English scholars with regard to French
poetry.

The series of lectures on Racine which have just
been collected in a volume and published by Jules
Lemaître should prove useful to those of our professors who make such amazing and childish state-
ments about French verse. It should prove as useful
as books like Professor Raleigh's works on Shakespeare and Milton would be to Frenchmen, who,
although acquainted with the English tongue, were
finding it difficult to understand why the English
thought that Shakespeare and Milton were writers of
merit.

Jules Lemaître's lectures were delivered to a French
audience : it was not therefore necessary for him
to discuss the questions whether or not Racine was
(a) a dramatist, (b) a poet, (c) a great writer. These
three questions the French imagine that they have solved
long ago, just as we think we have solved similar questions
with regard to Shakespeare and Milton. What Jules
Lemaître does is to tell the story of Racine's life, to trace
the growth and development of his genius, the birth
and origin of his successive works, their relation to his
epoch and his contemporaries, the effect they produced
on his contemporaries, and the effect they continue to
produce on Frenchmen of the present day. He makes
Racine, the man, live for us, and with the utmost
skill he paints the environment of the poet's soul,
and holds as it were a radiant taper before the serene
architecture of verse in which that soul expressed
itself.

Jules Lemaître is the most French of all the modern writers of France. His style is the purest, the most limpid, the most perspicuous, and the most nimble that is to be found in modern French literature, and in these lectures it is conversational. This book is like a gramophone, on which the record of French talked at its best is heard : talk as light in form as a gossamer, as well-knit in substance as a shirt of mail. One seems in listening to it to be looking into a clear stream, so clear that you think you would only have to dip your finger into it to touch the gravel which you see at the bottom. But this illusion of shallowness is caused by the extreme limpidity of the water, the stream is in reality deep, and were you to-leap into it you would find yourself out of your depth. No modern writer is therefore so well equipped to write about Racine as Jules Lemaître, and no better book could ever be written on Racine than this one. It does not contain a tedious page, and with extraordinary skill the author, in dealing with the events in the life and the factors of the works of the poet which are best known, while pointing out that his audience doubtless knows all this by heart, yet manages to relate them as if they did not know them, and in such a way that if they do know them, the story nevertheless appears to be a new one.

The dramas of Racine, Lemaître points out all through this book as well as in his final summary of the poet's work, were the fruits of the influence and the atmosphere of Port Royal and the Jansenists. In pages 9 to 14, Jules Lemaître explains exactly what Port Royal and the Jansenists were. He says :

" Le jansénisme, c'est la restauration, par deux théologiens passionnés, Jansenius et Saint-Cyran, de

la doctrine de Saint Augustin, le plus subtil des dialec-
ticiens et le plus tourmenté des hommes."

Psychologically, he adds, and not theologically the
Jansenist is the man whose relations with God are
the most dramatic. The Jansenist is the man who has
the least illusions about human nature ; he is therefore
the man to whom faith in the Redeemer is the most
imperatively necessary. In his summing up at the end
of the book, Lemaître writes that not only was Port
Royal the cradle of Racine and the sheltering home of his
old age, but that the drama of Racine was the unexpected
and secular flower of the great labour of religious con-
templation and " perfectionnement intérieur " which
took place in Racine's soul at Port Royal during his
early years. For it is the painting of the natural man,
according to the standards of Port Royal, which forms
the solid basis of the secret energy of Racine's harmonious
tragedies, just as it is the beauty, the harmony, and
the rhythm of the Greeks which lent them their beautiful form, so that Racine unites in himself the two
greatest traditions of our race — the Greek and the
Christian.

Racine, says Lemaître, is the diamond of French
classical literature, for there is no drama in his opinion
which contains at the same time so much ordered discipline, so violent an inward crisis, so much psychological
truth, and so much poetry. He points out that the action
in the drama of Racine arises simply from the clash and
the conflict of the passions of the persons brought together. These are the forces which are the factors
of the dramas, and these alone. The dramatic method
of Racine consists in depicting the evolution of a crisis
in a tiny circle of action, space, and time. He takes
Pyrrhus twenty-four hours before he declares his passion

to Andromache, Nero twenty-four hours before his first crime, Bérénice twenty-four hours before she leaves Rome. The sentiments and the passions of the characters taken at a short distance from the catastrophe are violent at the start, and this violence goes on increasing until the catastrophe is reached. This method is the result of the peculiar nature of the soul of Racine, which was extraordinarily sensitive and extraordinarily violent.

Racine was the first Frenchman who introduced psychology into drama : the first French dramatist to depict the passion of love—the love of ordinary men and women, and not the lofty sentiment of legendary heroes. The women in his dramas occupy the foremost place ; and the majority of these women are creatures of wild impulse, possessed either by ambition or by passion, driven by love to either murder or suicide through currents and counter-currents of alternating fear, rage, and jealousy.

The second great fact with regard to Racine's drama which Lemaître brings out is its truth. The tragedy of Racine, he says, is neither idealistic, nor optimistic, nor edifying ; it is *true*, and the reason is that, although Racine was a devout Christian, he was at the same time a fearless painter and psychologist.

Thirdly, Lemaître speaks of the poetry of Racine's drama. The dramas of Racine are poetical by their setting, their atmosphere, by what he calls the dignity of the persons who move in them. Every one of his tragedies has an historical, legendary, and mythological background which belongs to it and is poetical.

Finally, and this is what English critics find most difficult to realise, the dramas are poetical, poetical in

diction, style, and verse. No purer French has ever
been written, and should any one ask how it is that the
language of Racine is considered poetical, no better
answer could be found than that which Lemaître gives
in the following sentences :

" Et c'est la versification la plus souple, et le rhythme
le plus varié ; les mots importants à la rime ; rimes
souvent modestes parce que l'harmonie est dans tout le
vers et non dans la rime seule. Et c'est le style le
plus beau de clarté, d'exactitude, de justesse, de pro-
priété (qualités redevenues si originales et si rares !).
Et ce style exprime tout par des moyens si simples !
Souvent, nu et familier, il rase la prose, mais avec
des ailes. Et ces vers ont toutes les diverses sortes de
beauté."

The verse of Racine, he says, is sometimes charmingly
picturesque, sometimes audacious in ellipse and anti-
thesis ; at other times it enchants by the sustained grace
of rhythmical periods.

But in all its various phases of beauty it has certain
characteristics and qualities which are permanent :
taste—the subordination of feeling and fancy to tact—
and never-failing lucidity. I have seen it argued that
French verse is not poetry just because it possesses these
very qualities ; but if such qualities result, as they do
in the case of Racine, in verse which is full of tender
thought, delicate imagery, exquisite grace, high dignity,
and subtle music, why should French verse be less
entitled to the name poetry than that of Tennyson or that of Milton, whose ideal was that verse
should be simple, sensuous, and impassioned ; or that
of Coleridge, who talked of the best words in the best
order ?

Besides, if this argument were sound, then neither

is the verse of Catullus or of Horace or of Virgil poetry. But I think there is a simple explanation why learned men, who are otherwise sane, argue thus childishly about French verse. Very few Englishmen know how French verse scans.

SULLY-PRUDHOMME

SULLY-PRUDHOMME was born in Paris on the 16th March 1839, and educated at the Lycée Bonaparte, where, after a time, he gave himself up entirely to the study of science. He took his degree as *Bachelier ès Sciences*, and he was preparing for the entrance examination to the Polytechnic School when an attack of ophthalmia prevented him from competing. The course of his career was entirely changed by this prolonged interruption of his studies; but the scientific habit of mind which he acquired from his years of study never left him; and it is in the combination of this scientific bent, this love of exact reasoning, this delight in mathematical concepts, with aspirations towards the things which lie above and beyond science, and with a perpetually troubled conscience, that the striking originality of Sully-Prudhomme's character is to be found. When he definitely gave up all idea of entering the Polytechnic School, he found employment for a time in the Schneider factory at Creuzot; but he soon abandoned an occupation for which he was eminently unsuited. He then decided to read law, and entered into a notary's office in Paris. During this period he composed his early poems, which soon became famous in an ever-widening circle of friends. In 1865, he published his first volume of poems, which had for subtitle *Stances et Poèmes*. This volume attracted considerable attention in the literary world, and was favourably noticed by Sainte-Beuve. Sully-Prudhomme's family understood that his true vocation was not the Bar ; leisure was assured him, and he was relieved of the necessity of taking his degree in law. It was at this moment that the small circle of which Leconte de Lisle was the centre were preparing the *Parnasse*, to which Sully-Prudhomme contributed several pieces. In 1866 Lemerre published a new edition of the *Stances et Poèmes* and a sheaf of sonnets called *Les Épreuves*. From this time forward Sully-Prudhomme gave up his life entirely to poetry. It was in a volume of *Les Épreuves* that the note of melancholy which was to dominate the whole of his life's work was first clearly audible. In 1869 he published a translation of the first book of Lucretius with a preface, and *Les Solitudes*. In 1870 a series of domestic bereavements, and a serious paralytic illness, which was due to the strain and fatigue of the winter of 1870, during which he served in the *Garde Mobile*, shattered his health in a way which made entire recovery impossible. Between 1872 and 1892 he published various volumes of poems which were collected and republished first of all in 1886, and then later under the title *Poèmes*. He also published two volumes of prose criticism, and various monographs from time to time in the philosophical reviews, and among them a remarkable series of essays on Pascal—these essays were portions of a larger work which was unfinished when he died. After 1870 there were no remarkable incidents to chronicle in his life save his election to the Academy in 1881, and the award made to him of the Nobel Prize for Literature by the Swedish Academy in 1901. In later years he lived at Volnay and then at Châtenay in great isolation, a victim of perpetual ill-health, mainly occupied with his work on Pascal. He had been partially paralysed for some time when he died in September 1907.

What strikes the reader first and foremost in Sully-Prudhomme's poetry is that he is a thinker, and, moreover, a poet who thinks, and not a thinker who turns to rhyme for recreation. What is most strikingly original in his work is to be found in his philosophic and scientific poetry. If he had not the scientific genius of Pascal, he had at least the scientific habit of mind, and found delight in the certainties of mathematics. He wrote before the days of relativity. In attempting to interpret the universe as it is revealed to man by science, he succeeded in creating a form of poetry which seemed to be new, and which was not without a certain grandeur. One of his most beautiful poems, " L'Idéal " (*Stances et Poèmes*) was inspired by the thought which is due to scientific calculations, of stars so remote from our planet that their light has been on its way to us for thousands of centuries and will one day be visible to the eyes of a future generation. Even if this is untrue, even if it is only one of the fairy tales of science, it is a good subject for a poem. The second chief characteristic of Sully-Prudhomme's poetry is the extreme sensibility and the profoundly melancholy note of his love lyrics and his musings. Sully-Prudhomme was above all things introspective ; he penetrated into the hidden corners of his heart ; he laid bare the subtle torments of his conscience, the shifting currents of his hopes and fears, belief and disbelieving, when faced by the riddle of the universe, in so poignant a manner as to be sometimes almost painful. To render the fugitive phases and tremulous adventures of his spirit, he lit upon incomparably delicate shades of expression and an exquisite and sensitive diction. In his poems there is a striking nobility in the ideas and a religious elevation like that of Pascal ; and there is something of Lucretius as well. Yet he was neither an Epicurean nor a Jansenist ; he was rather a Stoic to whom the disappointments of life brought pity instead of bitterness.

In Sully-Prudhomme's work all oratorical effect is conspicuous by its absence ; it has an extreme simplicity and fastidious precision of diction. Other poets have had a more glowing imagination ; his verse is neither exuberant in colour nor rich in sonorous combinations of sound. The grace of his verse is one of outline and not of colour ; his compositions are distinguished by his subtle rhythm ; his verse is as if carved in ivory, his music is like that of a unison of stringed instruments. His imagination is inseparable from his idea, and this is the reason of the extraordinary perspicuity of his poetic style. His poetry extends to two extreme limits : on the one hand, to the borderland of the unreal and the dreamlike, as in a poem such as " Le Rendezvous " (*Vaines Tendresses*), in which he seems to express the inexpressible ; on the other hand, in his scientific poems he encroaches on the realms of prose. His poetry is plastic in the creation of forms which fittingly express his fugitive emotions and his lofty ideas. Both on account of the charm of his pure and perfect phrasing and by the consummate art and the dignity which informed all his work, Sully-Prudhomme deserved the rank which he held amongst the foremost French poets of the nineteenth century.

1900.

THE POETRY OF CRABBE

TO obtain justice for an unfairly forgotten poet is no mean final contribution to literature for a scholar-Churchman and a man of letters. When Canon Ainger's *Crabbe* was published, sorrow that this should be his last work overcame all other feelings ; but later we were able to appreciate its other aspect, and now we are glad that he lived to finish it. The book, at the time of its appearance, once more set us wondering as to the reason of the neglect into which the poet of the *Village* had fallen. When Crabbe's son was editing his father's poems in 1834, Wordsworth wrote to him that because of their combined truth and poetry these poems would last as long as any that had been written since, including his own. The reason for this unmerited forgetfulness which most readily occurs to the student of poetry is that Crabbe's carelessness as to form, his lack of technique, is distasteful to a generation which cares above all things for exquisite workmanship. It has been stated that the " Parnassian " epoch of modern poetry has seen its close, the epoch which produced Rossetti's sonnets and Tennyson's idylls. The wave of symbolism which has passed over Europe, bringing with it " impressionism," " art nouveau " and the rhymeless rhythms of the French decadents, is said to have been felt in England also ; and we are told that the influence of the school whose ideals are lawlessness

and emancipation from all discipline has left its mark
on contemporary English poetry. Whether this be true
or not, the fact remains that the poetry of to-day is far
more remarkable for its manner than for its matter.
The work of the more prominent writers of verse of
to-day, that of Mr. Watson, Mr. Yeats, Mr. Arthur
Symons, and Mr. Binyon, is all of it distinguished by
the excellence of its technique, and in none of it is
the subject-matter so impetuous and exuberant as to
bubble over and shatter the delicate vessel in which it
is contained.

Whenever a discussion as to the comparative merits of
matter and form arises, the defenders of both ideals are
prone to fall into exaggeration. The preachers of " art
for art's sake " tell us that subject-matter is of no account,
while those to whom the substance is all-important
reply that the purely literary artists are mere jugglers
who divert our attention from their poverty of thought
by the ingenuity of their metrical effects. One need
only point to Sophocles, Dante, and Milton for the
perfect combination of the two qualities. They afford
us an ideal which should silence all discussion. Yet if
the choice is offered between poetry pregnant with
thought and feeling, but deficient as to form, and poetry
perfect in form and devoid of content, is not the former
preferable ? Is not mere vocalisation apt to become
tedious, be it that of Apollo himself ? The poetry of
Crabbe belongs to the former class. When Wordsworth
reproached him with his careless workmanship, he merely
replied : " It does not matter." But he was not merely
deficient in form ; he chose for his vehicle the heroic
couplet, which, of all vehicles, owing to the consummate
mastery with which it has been handled by Pope and
others, leads us to look for exquisite manipulation. This

is why there is at times in the poetry of Crabbe a positive incongruity between the matter and the form. The late John Murray used to say in conversation that Crabbe often said uncommon things in so common a way that they passed unnoticed. The remark, Canon Ainger adds, applies equally to much of Crabbe's poetry. A second reason (in reality a part of the first) which accounts for the neglect of Crabbe is the length of his poems. It is impossible to do justice to Crabbe in selections. " The abiding impression " left by the poetry of Crabbe, as FitzGerald says, " results from being, as it were, soaked in through the longer process by which the man's peculiar genius works." The present generation are particularly averse to this soaking process. An example of this aversion is their contempt for the poetry of Byron, which, similarly, can only be appreciated in the mass.

But now the question arises—had Crabbe sufficient of the true poetic gold to compensate for the dross with which it is so negligently mingled ; and in what does the peculiar merit of his genius consist ? The first question can only be answered by referring the reader to the works of Crabbe ; to the *Village*, the *Parish Register*, the *Borough*, and the *Tales* ; but can also be partially answered by quotation.

As to the peculiar character of his genius, Crabbe was first and foremost an observer ; he studied human nature with profound insight and penetrating analysis, and depicted what he saw with the minuteness and mastery of a Dutch painter : his works are *choses vues*. It has been said, and Canon Ainger repeats the statement, that Crabbe was scarcely a perfect realist ; for if he saw life steadily, he failed to see it whole, and laid too great a stress on its sordid side, on details of brutality and coarseness. But Crabbe by no means ignores the brighter side of things, and Canon Ainger quotes some charming examples of his sunnier pictures ; these are by no means exceptional (especially in his later writings), and are found side by side with the gloomier pictures of life throughout all his work ; but if in his experience the scale of misery seemed to outweigh the scale of joy, must he be called a cynic for not having concealed the fact ? Job and Shakespeare seem to have shared his beliefs. I should indeed be inclined to adduce the work of Crabbe as that of the perfect realist, who, although he saw life without illusions, and did not flinch from describing all that he saw, nevertheless did not do so with the callousness of a vivisector, but was filled with the sense of the pathos of life and with pity for the

> " Poor, blind, bewildered human race
> Who, a short time in varied fortune past,
> Die and are equal in the dust at last."

Crabbe can only be accused of being a cynic by a misuse of the word. Nevertheless the accusation has been made, and will in all probability be made again, as no word in the language is more frequently abused than the word cynic.

It is easy in the case of Crabbe to show up the error. Nobody would dispute the patent fact that Crabbe was a philanthropist. But a cynic is essentially a misanthrope ; and whether he barks, or snarls, or sneers, or laughs, or blights, his disbelief in human sincerity or goodness is based on a fundamental hatred of mankind. Now Crabbe had—it is evident from his writings—a fundamental *love* of mankind. But he was acutely aware of the wickedness and folly inherent in human nature, and he spared no pains to depict them without gloss or disguise and to censure them. This makes him a satirist but not a cynic.

Had he laughed at wickedness and folly, and implied that they were inevitable phenomena and of no consequence, deserving only a sneer, or a snarl, or a contemptuous knowing chortle or chuckle, he would have been a cynic. The word cynic, it is worth while pointing out, is derived from the Greek word *kuon*, and is defined by Dr. Johnson as one who has " the qualities of a dog, currish, brutal, snarling, a misanthrope."

At his best his pathos and feeling find expression in terse and forcible language, as in the following lines describing a compulsory marriage brought about by the pressure of the parish authorities :

> " By long rent cloak, hung loosely, strove the bride
> From every eye, what all perceived, to hide ;
> While the boy-bridegroom, shuffling in his pace,
> Now hid awhile, and then exposed his face ;
> As shame alternately with anger strove
> The brain, confused with muddy ale, to move.
> In haste and stammering he perform'd his part,
> And look'd the rage that rankled in his heart :
> (So will each lover inly curse his fate,
> Too soon made happy, and made wise too late :)
> I saw his features take a savage gloom,
> And deeply threaten for the days to come.
> Low spake the lass, and lisp'd and minced the while,
> Look'd on the lad, and faintly tried to smile ;
> With soften'd speech and humbled tone she strove
> To stir the embers of departed love :
> While he, a tyrant, frowning walk'd before,
> Felt the poor purse, and sought the public door,
> She sadly following in submission went,
> And saw the final shilling foully spent ;
> Then to her father's hut the pair withdrew,
> And bade to love and comfort long adieu !
>   Ah ! fly temptation, youth, refrain ! refrain
>   I preach for ever   but I preach in vain ! "

In this passage the fine qualities of Crabbe's poetic style are apparent. His lines have the force, the directness, the quality of inevitableness which can only result from perfect simplicity and sincerity ; and it should be remembered, in bewailing Crabbe's frequent carelessness and lapses into the prosaic, that these great qualities might have been impaired had he attempted to chisel and polish his verse. His qualities were probably, as in the case of most writers, inseparable from, if not the result of, his defects.

Crabbe's descriptions of Nature have not been surpassed by any English poet ; he has not, it is true, that combination of " felicity of diction " and " natural magic " which gives to certain lines of Shakespeare and Keats a spell that " teases us out of thought." His descriptions are detailed and minute ; but so vivid, that they leave in the mind the impression that we have actually seen what he describes, just as after reading Tolstoy's novels we feel that we have actually known his fictitious characters in the flesh. Such is the description of the autumn day in the *Maid's Story* :

> " There was a day, ere yet the autumn closed,
> When, ere her wintry wars, the earth reposed ;
> When from the yellow weed the feathery crown,
> Light as the curling smoke, fell slowly down ;
> When the wing'd insect settled in our sight,
> And waited wind to recommence her flight ;
> When the wide ocean was a silver sheet,
> And on the ocean slept the unanchor'd fleet ;
> When from our garden, as we looked above,
> There was no cloud, and nothing seemed to move."

Sometimes he approaches something very like the achievement of which Dante is the greatest master,

15

of presenting in a single line a whole landscape and the atmosphere of a scene, as in :

> " Ships softly sinking in a sleepy sea."

But the following passage taken from one of the *Tales of the Hall* is perhaps the most characteristic example of Crabbe's work at its best, combining, as it does, his descriptive power, his pathos, and his charm :

> " The morning breeze had urg'd the quickening mill ;
> Assembled rooks had wing'd their seaward flight,
> By the same passage to return at night.
> While proudly o'er them hung the steady kite,
> Then turn'd him back, and left the noisy throng,
> Nor deign'd to know them as he sail'd along.
> Long yellow leaves from oziers strew'd around
> Choked the small stream, and hush'd the feeble sound ;
> While the dead foliage dropt from loftier trees.
> Our squire beheld, not with his wonted ease,
> But to his own reflections made reply,
> And said aloud, ' Yes ! doubtless we must die.' "

It is impossible to read these lines without feeling that the judgments of Johnson, Burke, Fox, Scott, Byron, Miss Austen, FitzGerald, and Tennyson with regard to Crabbe are just, and that the generation which neglects him is one, if not of vipers, at least of deaf adders.

The portrait which Canon Ainger has drawn of Crabbe the man is vivid and sympathetic ; perhaps what strikes one most forcibly in his life is the deep impression Crabbe made on his contemporaries ; Burke after his first brief interview with the poet became his patron and protector, and rescued him from starvation ; he afterwards helped him in his work with criticism and suggestions ; Dr. Johnson and Charles James Fox did the same, and actually revised and corrected his poems. It is as if at the present day the Prime Minister revised the poems of Mr. Austin Dobson.

At the conclusion Canon Ainger says that within the last twenty years there has been a marked revival of interest in the poetry of Crabbe. This interest must inevitably be fostered and increased by this delightful volume. It is to be hoped that it may lead to the reissue of Murray's edition of 1834, which would thus in a sense be a double monument, to Crabbe and his biographer.

1904.

MR. YEATS'S POEMS

IN this, his latest volume,[1] Mr. Yeats has given us the harvest of seven years' labour. The book contains three short plays and fifteen poems. The harvest is slender, but it is all pure wheat and there is no chaff at all in it. The plays are written for the stage, and they have all of them already been played and have successfully held an audience, although since then they have been considerably revised and altered by the author. They are not the kind of plays we see lavishly mounted (with real water and live camels) at His Majesty's Theatre or elsewhere in London. They depend for their interest, not at all on external things, and but little on their action. But it would be untrue to say they have no action. They display the development of the most interesting kind of action : the action of souls, or rather what Mr. Yeats in his preface calls the " subtle consequence of cause and effect that moves through vast sentiments and intricate thoughts that accompany action but are not necessary to it." The action, as in the case of Maeterlinck, is less important than the atmosphere in which the players are plunged. " Plays are plays and books are books," said a character in Mr. Wells's *Kipps*. And Mr. Yeats's plays are plays ; they have stood the test of performance ; if we had a national theatre where Shakespeare's plays would be played and not turned into an elaborate music-hall turn, where the words seem to interrupt the main business in hand, namely, the scenery,

[1] *Collected Works.* Vol. I. Poems published by E. A. Bullen. 1908.

the dresses, and the incidental music, Mr. Yeats's plays, would be performed at it, so would Swinburne's *Atalanta in Calydon*, and many other beautiful things. But we have not the thing, although a band of young people are now in many directions and in various ways struggling to obtain it, and assuredly one day they will succeed. To go back to Mr. Yeats's plays : they take hold of the reader ; they touch you with the desire to know what is going to happen next, and they suggest to you that what you see happening is a small thing compared to what you do not see ; that the actors are at once the sport and the interpreters of mighty forces, of wind and wave, of lake, mountain, and forest, and the calm, immutable powers that are hidden behind them. They are written in verse of which to say it is " musical " or " skilful " would be a poor and bald compliment. It is the verse of a master, full of subtle cadences, and sub-servient always to an invisible rhythm that is handled with the power of a wizard. The dramatist is not swamped by the poet. There are no purple patches and bravura passages, but every now and then a beautiful image blossoms in the right place and at the right time ; every now and then we get a glimpse into something illimitable or terrible or entrancing. Nothing is here solely for the sake of ornament, although everything serves to adorn. It is difficult to quote from plays such as these : but here are some lines from the *King's Threshold*, some jewels which should tempt the reader to the enchanted treasure-house :

> " O silver trumpets ! Be you lifted up,
> And cry to the great race that is to come.
> Long-throated swans, amid the waves of Time,
> Sing loudly, for beyond the wall of the world
> It waits, and it may hear and come to us."

Besides plays, there are in this book fifteen poems.
There are, thank goodness, a great many different kinds
of good poets in the world. When a new one appears,
people try to class him and to " place " him, as if he
were a schoolboy competing in an examination. This
is at the best rather a fruitless task, since every true poet
is simply himself, and he is himself because he is unlike
all others. But just as one can say that between certain
artists there are affinities, that Tennyson is related to
Virgil, Racine to Mozart, and Swinburne to Wagner, so,
for the sake of convenience merely, the convenience of
the reader who wishes to know what to expect, although
we cannot say what Mr. Yeats's poetry is like (to do that
you must simply read it), we can point out what it is not
like. Mr. Yeats's poetry is not at all like that of other
masters, whose contact with everyday life has been
intimate, whose poetry has arisen from the clash of
their personality with the everyday world. It is not
like the poetry of Mr. Kipling or Monsieur Rostand,
full of life, glitter, and the sound of a " world of men " ;
it is not like the poetry of a reflective meditator on human
affairs such as M. Sully-Prudhomme or Mr. William
Watson ; but it belongs to the world of those who,
while withdrawing themselves from the busy market-
place, have looked into their own souls and understood
the passions and the dreams of mankind, of those who
have wandered in the secret places of nature and have
gone beyond into the " unknown land " which reaches
right up to the shore of Lethe, where, as Catullus said
in a divine line :

" Pallidulum manans adluit unda pedem,"

and whose hills and plains and forests and valleys are
full of the shadows of dead kings and beautiful witches

and of heroes : Roland of Roncevaux, and Sigurd, with
the eyes like lightning. Mr. Yeats lives in this country,
and with the strains of his mysterious harp summons
up for us the holy vision, the wizard glimpse. Here is
an instance :

> " What were our praise to them ? They eat
> Quiet's wild heart, like daily meat ;
> Who when night thickens are afloat
> On dappled skins in a glass boat,
> Far out under a windless sky,
> While over them birds of Aengus fly,
> And over the tiller and the prow,
> And waving white wings to and fro
> Awaken wanderings of light air
> To stir their coverlet and their hair."

These lines occur in a poem called " Baile and Aillinn,"
which seems to me intoxicatingly beautiful. Here is
an image from " Adam's Curse " :

> " A moon, worn as if it had been a shell
> Washed by Time's waters as they rose and fell
> About the stars, and broke in days and years."

There is also another note which Mr. Yeats is master of,
that is, a kind of quaint and delicious humour, as, for
instance, the poem, " The Happy Townland." Here
is a stanza :

> " The little fox he murmured,
>   ' O what of the world's bane ? '
> The sun was laughing sweetly,
>   The moon plucked at my rein ;
> But the little red fox murmured,
>   ' O ! do not pluck at his rein,
> He is riding to the townland
>   That is the world's bane.' "

Critics, I believe, are supposed to point out the faults
as well as the qualities of a book. To me personally
there are no faults in this book ; there are things I do not

understand, but that is, I am sure, my own fault. " I do not always heed the sense," and am happy not doing so. Again, it is just possible that Mr. Yeats might incur the danger of imitating himself and falling into mannerism. In reading the lines which form the dedication one feels that one more touch, another inch, and we should be reading a very clever parody of Mr. Yeats.

1908.

THE SENTIMENTAL TRAVELLER

MODERN literature is like a display of fire-works. The rockets shoot up into the sky, and after they have burst in a splutter of many-coloured fires drop on to the ground, mere charred sticks, and attract no further attention. The rocket is the novel whose edition of many thousand copies is sold before the day of publication. Then there are Catherine wheels of sensationalism, Roman candles of verse, which are mistaken for poetry, squibs of abuse mistaken for satire, and crackers of familiar personality, which are equally conspicuous and ephemeral. The whole spectacle is so noisy and amusing that one no longer notices the permanent stars in the quiet sky beyond, and still less the calm tapers that burn unnoticed, save by rare worshippers, in the little wayside chapels. These chapels, however, exist. They belong to those who write well, and they are consecrated to the Deities of beauty, of tranquil thought, and of style.

The work of Vernon Lee constitutes just such a chapel. It has nothing to do with the daily display of fireworks. It is dim, and supported by delicate columns, incongruous pillars, some being Byzantine, some Doric, some Corinthian, as in the Roman Church by Tiber—I have forgotten its name—opposite the Temple of Minerva, and it is paved with marble the colour of seaweed and lit with tall waxen tapers.

It must not be thought that Vernon Lee is a priestess

of the art-for-art's-sake theory. It is now plainly visible in everything she writes that she considers life to be more important than art, and what she says leaves one with the feeling that she is giving you certain fruits from a large garden of thought, feeling, and experience, which is her life, whereas with the writers of the art-for-art's-sake school we feel they have poured the whole of the wine of their substance into their art, reserving for their life nothing but the dregs of the bottle.

This book by Vernon Lee, *The Sentimental Traveller*, is a series of glimpses, a kind of spiritual cinematograph, bringing before the reader definite visions of romantic, out-of-the-way, often obscure places ; and these visions in their turn reveal further glimpses, and open on to an enchanted beyond of memories, histories, forgotten epochs, quaint fashions ; and in all these evocations you hear, like the humming of a small stringed orchestra, the music of humanity, cheerful and pathetic. To say that these essays are well written would be as inadequate as it would be to say that Whistler's pictures are well painted. Vernon Lee's mastery of her vehicle of expression is absolute. She not only says exactly what she wants to say, but she leaves out a hundred things which she might say, but which would not be worth saying at a particular moment. She manipulates language as a consummate conductor directs an orchestra. By the use of one word, by the mention of one object, she evokes a landscape. Here is an example :

" When I came down to tea the peasants in the castle chapel were singing the psalm *Magnificat* in those tones which seem to have grown hoarse and false even as other things get chipped or stained in coming through the centuries ; our perfect church-singing sounding by comparison as if it had been renewed, cleaned up but yesterday. I remembered it was All Souls' Eve—the Vigil of the Dead, as the Italians express it. The sun was setting behind the wooded ridges ; curls of smoke hanging heavy among the yellow poplars of the river below. From that paved yard one could see into the church, see the tapers lit and the illuminated faces of the women holding them. In the middle of that former castle yard, now open to the landscape, stands an ilex overhanging the well, and a wine-stained cart and barrel stood by."

Again, she feels intimately the poetry of place, the meaning of mythology, and the legendary romance that clings to certain spots and names. In a beautiful paper called the *Hills of the Setting Sun* she evokes the poetry of what was the first haunt of the Three Hesperides, and she reproduces the magic of the Euganean landscape :

" Yesterday, in the sad journey south, my dear Hills of the Setting Sun, as I passed by in the train, seemed very distant and unfamiliar in their disembodied autumn blue ; . . . The yellow plain of faded vines wrapped itself in vapours, with faint precocious sunset flushings, lasting till dark. By twilight we were crossing the Po, brimful, the black bridge of boats spanning it. A little lurid red still lingered in the clouds and in the turbid water : the blood of Phaethon, maybe, or Icarus's scattered feathers."

By a sentence such as this last one, she opens a window on to the mythology of Italy and Greece. But perhaps her most pleasing papers are those in which the human note is most distinctly heard. The paper, for instance, on " Goethe at Weimar " which is singularly moving, that on " Säckingen and the Trumpeter " with its charmingly told reminiscences of childhood in Germany, " The Bead-Threader's Funeral " in Venice, and the description of Narni with the episode of the discharged convict. Indeed, the glimpses of personal reminiscence which we get every now and then in the delicate jottings of this "sentimental traveller" give one a thirst for more. Vernon Lee now has written five books almost entirely devoted to the *genius loci*, and among these *The Sentimental Traveller* is as delightful as any; it will be read, as all her books are read, all over Europe—in Austria, in Germany, in Russia, with delight. It is a beautiful book, an oasis of leisure and beauty amidst the noisy literature of the day. It is therefore in no carping spirit that one suggests to her that for her next volume she should seek for something a little different. The glimpses of personal reminiscence and biography to which I have alluded are so delightful that one would like a whole book of them. Why should she not write a book of personal reminiscences : *A Sentimental Diary* or *Biography*. One feels certain it would be a beautiful book, and eagerly devoured by her many admirers in many lands.

1908.

ARIADNE IN MANTUA

A FEW years ago a short play in five acts was published in Oxford by Mr. Blackwell bearing this title and signed Vernon Lee. Although the works of Vernon Lee are known and appreciated throughout Europe, this little paper book attracted scant attention. It was scarcely mentioned in the Press, and when it was mentioned it was classed with the ephemeral rubbish of the day, and given a few lines of hurried comment. " J'ai toujours pensé, peut-être bien à tort," says M. Anatole France, " que personne ne fait des chefs-d'œuvre, et que c'est la une tâche supérieure aux individus quels qu'ils soient, mais que les plus heureux d'entre les mortels produisent parfois des ouvrages qui peuvent devenir des chefs-d'œuvre, avec l'aide du temps, qui est un galant homme, comme disait Mazarin." I cannot help thinking that *Ariadne in Mantua* will run a considerable risk of becoming a masterpiece with the aid of courteous Time. About five years have elapsed since its first appearance, and these five years, which have touched so much prose with incurable decay, seem merely to have revarnished the colours of this masterly painting.

The Palace of Mantua and the lake it sleeps in (about which Vernon Lee once wrote a beautiful paper) and a certain song of the early seventeenth century, " Amarilli," by Caccini, suggested this drama to its author. The action takes place during the reign of Prospero I. of Milan, and shortly before the Venetian expedition to Cyprus under Othello. This little note telling us the place of action already opens a window on that most enchanting of periods, when the sea was in Bohemia and Giulio Romano painted a statue of Hermione, daughter of the Emperor of Russia, for Leontes, King of Sicilia, and contemporary of the Oracle of Apollo. The expectations raised by the opening note, so far from being disappointed, are realised beyond our dreams. One expects after it, and, indeed, in any work of Vernon Lee's, a subtle understanding of the past, a magical evocation of gorgeous spirits, of stately music, and courtly phrase. But in this drama there is all that, and more ; there is, besides, the potent imaginative spell which resuscitates a past with all its glowing atmosphere and its train of splendid phantoms, a rich and poignant vein of feeling and trembling thought, a suggestion of fundamental conflicts and a presentation of eternal passions.

Each of the stage directions describing the scenery of each act is a jewel in itself. Nobody but Vernon Lee could have written them. Here is the stage-direction which precedes the second act :

" *Another part of the Ducal Palace of Mantua. The Duchess's closet ; a small irregular chamber ; the vaulted ceiling painted with Giottesque patterns in blue and russet, much blackened, and among which there is visible only a coronation of the Virgin, white and vision-like. Shelves with a few books and phials and jars of medicine ; a small movable organ in a corner ; and in front of the ogival window a praying-chair and large crucifix. The crucifix is black against the landscape, against the grey and misty waters of the lake ; and framed by the nearly leafless branches of a willow growing below.*"

Such brief lines of description are the fruit of a whole lifetime of culture and erudition and of rare skill in the use of words.

The fundamental idea of this drama is, as Vernon Lee says in the preface, the conflict between the contending forces of history and life; between impulse and discipline; between blind, selfish, magnanimous love and tradition and civilisation. The hero of the drama is Ferdinand, Duke of Mantua, who has been a prey to an inexplicable malady ever since his return from many years' captivity among the Infidels. The Cardinal, his uncle, engages Diego, a Spaniard of Moorish descent, and a most expert singer and player on the virginal, to win access to his Highness's confidence; to understand and compass the Duke's strange malady. The Duke's moodiness is marked by abhorrence of all womankind. And the mere name of his young cousin and affianced bride, Princess Hippolyta, throws him into paroxysms of rage. Diego is told that the Duke is of those who are apt to love once, and, as the poets say, to die of love; Diego is to keep to his part of singer, and not to let the Duke suspect anything. He is to be a mere singing creature, having seen passion, but never felt it, yet capable by the miracle of art of rousing it and soothing it afterwards. Now Diego is in reality none other than Magdalen, a courtesan, whom the Duke loved passionately, who saved his life and brought about his escape from among the Infidels by sacrificing herself. At the beginning of the second act, which is a duologue between Diego and the Duchess Dowager, Ferdinand's mother, the Duchess thanks Diego for having been chosen of Heaven to work a miracle and to cure her son. She wishes to thank Diego, and he receives her thanks with irony. At last she touches him.

" Do not tempt me, madam," he says, " O God, I do not want your pity, your loving-kindness. What are such things to me ? As to understanding my sorrows, no one can save the very one who is inflicting them. Besides, you and I call different things by the same names. What you call love to me means nothing : nonsense taught to children, priests' metaphysics. What I mean you do not know. But woe's me, you have awakened the power of breaking through this silence—this silence which is starvation and death by thirst and suffocation. And it so happens that if I speak to you all will be wrecked."

Yet Diego reveals his secret. But the Duchess, instead of ordering his arrest, as he expects, is merely plunged in thought. At last she speaks thus :

"Then it is he who, as you call it, spurns you ? How so ? For you are admitted to his close familiarity ; nay, you have worked the miracle of curing him. I do not understand the situation. For, Diego—I know not by what other name to call you—I feel your sorrow is a deep one. You are not the woman who would despair and call God cruel for a mere lovers' quarrel ; you love my son ; you have cured him — cured him, do I guess rightly ? through your love. But if it be so, what can my son have done to break your heart ? "

Then Diego explains that the Duke does not recognise him. He is fully cured. " The Duke," he says, " remembers everything save me." The Duchess asks Diego to pray with her. " I cannot pray for light, most gracious madam," he answers, " because I fear it. Indeed I cannot pray at all ; there remains nought to pray for, but among the vain and worldly songs I have had to get by heart there is by chance a kind of little hymn, a childish little verse, but a sincere one." And while the Duchess kneels in silent prayer Diego sings this snatch of song :

> " Mother of God,
> We are thy weary children ;
> Teach us, thou weeping Mother,
> To cry ourselves to sleep."

The third act is a duologue between the Duke and Diego. It takes place in the hanging gardens of the

Duke's apartments in the darkness of the first warm night of spring. The Duke tells Diego that he owed his liberation from captivity to the most faithful, the most beloved, intrepid, magnanimous, and loving of women.

" The poets," says the Duke, " fabled many things concerning virtuous women " (he cites Arria, Antigone, and Alcestis), " whereas here, here was a creature infinitely humble, a waif, a poor spurned toy of brutal mankind's pleasure . . . who had never heard such words as duty or virtue, and yet whose acts first taught me what they truly meant."

Here the crisis of the drama is reached. The Duke explains the magnanimous conduct of Magdalen, and on Diego's saying that perhaps Magdalen realised that his love was turning stale and therefore set him free, the Duke breaks into passionate outburst :

" Stale ! My love grown stale ? You make me laugh, boy, instead of angering. Stale ! you never knew her. She was not like a song—even your sweetest song. . . . She was like music—the whole art : new modes, new melodies, new rhythms with every day and hour, passionate, or sad, or gay, or very quiet. . . .

DIEGO. You loved her then sincerely ?

DUKE. . . . Loved her, boy ! I love her."

And the Duke tells him how it is not music, but love and love's delusion that has cured him, since by Diego he has been somehow reminded of Magdalen. Diego asks what would have happened if Diego had turned into Magdalen. The Duke answers that he would have taken Magdalen's hand and said, " Welcome, dear sister. This is a world of spells ; let us repeat some. Become henceforth my brother. . . . Be the Duke of Mantua's best and truest friend ; turn into Diego, Magdalen."

16

But in saying all this to her, has he recognised her ? That is the question, and I doubt whether the author herself could give us an answer. Has he recognised her, and is he saying all this, meaning her to understand that he *has* recognised her ; and that they are both of them to leave it at that ? That is to say : is he veiling any feelings he still may have and avoiding the expression of them, avoiding all possible expression of all possible feeling, on both sides, and simply behaving as a perfect man of the world and wishing her to understand this, once and for all ? or, is he groping blindly and desperately like a man awakening from a dream, too wide awake for dreamland, and still too dream-dizzy and spellbound for reality ?

We don't know ; possibly, I say, the author does not know ; and it is this doubt, this uncertainty that constitutes, I will not say, the originality (for *Hamlet* and other works are original in just the same way), but let us say the poignancy, the drama of the situation.

Of course, if the play were to be acted on the stage, the actor who plays the Duke would have to make up *his* mind what he imagines was the Duke's state of mind, and let the audience feel that he meant to portray either one thing or the other, either this or that, either that the Duke recognised Magdalen, or that he did not. Or rather, it would be his task to let the audience be pleasantly mystified, just as when they see *Hamlet*.

I mean, when an actor plays Hamlet, he must make up his own mind as to whether he thinks Hamlet was mad or not, and yet he need not let the audience into the whole of his secret ; he may still allow the audience to be mystified—mystified, that is to say, as far as mystification is a pleasure, but not one inch farther. He must act in such a way that every member of the audience may be able to say, " he means Hamlet to be mad," or again, " he means Hamlet *not* to be mad." And every member of the audience must think that he and only he himself is right. It is the same here. Every member of the audience should be led to say, if he sees this play acted, " the Duke does," " the Duke does *not* recognise Magdalen," just as the reader does ; and every member of the audience should, just as every reader, think he is right.

It is only a rare artist who creates and successfully deals with these complex poignant situations.

The fourth act is a duologue between Diego and Princess Hippolyta, the Duke's affianced bride ; but in reality it is a dialogue between impulse and discipline, between blind love and civilised tradition, in which tradition carries off the victory. In the fifth act comes the catastrophe. The wedding-day of the Duke is being celebrated by the performance of a masque in a Grecian temple overlooking the lake. The masque performed is the story of Ariadne in Naxos : the desertion of Ariadne by Theseus. Diego plays Ariadne, and sings at the end a little song which the Duke had loved when Magdalen sang it. He recognises the song. Ariadne flings herself into the lake and is drowned in earnest. The dripping body of Diego is brought and the Duke, stooping over it, says : " Magdalen ! "

The beauty and power of the play depend entirely on subtle gradations of thought and feeling answering to each other and playing upon each other, built up note by note. Quotations from this play are like bars of music torn from a song, or squares of canvas cut out of a picture. To touch the play is to mutilate it ; to appreciate it one must read it all. A company such as that of the Art

Theatre at Moscow would make something gorgeously effective with it on the stage ; but it is a play which does not call for star actors, but for whole-hearted co-operation, perfect *ensemble*, and above all things for an intelligent and courageous producer.

1908.

IBSEN

IT is a singularly fortunate dispensation of Providence that it should have fallen to the lot of Mr. Edmund Gosse to write the first complete biography of Ibsen which has appeared in Europe. Mr. Gosse is not only the first Englishman who discovered Ibsen, and introduced him to the English public so far back as 1872, nearly twenty years before there were such things as " dolorous Ibsenites," but he has made a special and lifelong study of Northern literature ; he is steeped in the atmosphere, the language, the manners, and the customs of the native country of his subject ; he has a first-hand knowledge of the soil and the air which nourished and supported the portentous tree. Other critics have likewise known Ibsen personally ; the point is that Mr. Gosse conversed with him in Norwegian, and saw his dramas played in their native tongue without the veil of a translation. If I were Mr. Chesterton, I should say the important thing about Mr. Gosse as a biographer of Ibsen was not that he knew Ibsen, but that he knew Björnson. He has an intimate knowledge of the works and the personalities of all the great Northern writers the contemporaries of Ibsen, the trees of the forest in which Ibsen grew, and he is equally familiar with the predecessors of the poet (with Holberg, Hertz, etc.) in the domain of Norse literature. That this makes a substantial difference any one who has lived in Denmark or Norway can testify. A great deal that seems to be extravagant in the plays of Ibsen is less extravagant than what occurs every day in real life in Copenhagen. Ibsen's mirror attenuates rather than exaggerates the phenomena of Norse life. But Ibsen is fortunate in his biographer, not only on account of Mr. Gosse's unique and first-hand knowledge of his subject, but also by reason of his unique biographical gifts. It is scarcely necessary to point this out at a moment when the whole literary world is ringing with the praise of Mr. Gosse's *Father and Son*, which has been instantly and universally recognised as one of the finest pieces of portraiture ever written, and as a book to which only one epithet is applicable, but one which renders all further praise superfluous, namely, " classic."

In his life of Ibsen the qualities which delighted us in *Father and Son* are once more present : the same *sensibilité*, the same gift of delicate portraiture, the same lightness of touch, the same rippling undercurrent of inimitable humour. (Oh, what a relief when Ibsen is the subject !) One cannot help thinking, however much one admires the giants of the North, that it would be a fatally easy achievement to write an unreadable book about Ibsen ! What makes the lives of poets, as Dr. Johnson said, as cheerless reading as *The Newgate Calendar* is perhaps this : they tell what they wish to tell to the whole world, only they tell it in poetry, and the world does not understand them ; and having made this great public and impersonal confidence they shut the gates of their soul on individual human feelings and deny the secrets which their poetry is shouting to the world, even to their nearest and dearest friends. One is particularly conscious of this in reading Ibsen's life. Because the great fact about Ibsen, by far the most important thing about him, is that he is a poet. All great poets are isolated from the world ; they dwell

> " In the cold starlight where thou canst not climb";

and Ibsen seems to have gone through the world like a solid ghost, a somnambulist, merely opening his lips to bark at the people who disturb his dream. Certain things affected him, the presence of Björnson, for instance, because even in the cold starlight an orb cannot be unconscious of the inrush of a comet, and in the super-human spaces Lucifer still bows to St. Michael ; but what was said about Ibsen in the daily Press, what the man in the street thought about him, never reached the spaces of sun and storm in which he lived, the snowy pinnacles, the thunderous avalanches, and the gleaming fjords of his soul. Mr. Gosse has made what is generally the most tedious part of biography entertaining in the highest degree. The record of Ibsen's youth as told in this book is intensely fascinating ; his childhood in Skien, the city of marine merchandise, by the waterfalls and the " screaming saws " ; his apprenticeship to an apothecary at the little town of Grimstad, where for nearly six years, in Mr. Gosse's phrase, one of the acutest brains in Europe interested itself in fraying ipecacuanha and mixing black draughts ; his excruciating poverty ; his spectral appearance ; the awakening of his soul to the convulsion of 1848 ; his first drama, *Catalina*, inspired by Sallust, in which the voice of the great rebel is heard for the first time (from which Mr. Gosse quotes some extremely interesting and characteristic passages) : all this is painted vividly, lightly, and sympathetically, with infinite intuition and unerring tact.

Then comes the period when, in 1851, Ibsen went as a sort of literary manager to the theatre at Bergen, and for a second time became an apprentice, only this time in the art of the dramatist. And here he learnt to make the " rainbow-coloured pills " which fell like dynamite on the modern stage, and convulsed Europe.

It would be too lengthy a business here to follow Ibsen's career from start to finish under the delightful guidance of Mr. Gosse. The reader will find in his book every phase of Ibsen's life and each new factor and manner of his work delicately evoked and underlined with a thin line of luminous comment.

Some of the remarks he makes by the way are extraordinarily acute. This, for instance : " Ibsen, whose practice is always better than his theory " ; and again : " He was always an observer, always a clinical analyst at the bedside of society, never a prophet, never a propagandist." Here, too, is a remark made about Ibsen's see-saw relation of friendship and feud with Björnson : " Nothing exasperates a friendship more fatally than public principle grafted on a private slight." About Ibsen's renunciation of verse, Mr. Gosse writes the following exquisitely apposite sentence : " If in the second portion of his career he resolutely deprived himself of all indulgence, it was a voluntary act of austerity. It was Charles V. at Yuste wilfully exchanging the crown of jewels for the coarse brown cowl of St. Jerome."

But the keynote of this biography is the great dominant fact, which all students of Ibsen feel, but which those who know the Norwegian language feel intimately, that Ibsen was from the beginning to the end of his life a poet. He learnt the business of Scribe, and this enabled him to present the human beings he created on the stage, a thing which Goethe confessed himself he had tried and failed to do all his life. But the reason why Ibsen was able to create his human beings, to know all about them, to be the " clinical analyst at the bedside of humanity," was because he was a poet : because his knife was intuition and his diagnosis the art of divination, which the great poets alone possess. After Ibsen deliberately renounced verse as a vehicle, and set about inaugurating a new era in theatrical realism, still the poet in him subsisted. Mr. Gosse does not agree with Georg Brandes when he talks of the " poetry " of *Ghosts*. One cannot help thinking, however, that the man who bade so tremendous a tragedy arise, develop, and burst like a crash of thunder in such intensely commonplace surroundings, was indeed writing a poem. In Ibsen's later plays the poet triumphed in a riot of symbolism, which ended in that blaze of unintelligibility and—Ibsenites all, forgive us !—boredom : *When we Dead awaken*.

Mr. Gosse not only paints for us a vivid portrait of Ibsen the man, but he provides us with an illuminating commentary on the prose plays. He is sometimes heretical ; for instance, when he says that *Rosmersholm* is sometimes scarcely more credible than a Gilbert and Sullivan opera, and much less amusing, a remark which will elicit sympathy amongst hundreds of genuine admirers of Ibsen. A religion has been made around the realistic prose plays of Ibsen, but one doubts whether they form the most enduring jewel of his crown. The present writer assisted at a great revival of *The Doll's House* at Copenhagen some years ago, when Nora was interpreted by the celebrated Danish artist, Fru Hennings. The next day the Press pointed out what the public had felt, namely, that the last act, which when the play was first produced had seemed so startling and audacious, now seemed commonplace and dull. Such is the fate of advanced ideas in prose. With poetry it is different. Euripides' advanced ideas are still fresh. *Brand* and *Peer Gynt* will for ever endure. And on the strength of these two huge, glorious poems, Ibsen must have marched straight to the Valhalla of the Immortals ; there where the serene Olympians—Sophocles, Virgil, Goethe, Pushkin, and Racine—sit on the right ; and the sombre Titans—Aeschylus, Dante, Byron, Baudelaire, and Dostoyevski—on the left ; Shakespeare and Homer presiding in the middle in serene impartiality. There he no doubt exclaimed, " All or nothing," and asked for the best place ; but the ghosts gave him a high throne, like that of Satan, among the Titans, and some one of them (perhaps it was the disrespectful Heine) chanted the words of Carducci :

> " Salute, O Satana,
>   O ribellione,
> O forza vindice
>   De la ragione ! "

1908.

MARY COLERIDGE

(*To R. B.*)

UNDER the pseudonym of "Anodos" Mary Coleridge gave a few of her poems to the world during her lifetime. At different times she published a few more. But she refused to publish under her own name an edition of these poems, which now that she is dead, have been collected and given to the world. Poetry with Mary Coleridge was not the recreation of a dilettante, but the record of imperative visions, the expression of "thoughts that breathe," and cannot be stifled. In a poem called "Confidence" she writes :

> " Even to one I dare not tell
> Where lies my Heaven, where lies my Hell ;
> But to the world will I confide
> What's hid from all the world beside."

Her poems are the confidences and confessions of what is too intimate save for poetry. Clothed in the intangible veil of verse, she lets her thoughts loose like dragon-flies on a summer field ; they have the transparence and mystery of dew, they are as perspicuous and enigmatic as a crystal with a rainbow in its heart. Her poems are completely personal, utterly unlike those of any one else, and show no traces of alien influence, contemporary, past or present. She has, of course, Coleridge blood in her veins, and her poems are like Coleridge's in kind, without being in the least imitative ; that is to say, her poetry has more affinity with her ancestor than with Dryden or Leopardi ; but, on the other hand, her verse is not more like Coleridge than it is like Heine.

Many poets seem to get half a vision, a glimpse, a hint of what is behind the veil. Others—a very small number—seem to have the veil lifted for them and to see as clearly in the land of dream as they do in the broad day. Mary Coleridge records visions as direct and enigmatic as those of " Christabel." For instance, this unforgettable beginning of a song :

" We were young, we were merry, we were very very wise,
    And the door stood open at our feast,
When there passed us a woman with the West in her eyes,
    And a man with his back to the East."

Here we have a record of something seen in a crystal in which the mists have dissipated. Perhaps they descended once more before she finished the poem, the end of which seems to be superfluous, since all is said in these four haunting lines. Sometimes the vision strikes a chill by its supernatural quality : as in the " Witches' Wood," or the poem called " Wilderspin," which begins :

" In the little red house by the river
    When the short night fell . . ."

Sometimes it bids one hear the horns of romance, as in the song of the Seven that fought with Four :

" There were three that bled, there was one that led,
    Where they fought with four and three.
The silvery swords were crimson red,
    And the grass was a sight to see."

She has the gift in a few short lines of evoking a picture which suggests a whole story, enough to furnish a playwright with a drama or a storyteller with a romance.

An instance of this is " The King " :

> " It was but the lightest word of the King,
>   When he was neither merry nor sad ;
> It was but a very little thing,
>   Yet it made his servant glad.
>
> He gave a look as it befell,
>   Between a smile and a smothered sigh.
> Whether he meant it, who can tell ?
>   But the man went out to die."

Perhaps the finest of her imaginative poems is " Master and Guest." But there are a great many poems in this book where this kind of romantic second sight is in abeyance, and she merely crystallises the lyric impulse of the moment. Here is an example in which there is a note of ecstasy :

> " Love went a-riding over the earth,
>   On Pegasus he rode,
> The flowers before him sprang to birth,
>   And the frozen rivers flowed.
>
> Then all the youths and the maidens cried,
>   ' Stay here with us, King of kings ! '
> But Love said, ' No ! for the horse I ride,
>   For the horse I ride has wings.' "

The following also seems to me not only characteristic but undefinably beautiful :

> " The sense of fellowship is grown
>   A radiant mystery.
> The dusk is shot with light ; the stone
>   Is like unto the eyes that see.
>
> " No more the wild confusèd main
>   Is tossed about with storms of fear.
> The sea is singing ; and the rain
>   Is music in the ears that hear."

Very beautiful, too, in quite a different manner are the lines " To a Tree " and those " On an Ink-Bottle." In all these poems, whatever they may be about, whether they are supernatural, romantic, or personal, we are in communication with a radiant spirit, a seer of marvellous things, a worshipper in the inner shrine. Combined with this vision, Mary Coleridge had a gift of expression which above all others is precious, namely, perfect simplicity and limpidity of style. It is the gift which Heine and Coleridge possessed in the highest degree, and Goethe in his finest lyrics. I have seen it said in the Press that he who seeks for graces of style must not go to Mary Coleridge. Greater nonsense was never penned. It is true that you will not find ornament here for the sake of ornament, but the perfection arising from the utter absence of unnecessary ornament and out-of-the-way words. If any one should doubt this, let them read the following sonnet :

ALCESTIS TO ADMETUS.

" Build over me no marble monument,
  To stand for ever high above the throng ;
  Weave not my name in any wreath of song,
Hang up no picture of my life's event.
The lasting stone would mock thy brief lament,
  Witness thy short affection over long,
  The steadfast words thy changing passions wrong.
The painted features cry : ' Repent ! repent ! '
Live and forget me. Farewell ! Better so,
Than that I should be made the scorn of men,
  Who mark the pageantry of grief, the show
Of feeling lighter than the wind, and then,
  With lifted eyebrows, smile and whisper : ' Lo !
A year is passed, Admetus weds again.' "

1908.

EDWARD LEAR [1]

NO one can have read Lear's *Book of Nonsense* without feeling that its author must have been a delightful person. His biography, edited by Lady Strachey, confirms that suspicion. It reveals the personality of the author of " The Owl and the Pussy Cat." It also bears witness to the general rule that whimsical nonsense is the offspring of permanent sadness. " Out of my big sorrows I make my little puns," Lear might have said. Lear was whimsical but not eccentric. He jingled the jester's bells ; but Ariel, and not Chicot, was his master. There was in him a vein of delicate music. He composed tunes for Tennyson's lyrics and sometimes for his own verse, but he did not know how to write them down. Like all those singers who give the most pleasure (if one may not call them the best), he had no voice, but his singing made his listeners cry. Once when he was singing " Home they brought her Warrior Dead " to a large party in 1851, Archibishop Tait, then Bishop of Carlisle, said to him : " Sir, you ought to have half the Laureateship." Sir Percy Florence Shelley once transcribed the tune Lear had composed to the lyric, " O World, O Life, O Time." His extraordinary mastery of rhythm is, of course, the most remarkable thing about his verse. It is quite different from the neat clashing rhymes of

[1] *Letters of Edward Lear.* Edited by Lady Strachey. (Fisher Unwin. 1907.)

most writers of humorous poetry. Poems like " The Owl and the Pussy Cat " have an *organic* rhythm. That is to say, the whole poem (and not merely the separate lines and stanzas) forms a piece of architectonic music. The only other poet who has achieved the same thing (in a serious vein) is Edgar Allan Poe, and sometimes— in a lesser degree—William Morris. Edward Lear was also a painter. Painting was the main business of his life ; and by his brush he earned his daily bread. " Lear never seems," Mr. Henry Strachey tells us in an interesting estimate of his painting, " to have had complete sympathy with any aspect of Nature except one which showed him the greatest number of topographical details." He was a topographical artist. At the same time he had a real and true sense of beauty which enabled him to depict with the brush the amethyst mountains and the blue valleys above Thermopylæ. What is perhaps most striking in his water-colours, his humour, and his verse, is their essentially English quality and character. Nobody but an Englishman paints this kind of water-colours ; nobody but an Englishman could have thought of the young lady of Sweden who went by the slow train to Weedon, or invented the " Yonghy-Bonghy-Bò."

Lear was born in 1812. He began to draw " for bread and cheese " in about 1827, shop sketches, screens and fans, and " morbid disease drawings for hospitals." In 1832 he published *The Family of the Psittacidæ*, the first complete volume of coloured drawings of birds on a large scale published in England. In 1835 he turned to landscape painting, and in 1837, finding his health to be affected by the climate, he went abroad, wintering in Rome till 1841, when he came to England and published a volume of lithographs called *Rome and its Environs.* In 1845 he gave Queen Victoria some drawing lessons. In connection with this, Lady Strachey tells an amusing anecdote. The Queen was showing Lear some of the treasures at Windsor, and Lear, carried away by the interest of what he saw, exclaimed : " Oh ! how *did* you get all these beautiful things ? " " I inherited them, Mr. Lear," was the Queen's answer. From 1847 until 1850, Lear visited Calabria, Sicily, Malta, Greece, Constantinople, and Mount Sinai. The first edition of the *Book of Nonsense* was published in 1846, a second edition in 1862. The letters published in this book cover the period from 1847 to 1864 ; but Lear lived until 1888, when he died at San Remo, at the age of seventy-six. He spent most of his winters abroad, chiefly at Cannes ; his summers he spent in England, where he busied himself in having exhibitions at 15 Stratford Place. During the whole of his life he continued to paint with sedulous industry, in spite of bad health and other difficulties. In 1874 he visited India, and from 1870 until he died in 1888, he lived at San Remo, never returning to England after 1877.

The interest of the letters now published is twofold. First of all, they reveal Lear's character, and enrich the world with fresh examples of his unique humour ; and, secondly, since Lear had a large number of friends, they paint the period. Lear was an intimate friend of Tennyson, a friend of Robert Browning, Holman Hunt, Lord Stratford de Redcliffe, and many other notable men of the time, and he was a unit in the society of brilliant people who centred around Lady Waldegrave at Nuneham. Lady Waldegrave, to whom so many of these letters were written, was the daughter of the greatest of English[1] tenors, John Braham. She was one

[1] Or Anglo-Jéwish.

17

of the most remarkable women of her day—remarkable not only because she was beautiful, kind, and amusing, but, so I have been told by some one who used to take part in the theatricals at Nuneham, because of the fundamental independence of her character. She followed the ideal which Sarah Bernhardt set up for herself : " Faire ce qu'on veut." And when people carry such an ideal into practice, they find that the world, which consists so largely of sheep, follows them. All that was most amusing and brilliant in the 'sixties was to be found at Nuneham. She ultimately married, when her second husband, George Harcourt, died, Chichester Fortescue, to whom the greater part of these letters are written.

Lear's letters are distinguished by absolute natural-ness ; and by what is the greatest charm of letter-writing !—the gift of relating the trivial incidents of everyday life.

Here is an example taken from a letter written to Fortescue from Corfu :

" Colonel Campbell has a celebrated horse, a stallion, called Billy. I hate the sight of him myself, in as much as he bites and kicks whoever he can. The other day, being loose, and seeing a helpless horse in a cart, he pounced on him and began to oppress him horribly, the two making any amount of row. This happened opposite Lady Buller's window, whereon the lady, being of a tender heart and a decided manner, opened the window and called out, ' Sentinel ! '" (Sentinel shouldered and presented arms.) ' Shoot the horse directly ! ' (Sentinel looks horribly bewildered but does nothing.) ' Why don't you shoot it ? ' Sentinel : ' Lord, Madam, it's Billy ! ' Lady B. : ' What's Billy. What do I care for Billy ? Shoot it, I say.' (Billy

all the time tearing and biting the prostrate horse.)
Sentinel : ' Can't nohow, Madam, my Lady, 'cause it's
the colonel's Billy.' "

Here is another example in his most fantastic
punning vein :

" MY DEAR SIR JOHN,—I send you in this letter
2 Corpses of the most abominable—or rather bee-
bominable insects that ever made a florist miserable.
The plague of black bees has multiplied here so horribly,
and they are so destructive, that there is not a seed of
my beautiful Grant-Duff Ipomœas anywhere, as the
beastly bees pierce all the flowers and no seed is matured.
We are driven mad by these bees, and have bees on the
brain ; we kill them by scores and the ground is bee-
strewn with their Bodies. Even the broom we use to
sweep them away is call a Beesom. Can you at all
enlighten me as to where these creatures build, or
if they live more than a single summer ? Or is there
any fluid or substance which may kill them and save
me the trouble of running about after them ? I
bee-seech you to do what you can for me in the way of
advice. . . ." [1]

Lear's faithful Suliot servant, Giorgio, who appears
from time to time in the book, is a delightful character.
He detested Rome, saying : " Almeno in Gerusalemme si
poteva vedere un camelo morto e qualche Arabi,[2] ma qui
non c'è nulla." (In Jerusalem there were at least a dead
camel and a few Arabs to be seen, but here there is
nothing.)

In the stream of Lear's gibes and puns there is nearly

[1] This letter occurs in the *Later Letters of Edward Lear*. Edited by
Lady Strachey. Published by Fisher Unwin. 1911.
[2] *Sic*.

always an undercurrent of wistful sadness, but there is
nothing so pathetic in the book as the letter he writes on
the death of his sister, in which he says :

" I went to Oatlands after the funeral—but have come
to-day to this place, hoping to get to A. Tennyson, but
there was no steamer.

" I am all at sea and do not know my way an hour
ahead. I shall be so terribly alone.

"Wandering about a little may do some good, perhaps."

His letters are interlarded with sentences in modern
Greek. The Greek, the editor writes in the preface, is
incorrect. I profess I find the Greek perfectly intelligible, but the footnotes which explain it are puzzling
in the extreme ; for instance, Δὲν ἐξεύρω τίποτες does
not mean " Perhaps I shall discover something," it
means the opposite, " I shall not find anything " ;
ὁμιλῶ in modern Greek means to converse, and not to
meet. This is a mistake which occurs several times,
and in one place (the footnote on p. 240) makes nonsense
of the text ; but the most startling rendering is one (p.
253) where the Greek for " We will discuss the matter
to-morrow at luncheon " is rendered, " Until we meet
to-morrow to eat raw flesh." This has an almost
(Fourth Form) Etonian flavour !

In writing to the Under Secretary for the Colonies,
Lear says he is nearly half through Οἰδίπους ἐπὶ Κολώνῳ
(Sophocles' Oedipus in Colonos), which is translated in
the editor's footnote " Oedipus on Colonies." If the
footnote had been included in the text the results would
have been extremely characteristic of Lear.

1907

THE BALLAD OF THE WHITE HORSE

*T*HE *Ballad of the White Horse* is the record of a noble vision flung on to the canvas with bold, strong colours. Like most records of visions it is incomplete, not because the seer has not seen enough, but because he has seen too much. Mr. Chesterton has so many ideas that his difficulty consists, not in expressing them, but in rejecting the overflow.

The poem is an historical ballad, one of the few attempts in modern times at a big historical poem. It is historical in the true sense of the word, in that it aims at and achieves seizing the spirit if not the letter of history. It is the legend that passes from lips to lips until it reaches our own times, and not one of the fantastic concoctions, of a purely negative character, which are made up in the studies of pedants, and solemnly repeated in the middle of the night by journalists who wish to give an air of scholarship to the shallowness of their threadbare phrases. The poem is a ballad. It is in reality more than a ballad ; it is what Matthew Arnold said poetry should always be : " A criticism of life." If a ballad should be merely a story, told in the simplest possible manner, it may be held that to charge it with philosophy diminishes its power as a ballad. On the other hand, a poet has the right to choose what vehicle he pleases for his message ; and for this particular message Mr. Chesterton obviously found that the ballad form was what he needed.

The result certainly justifies the choice. There are not only stanzas, but whole passages in this poem which, judged simply as narrative ballad poetry, are of the very highest possible order.

Here is an instance of a single stanza which stands out like a shining face in a fresco :

> " The Northmen came about our land
>   A Christless chivalry :
> Who knew not of the arch or pen,
> Great, beautiful, half-witted men
>   From the sunrise and the sea."

And here is a passage which reaches the high-water mark of ballad poetry :

> " And he saw in a little picture,
>   Tiny and far away,
> His mother sitting in Egbert's hall,
> And a book she showed him, very small,
> Where a sapphire Mary sat in a stall
>   With a golden Christ at play.
>
> It was wrought in the monk's slow manner,
>   From silver and sanguine shell,
> Where the scenes are little and terrible,
>   Keyholes of heaven and hell.
>
> In the river island of Athelney,
>   With the river running past,
> In colours of such simple creed
> All things sprang at him, sun and weed,
> Till the grass grew to be grass indeed
>   And the tree was a tree at last.
>
> Fearfully plain the flowers grew,
>   Like the child's book to read,
> Or like a friend's face seen in a glass ;
> He looked ; and there Our Lady was,
> She stood and stroked the tall live grass
>   As a man strokes his steed.

> Her face was like an open word
> When brave men speak and choose,
> The very colours of her coat
> Were better than good news."

These are lines which no one who has read them will ever forget. They will become a part of the permanent furniture of his mind.

Equally beautiful is the vision of Our Lady which comes to King Alfred in the final battle of Ethandune, of which I will only quote one matchless stanza :

> " The Mother of God goes over them,
> Walking on wind and flame.
> And the storm cloud drifts from city and dale,
> And the White Horse stamps in the White Horse Vale,
> In the village of our name."

Mr. Chesterton tells the story of Alfred, following, and rightly following, the popular legend. The story of how he played the harp and sang in the Danish camp, of how he burnt the cakes in the herdsman's hut, and how his ultimate victory came about in the Valley of the White Horse. These are the bones of the story, and they, I repeat, are treated in the true ballad form by a masterly hand, and with driving inspiration. Besides this, there is the philosophic import and significance of the poem, the " Criticism of Life," which is so large that it almost swamps the ballad element. The point is the contrast between Pagan and Christian ideals. Alfred, in the poem, is the incarnation of the Christian tradition. The Danes Mr. Chesterton represents as the types of Paganism, and here Mr. Chesterton takes a hammer and hammers hard on the idea, as on a nail, that while the Pagans may have lived in a gayer world than the Christians, they inhabited a more dismal universe. The story of the singing of Alfred in the camp of the Danes is made the opportunity for a fine outburst of lyric imagination. First Alfred sings, then four of the Danes; each, in a subtly differentiated manner, nobly voices the majestic but desperate creed of Paganism.

> " For this is a heavy matter,
>   And the truth is cold to tell;
>   Do we not know, have we not heard,
>   The soul is like a lost bird
>   The body a broken shell? "

When they are silent, Alfred smites the lyre once more, and sings the triumphant hymn of the defeated Christian :

> " That though you hunt the Christian man
>   Like a hare on the hillside,
>   The hare has still more heart to run
>   Than you have heart to ride."

Another idea which lies behind Mr. Chesterton's poem is one which lies at the root of all his books—that the battle is not to the strong, that Jack kills the giant. Alfred is beaten by the Danes, but in the moment of defeat something is kindled in him, he does better than his best, and he wins.

This philosophy not only broods behind the whole poem like a flame behind the cloud, but is finely expressed again and again, sometimes epigrammatically, sometimes simply, sometimes rhetorically, sometimes gorgeously, sometimes metaphorically—in a thousand ways. It lends interest to the poem. It *might* be said to detract from the value of the ballad if the ballad were regarded as a ballad and nothing else. Of course no poem can exist that has not either consciously or unconsciously some fundamental moral root-idea; but it might be argued, that it is for the reader and the critic to discern and expound that fundamental idea, and not for the poet to point it out and underline it again and again. It might be argued that the moral of such a poem should be there in spite of the poem ; that it should proceed from the facts and the manner of telling, but that it should not be explicitly explained. On the other hand, there is no reason why one should dogmatise as to how a particular poem should be written. One should accept the poem as it is. Nearly half of modern criticism consists of saying that a wine-glass ought to have been a bottle, whereas the point is, if a wine-glass is a wine-glass, what sort of wine-glass it is. Therefore it is absurd to say that Mr. Chesterton's ballad ought to have been different, that it ought to have been more like " The Ancient Mariner " or " The Border Ballads " or Heine, the point is that it is *The Ballad of the White Horse*, written by G. K. Chesterton, and written as no one else could have written it. The wise reader will read it, re-read it, remember it, and be thankful.

1911.

TCHEKOV

MRS. GARNETT has rendered another great service to English readers and to English literature (they already owe her an immense debt of gratitude for her translations of Turgenev and Dostoyeskvi and of Tchekov's stories) by translating a selection of Tchekov's letters.[1]

Tchekov's life was uneventful. He was born at Taganrog in 1860. His grandfather was a serf on the estate of Chertkov, the father of Tolstoy's friend. His father opened a shop at Taganrog and conducted its business until he migrated to Moscow in 1876. Anton Tchekov went to the university of Moscow in 1879. In 1886 he began to write for the *Novoe Vremya*. In 1887 he wrote his first play, *Ivanov*. It was performed at Korsh's Theatre in Moscow, and had a mixed reception. In 1889 the same play was performed in St. Petersburg. By this time his name was well known to the reading public in Russia. In 1889 he made a journey by road to the island of Saghalien, where he studied the convict system. On his return he went abroad with Souvorin, the editor of the *Novoe Vremya*, and visited Vienna, Venice, Rome, and Monte Carlo. In the winter of 1892 he bought an estate in the Government of Moscow near the village of Melihovo. Melihovo then became his permanent home, although he often paid visits to

[1] *Letters of Anton Tchekov.* Translated by Constance Garnett. Chatto & Windus. 12s. 6d. net.

Moscow and St. Petersburg. Early in life he had developed consumptive symptoms, and his health grew gradually worse. In 1896 his play *The Seagull* was produced at the Alexandrinsky Theatre in St. Petersburg, where it failed.

Owing to his ill-health he had to choose between spending the winters at Nice or Yalta in the Crimea. He chose Yalta, meaning at first only to stay there in the winter months, but the complications of life compelled him to sell his property at Melihovo and settle for good in the Crimea.

One of the reasons which made him disinclined to go abroad was the production of his plays at the Art Theatre in Moscow. On 17th December 1898 he writes : " As I write these lines *The Seagull* is being acted in Moscow." The production of *The Seagull* at the Art Theatre, Moscow, was the turning-point of his theatrical career as a dramatic author and of the fortunes of the Art Theatre. It was then that he entered his theatrical kingdom. For the first time his plays were understood by the actors and, consequently, by the public. In 1899 he went for the winter to Moscow, where his plays— *The Seagull* and *Uncle Vanya*—were enjoying a splendid success. In 1900 he wrote *Three Sisters*. In 1901 he married Olga Knipper, the leading actress of the Art Theatre. The doctors told him he ought to live in one place, Switzerland for preference, instead of which he was constantly travelling. The consequence was his health grew worse and worse. He was a prey to violent, exhausting hæmorrhages. In 1903 his health was so bad that his doctor advised him to give up even going to Yalta and to settle near Moscow. However, he went back to Yalta and there finished his last play, *The Cherry Orchard*, that year, and he went to Moscow to produce it himself. It was first performed on 17th January 1904, and although numbers of addresses were read to him, and he was called many times, the reception of the play in the Press and at first by the general public was less enthusiastic than that which had greeted his earlier plays. The Japanese War had begun. Tchekov's health was now shattered. He spent the spring at Yalta, but started for Moscow at the beginning of May. He was taken ill on the journey and laid up until June. He then went for cure to the Black Forest with his wife and settled at a watering-place—Badenweiler. There he died on 2nd July 1904.

His life, although uneventful, was feverishly active. He was the most hospitable of men, and liked to be surrounded by crowds of friends and guests. He could not live without people. He was active in the service of others, and keenly interested in Zemstvo work, in schools, roads, hospitals, and he presented a public library to his native town of Taganrog. He was constantly on the move. All this in addition to his literary activity, which continued until the end of his life.

The readers of these letters will have no difficulty in seeing what kind of man he was. They will be charmed by the pictures of his domestic life and follow with keen interest the career of his mongoose. He was, above all things, simple and lovable. The shibboleths of art criticism, the wrangles of schools, and all coteries, bored him to death. All he wanted was to work in peace and to enjoy the work of others.

" Of the word ' art,' " he writes, " I am terrified as merchants' wives are terrified of ' brimstone.' When people talk to me of what is artistic and inartistic, of what is dramatic and not dramatic, of tendency, realism, and so on, I am bewildered, hesitatingly assent and

answer with banal half-truths not worth a brass farthing.
I divide all works into two classes—those I like and those
I don't . . . all conversations about what is ' artistic '
only weary me."

Political and artistic cliques wearied him. " I am
sick," he says, " of theorising of all sorts." And again,
" I am not a Liberal, not a Conservative . . . I should
have liked to have been a free artist and nothing more—
and I regret that God has not given me the strength to
be one."

As an artist he knew his limitations, and never
attempted to overstep them. " An artist," he says,
" must only judge of what he understands ; his field is
just as limited as that of any other specialist."

Tchekov was a specialist in delicate portraiture. He
was a *paysagiste*. Tolstoy said of him, " A photographer,
a *good* photographer, but a photographer." And
another well-known Russian critic said of his work that
although in reading Tchekov's stories every character
seemed to you as living and as individual and as minutely
differentiated as the people you met in real life, the
impression after reading several stories was one of intense
monotony. He thought that the reason of this was that
although Tchekov was a master in the delineation and
analysis of the *outer* psychology of human beings, he
never let you into the secrets of the soul which were the
cause of these outer manifestations. In this he resembled
Maupassant, to whom he has been often compared by
Russian critics. He had the same gift which Maupassant
possessed of delineating a character by choosing only
two or three traits, which are then thrown into relief
with the aid of a delicate psychological analysis. But
if this is true, if Tchekov's work is a cinematograph of
miraculously rendered psychological pictures, it is a

unique kind of cinematograph managed by a celestial mechanic. It has the colours and the play of life, colours as delicate as those of an inspired water-colourist ; there is no vibration, no noise, no buzzing, no flickering, no exaggeration. His characters move and speak with subtly chosen gesture and accent against a background cunningly selected and always true. And if he is less vigorous than Maupassant, or than Mr. Kipling, he has done one thing which neither of these artists achieved, and that is to transfer his delicate pictures of life to the stage without any of the usual stage tricks and without sacrificing their delicacy.

Tchekov has put on the stage what we all feel like when we go away, when we say good-bye to friends or leave a place where we have lived. He has brought across the footlights that shadow of death which is in the partings of everyday life. As a rule, the leaves of life are turned over so quickly and so noiselessly by Time that we are not aware of the process. In the case of a sudden parting we hear the leaf of life turn over and fall back into the great blurred book of the past—read, finished, and irrevocable. It is the turning of the leaf which Tchekov has rendered.

Nearly all his plays turn on the partings of everyday life. *Three Sisters*—when the regiment leaves the provincial town (Oh, the melancholy of that band and the girls it leaves behind !). *Uncle Vanya*—when you see not only the people go, but those who remain behind going on with their avocations, and the servant comes in and achieves an unforgettably poignant effect just by saying, " They've gone." And *The Cherry Orchard*, which is about a parting of a family with its home . . . symbolising the end of an epoch and a chapter of history.

These plays require special acting, or rather special production, and long after Tchekov's plays were successful, *The Seagull*, as played in the ordinary competent professional manner at the Alexandrinsky Theatre (I am speaking of 1910), lost nearly all its effect. The limitation of this kind of dramatic work is the same as that of Tchekov's stories. There is a slight feeling of stagnation about it.

" There is a sort of stagnation in my soul," he writes in one of his letters. " I explain it by the stagnation in my personal life." But Tchekov was the child of a stagnant epoch, in which the whole of Russia had run to seed playing Vindt, as he said to himself.

But in his own sphere Tchekov is an incomparable artist, and even the footlights only bring out more clearly the perfection of his workmanship and the delicacy of his touch. In these letters, the charm of his personality, his love of landscape, his serene and kindly observation, and the quiet aura of goodness that surrounded him are apparent on every page. One may repeat his words, " My God, how rich Russia is in good people ! " Mrs. Garnett's translation is excellent. The English is natural and nearly always idiomatic. I think Mrs. Garnett will find a slip in translation (or, perhaps, it is a misprint) on page 559; and in 1904, in *The Cherry Orchard*, Stanislavsky played Gaev and not Lopachin. I think the part of Lopachin was played by Leonidov.

One sentence referring to Dostoyevski is translated, " It is fine, but very long and *indiscreet*." I have not the Russian text of the volume where this sentence occurs. If the Russian word is, as I guess it to be, " Nieskromni " (lacking in modesty), the translation is interesting, because Queen Victoria, we have been told, always used the word " indiscreet " in the sense of " Nieskromni," and when she feared So-and-so was not quite discreet, it meant not that they would blurt out a family or a State secret, but that they would be liable to overstep the limits of good taste, as Mr. Pooter remarked about Gowing, when they played consequences.

1920.

THE EPIC SONGS OF SERBIA

(Translated by Miss Rootham)

I WAS asked by Miss Rootham to write a few
words of introduction to her translation of some
of the Epic Songs of Serbia. No sooner had I read
them than I realised what I had already suspected,
that the poems spoke for themselves and needed no
introduction.

They have that quality which is common to all great
epic poetry; the quality we find in the *Iliad* and the
Odyssey, in the *Chanson de Roland* and in the *Word of the
Fight of the Prince Igor*, in the Bible, in Villon, and in
some of the very great poets when they are sufficiently
inspired to forget that they are poets — when their
" style " disappears. It is a quality which arises from
the natural and direct observation of life by man.

The writers of these ballads saw the world with the
eyes of a child and with the heart of man, as it is shaped
by life.

The similes used are such as any worker in the fields
would understand and recognise.

> " Like a cloud their battle-standards streaming
> And their tents stretched like the snow in winter."

> " If the gentle rain should fall from heaven,
> Not one inch of ground could then receive it."

> " And he threw the Turks into disorder
> As the falcon strikes the homing pigeons."

18

It is very seldom that modern poets succeed in achieving what Monsieur Anatole France calls " ces traits de nature qu'on dit le comble de l'art quand l'art a le bonheur de les trouver."

In the Slav literature these happy moments occur more often. Pushkin, thanks to his genius and to his old nurse, succeeded in catching in his fairy tales and sometimes in his poems the authentic *Volkston*, and a line such as

> " I morye gdye bezhali korabli,"

might have come out of these ballads.

Translate the line (and this is always the trouble in translating epic speech from one language into another), and you get a bald statement of fact,

> " And the sea where the ships were scudding."

In the original, the words are simple to nakedness but they are not bald, and they call up the picture like magic : they are the last word of felicity. Compare this with the treatment of a similar impression by a great poet who has not the gift of epic simplicity, and you will at once see the difference.

Tennyson—and Swinburne quotes the line as being a signal example of Tennyson's miraculous gift of evoking landscape—says :

> " And white sails flying on a yellow sea."

But Pushkin reaches a higher, a more magical effect without the aid of epithet or colour.

And so it is in these ballads. The colours are primitive like those of the primitive painters who painted the holy figures because they believed in them, and not because they wanted to make an arrangement of line and colour. The similes are taken from a first-hand communion with the sights and facts of nature. The emotions are the primitive emotions of man, " Not sicklied o'er with the pale cast of thought." But the mention of the emotions leads us to the second fundamental characteristic of these ballads : to the soul of them which differs from that of Grecian epics, and which is more akin to the *Chanson de Roland*, to the *Gestes* of the mediæval knights, and to the Celtic epics, but which has a quality and savour which is entirely its own and entirely Slav.

The soul of these ballads is saturated with Christian faith, the faith of the crusaders, of the Morte d'Arthur, of Villon ; the faith of the *gracieux galans* who stormed Jerusalem with young Lord Raymond. The " Ballad of the Fall of the Serbian Empire " gives us the keynote of all this song.

A message comes from Jerusalem to the King :

> " Say, dost thou desire a heav'nly kingdom,
> Or dost thou prefer an earthly kingdom ?
> If thou should'st now choose an earthly kingdom,
> Knights may girdle swords and saddle horses,
> Tighten saddle-girths and ride to battle,—
> You will fight the Turks and crush their army.
> But if thou prefer a heav'nly kingdom,
> Build thyself a church upon Kossovo,
> Let not the foundations be of marble,
> Let them be of samite and of scarlet. . . .
> And to all thy warriors and their leaders,
> Thou shalt give the sacraments and orders,
> For thy army will most surely perish,
> And thou, too, wilt perish with thine army."

And the king chose the Heavenly Kingdom, built the church, and went out to battle—and fell.

These ballads sing the lost cause ; the foredoomed loyalty ; the cause which is lost on earth but which triumphs in another world. The warriors go to war certain beforehand of defeat, but they fight to the last man nevertheless, certain of victory in defeat.

This is where these ballads remind us of the Celtic epics.

"They went out to battle, but they always fell."

Such is the burden of the Irish epics. It is a proud and triumphant burden like the music of a funeral march, which however piercing its melancholy, however poignant its sadness, soars nevertheless in triumph above the vain and transitory triumphs of the world.

But the grief is great, the anguish complete ; great and complete enough to break the hearts of those who are not killed in battle : the mothers, the wives, the sisters.

"And the mother's heart swelled big with anguish,
Swelled the mother's heart and broke with sorrow—
For her dead, the Jugovitch,—nine brothers,
And the tenth, the Jug Bogdan, their father."

In reading this we seem to look upon those tremendous blocks of living stone in which Mestrovitch has written the sorrow of Serbia ; the undying sorrow, the unspeakable anguish, the certainty of victory in defeat ; never so great as now, and never so triumphant.

July 1919.

HOW IT STRIKES A CONTEMPORARY

I

MR. SHANKS, MR. TURNER, AND " EVOE "

HOW it strikes a contemporary. That is the question, the delicate, puzzling, elusive question. And when the subject is verse, the question how it strikes the contemporary is more delicate and more puzzling still. Sainte-Beuve, who was a wise man, said that it was " chose délicate de parler des poètes surtout quand on l'a été un peu soi-même." I can't verify the reference, and I implore those many lynx-eyed readers who seem to have so much leisure, so wide an erudition, so many handy books of reference, and such well-stocked libraries, not to bother to write and say that I have a misquotation. Something was said to that effect by some one, and if not by Sainte-Beuve by some one else, and if by no one else, then by myself, now. It is a delicate, a very delicate and difficult affair for a man to criticise contemporary verse, especially if he has dabbled in verse himself, and dabbled to the extent of publishing volume after volume of verse—of a kind ; so delicate a question, so difficult, so likely to lead to misunderstanding on all sides that I wish with all my heart that there were no such thing as reviews of contemporary books of verse. What, after all, is the use of them ? What do they amount to, and how are they done ? The little books pour in to the editor's office, verse and more verse. They are sent out in batches for review, to overtired men or women of letters.

So many words must be written by next Monday, and if the article is too long it must be truncated with a foot rule, and if the article is too short it must be padded with parentheses. There is no time for the verse to be read, that is to say, it is read in a way, and in a hurry, but is that the way to treat a casket of dreams in which, as in Pandora's box, the poet has treasured his sorrows and his one many-coloured winged hope ?

That is not the way a bottle of wine is treated, that is not the way a cigar is smoked, and wine and cigars and verse are meant to be enjoyed at leisure, and in the right mood.

Again, it needs courage to state your opinion boldly and *ex cathedra* on anything contemporary, especially on verse. We, the contemporaries, cannot possibly judge it in perspective ; we see it through the distorted glass of a thousand prejudices and preoccupations ; who are we to judge ? Besides, we have behind us so many awful examples : the popularity of the poet Montgomery, the silence on Shakespeare, the things which were said of Shelley and Keats, not only by critics but by casual contemporary men in the street—that is to say, Fleet Street.

When Shelley's *Prometheus Unbound* fell almost stillborn from the press, an extremely witty writer, Theodore Hook, wrote this quatrain about it :

" Shelley styles his new poem ' Prometheus Unbound,'
  And 'tis like to remain so while time circles round,
  For surely an age would be spent in the finding
  A reader so weak as to pay for the binding."

Here, indeed, is a flavour to delight with bitter-sweet melancholy the connoisseurs in time's little ironies. For no age was spent in the finding of such weak readers. Only about fifty or sixty years. And then the readers spent hundreds and hundreds of pounds, both in the old and the new world, in devising expensive bindings for *Prometheus Unbound*. A further irony : precious as the bound copies are, the unbound copies are more precious still, and the boards that Hook scoffed at are now worth their weight in gold. Indeed, I once heard an American millionaire collector say that he considered no nursery complete without a *Prometheus* bound by Cobden Sanderson. That sentiment would have astonished Theodore Hook. And yet Theodore Hook was a clever man, much cleverer than you or me. So, my brothers, are we not a little rash when we say that the latest volume of Georgian poetry is trash, and are we not equally likely to be mistaken when we say that Mr. Jones's last epic in *vers libres* is the finest product of the human mind ? Yes, we are likely to be wrong either way. That being so, let us go ahead and courageously record our contemporary and, most likely, fallacious and absurd opinion of our contemporaries, and if by so doing we one day give posterity a good laugh, well, what does it matter ?

All this preamble leads me to the too, too solid fact that I have two books of verse to review, and a book of parodies which is replete with authentic wit, merciless observation, and an almost superhuman cleverness.

Well, I have read these books and, what is more, I have read all of them twice, and I have read them at leisure, just as if I never should have to say a word about them in print, and after one last word of preamble, which I meant to say before, I will try and record the impression they made upon me. My last word of preamble is this, and put in here belatedly because I think it is important. Reviews of verse and, indeed, of prose are generally written by authors of verse and of prose, who may be the friends, the enemies, or the indifferent fellow-writers of the writer. This is a pity, because if the review is written by an enemy he is inclined to be too spiteful or, worse still, too magnanimous : if it is written by a friend, the friend often feels obliged to press the soft pedal too frequently on the strong chords of loyal and genuine admiration lest the music should sound too extravagant ; and if the review is written by an indifferent, casual fellow-worker, that man, even if he escapes accentuating the discords with envious rivalry, will hardly be able to help reconstructing the whole in a different mode with the unconscious but conscientious criticism of the fellow artist, but of the artist who works in another way, and who sees the world of life and of art from a different angle.

In Mr. Shanks's book there is a long poem called " The Island of Youth." It tells of Achilles, who was conveyed to the island of Scyros by his mother, Thetis (she, being half immortal, should have known better), in the fond hope that she might thus, by disguising him as a girl, avert the destiny that had been foretold him—a glorious life and an early death. The poet tells how on this island Achilles loves Deidamia, and how Ulysses, with a simple gift of a sword, puts an end to the futile masquerade. But the poet tells us a great deal more than this ; he shows us the agony, the joy and the sorrow, and all the prophetic soul of Achilles, and he tells the story in so delicate a fashion that what might have been repugnant is beautiful, and what might have been coarse is befitting and seemly and right.

This verse made on this contemporary (I use the phrase

not to avoid the egoistic personal pronoun but to accentu-
ate the fact that I *am* a contemporary) the same kind of
impression as the music of Chopin ; it seems to me to
have the same blend of sureness and delicacy.   Here is a
fragment :

> " The sun dipped underneath a neighbour peak
> And suddenly the air was still and cool.
> Below him far, a bird on bough unseen
> Raised a night anthem in sweet jets of sound ;
> And further still, beyond the edge of foam,
> A little boat, as little as a leaf,
> Rocked on the falling swell, and from the bow
> A kneeling fisherman dipped in the wave
> His knotted line and watched, with back intent,
> While his companion with slow-moving oar
> Kept equal head against the gentle tide."

But I would refer the reader to a finer passage on page
81, which cannot be torn from its context without
too great laceration.   It begins :

> " O stars, shine kindly on them."

I challenge my fellow contemporaries to deny that this
page in its context is a fine piece of imagination, imagery
and deep feeling expressed in a masterly manner.   There
are many other beautiful things in this volume, notably
a poem called " Memory " and a poem called " The
Night-Jars."   But space is filling and time is creeping,
and neither of them allows me to quote more than two
lines from the latter poem :

> " A dark shape flaps out from the invisible trees,
> And slides across our path, a moving clot of night."

And now for Mr. Turner's poems.   They require a
more deliberate reading, a more leisurely mood for the
tasting of them, for there is something intoxicating and
heady about them.   If you drink them all at one draught

you will feel that you have pleasantly overdone things, and you will have no clear recollection of what you have been tasting. And yet here again this fallible contemporary is convinced that he has been tasting real poetry and reading good verse.

Mr. Turner has vision, if anything too much vision, so that the images and the atmosphere in his poems are sometimes almost overwhelming, but he has also a consummate technique.

He has the same kind of blend of voluptuous evocation, sonority, and tight utterance that distinguishes the verse of Baudelaire :

> " And if I dreamed, I dreamed of that far land,
>   That coast of pearl upon a summer sea."

Here is a Donne-like conceit :

> " Night's fishing fleets, the stars,
>   Dragged Time for aeons ere they found those eyes."

The following is perhaps most characteristic of all :

> " The shepherds in the lowland heard her cry—
>   Sitting like stones among their scattered sheep."

In every epoch writers of verse are apt to breathe a sigh or snort of contentment at having escaped the mannerisms of the epoch which precedes them. Those who came after Donne were happy in smoothing out his verse. The romantics rejoiced in being set free from the trim parterres of the eighteenth century : the pre-Raphaelites mocked at the rococo of the romantics, and now the Georgians laugh to scorn the rococo of the Victorians, and yet the Georgians have their own mannerisms, and the Edwardians of the future will probably make fun of them ; indeed " Evoe " makes fun of them already ; and in *Parodies Regained* you will find every note and cadence chord of contemporary verse consummately reproduced and good-naturedly bantered. One particular mannerism caught my ear in reading this verse, and that is the abuse of the unfortunate word *pale*. Mr. Turner uses the epithet thirty-five times in sixty-six pages, and sometimes more than once in the same poem, and once twice in the same short poem, and three times on two consecutive pages. Mr. Shanks is fond of the epithet, too. I did not count how many times he had used it, but a cursory examination showed me it occurred at least ten times.

" Evoe," in his parody of Mr. Turner, writes :

" Gathering pale flowers that grew beneath faint hoods,"

and uses five " pales " in four pages.

These poets should get a trusty friend to look through their proofs and cut out the word *pale* after it has occurred more than five times.

1922.

II

MR. BELLOC'S POEMS

NOTHING is more hazardous, more full of possible pitfalls and errors than to write a considered judgment on contemporary verse, as I have already said at some length in the preceding Essay. The question is further complicated when the contemporary author happens to be a personal friend ; not because, as I have also already said, the critic is too easily biased in favour of his friend's writing, but, on the contrary, because he is liable to check his spontaneous praise and admiration, to understate his case, thinking that he is obliged to discount the personal bias.

There is one thing to be said in favour of criticising a contemporary ; you may be affording great fun to posterity ; the chance student may look up what you write in the bound files of an old newspaper and have a hearty laugh over your judgments. I mean in this case to give posterity a chance either of having a good laugh or a sound clap of agreement.

In the year 1896, Mr. Hilaire Belloc published in London a small book of verse containing sixty-four hard pages of verse that, in a sense, was as hard as the paper on which it was printed. The verse was printed on cardboard, the pages are the stiffest to turn I have ever come across, and the verse had something which, at the time, appeared to be more durable than the kind of stuff which was appearing then ; and here I will say what I should have begun by saying : that it is easier to criticise a contemporary when some of his work has been in print for a certain number of years. It is not at all the same thing as writing about that same contemporary at the moment of his *début*. Mr. Belloc's book, I repeat, was published in 1896. That is a long time ago ; since then a great deal of water has passed under the bridges and a great deal of verse has blossomed and died. I turn over the leaves of the little book, and I notice that it contains some poems which Mr. Belloc has republished in his volume of collected poems, *Sonnets and Verse*, published in 1923, and before the publication of this latter volume Mr. Belloc published another sheaf of collected verse called *Verses* in 1910. That is the main fact I notice, that Mr. Belloc having reached the age of maturity has, in his considered judgment, reprinted some of the verse of his salad days, and I think that any lover of verse will say he has done well to do so.

There is, in the early volume, a poem called " Auvergnat " which has lived during all that period ; that is to say, it has been quoted in anthologies :

> " There was a man was half a clown
> (It's so, my father tells of it),
> He saw the church in Clermont Town
> And laughed to hear the bells of it."

and which ends thus :

> " He broke his heart in Clermont Town,
> At Pontgibaud they mended it."

It also contains some sonnets, noble for gleams of vision and fitful, strong chords of expression where rhetoric suddenly melts into poetry. It also reveals an undeveloped but decided gift for epigram ; and yet it seems to me that few people with this little book in their hands would have dared to prophesy great things of its writer. Or, had they prophesied, it is most likely that they would have foreseen a great prose writer and not a poet. And now, twenty-seven years later, appears a book of collected verse from an author who is known throughout the world as a writer of prose and verse, but chiefly known—to the large public, that is to say— as a writer on the War and as a writer of children's verse. This book of collected poems, to my mind at least, proves something else—I am not the least afraid of prophesying in this case, and I am quite willing to affront or confront and face the possible jeers of posterity—that Mr. Belloc has, in his collected volume, contributed to the permanent storehouse of English verse. Just as in a picture-gallery, which is full of old masterpieces by Holbein, by Rembrandt, by Velasquez, by Gainsborough, by Raeburn, you sometimes can hang a picture by a modern artist without there being a shock or jar ; so, when verse reaches a certain pitch of excellence—and this is the supreme test—you can transplant it into any epoch of English poetry, say the Elizabethan period or the Caroline period or the Georgian period or the Romantic period at the beginning of the nineteenth century, without a qualm, with the sure knowledge that it will not suffer from its surroundings nor from the comparisons and inferences which such a juxtaposition must necessarily bring with it.

Mr. Belloc is well known as a writer ; people have heard his name as a war critic all over the world ; lines from his satirical poems, his nonsense rhymes, and his poems for children are frequently quoted and misquoted. But the pundits have not yet done justice to him ; what somebody called " the fastidious fools " have not yet discovered him. Perhaps this only happens to an author when he is dead, when, as some one else said, " the gates of fame are opened and those of envy are shut." How this recognition comes about is a mystery ; sometimes it will happen instantaneously ; sometimes it will not happen for years. Mr. Belloc has probably retarded the moment by his versatility, by writing on so many and various topics. It takes a long time for it to penetrate the skull of public opinion that although a man may know a great deal about Roman roads, French, and mediæval history, ships, maps, and beer, and the way to cut hay, he may, at the same time write good verse ; but such is the case. Up to the present, Mr. Belloc has received about as much recognition for his verse as Keats received during his lifetime from his personal friends, and from one or two reviewers who happened to be his friends, namely, Leigh Hunt and Charles Lamb, and who probably from the very fact of being his friends understated their praise, for reasons which I have already alluded to. However that may be, I feel quite confident in asserting, with all the possibilities of change of taste before me, and knowing what the whirligig of time can do, and how sharp and how sudden revolutions of mind and taste may be, that in Mr. Belloc's volume of verse there are poems made of the kind of stuff that endures as long as any verse endures. Such duration is, of course, only relative; a short earthquake, and all the verse in the world may be annihilated; but as long as thêre are books, books of verse, and books of English verse— readers of various anthologies, old men and young men who read Chaucer, Shakespeare, Pope, Byron, Wordsworth, Keats, Crabbe, and any others you like to name —I am sure those same readers will read with admiration and delight a great deal of the verse Mr. Belloc has included in his latest volume.

There are, to begin with, thirty-one sonnets; and among them a few of the quite early ones of 1896. They are packed with " fundamental brain work "; they are carefully wrought; they are, if anything, over-wrought. You feel that some of them remained in the mind of the poet for years and years; that he has ruminated on them, chewed them, turned them over and over again, accepted this word and rejected that; and then once more rejected what he has accepted and reverted to what he had rejected. The result to my mind is a gallery of highly wrought works of art, if anything too highly wrought, like clothes that have been fitted and refitted until they fit too well. But, after all, that is of little consequence compared with the gleams of vision in these poems and the mastery, restraint, strength,

and beauty of the expression.   I will quote the beginning
of one :

> Your life is like a little winter's day
>   Whose sad sun rises late to set too soon ;
> You have just come—why will you go away,
>   Making an evening of what should be noon.
> Your life is like a little flute complaining
>   A long way off, beyond the willow trees :
> A long way off, and nothing left remaining
>   But memory of a music on the breeze " ;

and here is a whole sonnet :

> " But oh ! not Lovely Helen, nor the pride
> Of that most ancient Ilium matched with doom.
> Men murdered Priam in his royal room
> And Troy was burned with fire and Hector died.
> For even Hector's dreadful day was more
> Than all his breathing courage dared defend
> The armouréd light and bulwark of the war
> Trailed his great story to the accustomed end.
>
> He was the city's buttress, Priam's son,
> The Soldier born in bivouac praises great
> And horns in double front of battle won.
> Yet down he went : when unremembering fate
> Felled him at last with all his armour on.
> Hector : the horseman : in the Scæan Gate."

Personally—noble as the work in these sonnets is, stern
as is the stuff they are made of, and priceless their fitful
gleams of vision—I do not think that it is in the sonnet
that Mr. Belloc is most successful.   His sonnets have
sometimes the complexity of Shakespeare's without
their fundamental ease and lucidity, and at moments
the baldness of Wordsworth without the supreme sweep
of simplicity that in Wordsworth carries you off your
feet.   But you notice, and I hope he will notice, that
it is with Shakespeare and Wordsworth that one compares him, when talking of sonnets.

Next to the sonnets, there are the lyrical poems and ballads, one of which, " The South Country," is perpetually quoted and to be found in many anthologies. In this poem the technical mastery is just as sure, complete and complex, but the elf of poetry is definitely caught in the net ; for instance in these lines :

> " Comes surely from our Sister the Spring
>   When over the sea she flies ;
> The violets suddenly bloom at her feet,
>   She blesses us with surprise."

He does the same trick to my mind in a higher degree in the poem called " Ha'nacker Mill," which has not only lilt, but an undefinable, vague, haunting suggestion of poetry, sadness, and doom about it. It says what it has got to say quite perfectly, but it suggests at the same time a great deal more than it says. It has magic. The same could be said of the poem which follows it in the book, " Tarantella."   But if I were asked to quote an instance of Mr. Belloc at his very best, when his vision and his feeling are expressed at their highest pitch and are mingled, without being overladen or overcomplicated by his technical skill or by his sometimes too-active brain work, I should quote five stanzas from the *Dedicatory Ode* :

> " I will not try the reach again,
>   I will not set my sail alone,
> To moor a boat bereft of men
>   At Yarnton's tiny docks of stone.
>
> But I will sit beside the fire,
>   And put my hand before my eyes,
> And trace, to fill my heart's desire,
>   The last of all our Odysseys.
>
> The quiet evening kept her tryst :
>   Beneath an open sky we rode,
> And passed into a wandering mist
>   Along the perfect Evenlode.

19

> The tender Evenlode that makes
> Her meadows hush to hear the sound
> Of waters mingling in the brakes,
> And binds my heart to English ground.
>
> A lovely river, all alone,
> She lingers in the hills and holds
> A hundred little towns of stone,
> Forgotten in the western wolds."

These stanzas, it seems to me, are sufficient to put Mr. Belloc among the English poets.

There are, in the book, poems which belong to four other categories. First of all, the Drinking Songs ; the best of these are not in this book at all, but are to be found in a book called *The Four Men*, and will probably be included one day in a complete edition of Mr. Belloc's works. There are, however, some good drinking songs in this book. There is this to be noted about them ; they are songs that were written to be sung to definite tunes and which have been sung. It is quite wrong to call them *pastiches*. The poet probably had the tune ringing in his head to begin with, and wrote the words to suit the tune. In *The Four Men*, indeed, he gives us bars of the tunes themselves which suggested the songs.

Then there are the satirical poems. Of these one need say little, for Mr. Belloc is well known as a writer of satirical verse ; but what his readers, who read and so frequently misquote these happy lines of his probably do not realise is, that his skill in this line, his cleanness and neatness of touch, his unerring rhythm (like that of W. S. Gilbert's) are quite inimitable. Even the most skilful parodists, who try to parody Mr. Belloc's light verse, even Mr. Max Beerbohm and Mr. J. C. Squire, fail ; they cannot get either the requisite strength of swing, the underlying gusto, or the superficial neatness, the sharp, swift rapier play, to the same extent as their model. They try and try ; we all try and try ; we can't do it ; we can't achieve this kind of thing :

> " The daybreak on the failing force,
> The final sabres drawn :
> Tall Goltman, silent on his horse,
> Superb against the dawn " ;

or :

> " Dons different from those regal Dons !
> With hearts of gold and lungs of bronze."

Next to the satirical verse, there is one special gift of Mr. Belloc's which I think needs pointing out, and that is his peculiar gift for writing ballades. This is a very rare gift. You see it said that the ballade is a complicated artificial form which is used by people who juggle with rhyme :

> " And little masters make a toy of rhyme,"

a poet said. But in the history of literature when the ballade was first used by writers such as Villon, it was not used in this manner ; it was used to express deep and grave thoughts ; its expression was intensified by the monotonous iteration of the rhymes and the stern discipline of the whole vehicle. Nobody would call Villon's ballade on his comrades who were about to be hanged, or his ballade on " Our Lady," playthings or precious experiments in versification ; they are solemn as liturgies, as plangent, as sonorous, as reverberating as the *Dies Iræ*. But since the death of Villon, who has written ballades of that kind ? Well, Mr. Belloc has done it twice or three times in this book. Look at the last stanza of his " Drinking Dirge " :

> " In many a briny boat I've tried the brine,
> From many a hidden harbour I've set sail,
> Steering towards the sunset where there shine
> The distant amethystine islands pale."

He does it again more vehemently in his " Ballade to our Lady of Czestochowa," of which the last stanza is :

> " Help of the half-defeated, House of gold,
>   Shrine of the Sword, and Tower of Ivory ;
> Splendour apart, supreme and aureoled,
>   The Battler's vision, and the World's reply.
>   You shall restore me, O my last Ally,
> To vengeance and the glories of the bold.
> This is the faith that I have held and hold,
>   And this is that in which I mean to die ";

and again, in his " Ballade of Unsuccessful Men," which must be read in its entirety to be appreciated, but of which I cannot help quoting the last stanza :

> " You, the strong sons of anger and the sea,
>   What darkness on the wings of battle flew ?
> Then the great dead made answer : ' Also we
>   With Nelson found oblivion : Nelson, who
> When cheering out of port in spirit grew
>   To be one purpose with the wind and tide—
> Our nameless hulks are sunk and rotted through :
>   The Devil didn't like us and we died.' "

Finally, there are Mr. Belloc's epigrams, in which you get the quintessence of his poetical talent. I use talent in the German sense, in the sense which Goethe used it about Byron. In this book he has not published what are, perhaps, the most successful of his satirical epigrams, but of the serious ones nothing could be better than the lines " On a Dead Hostess " :

> " Of this bad world the loveliest and the best
>   Has smiled and said ' Good-night,' and gone to rest."

and " The Statue " :

> " When we are dead, some Hunting-boy will pass
> And find a stone half-hidden in tall grass
> And grey with age : but having seen that stone
> (Which was your image), ride more slowly on."

I saw it stated in a review that nothing of the kind had been written as good as this since Landor. To my mind, in these epigrams Mr. Belloc succeeds in catching in his no-less-perfect net an elusive elf that escaped the classical strands of Landor's snare although he set it never so wisely.

1923.

THE STAGE

L'AIGLON. EDMOND ROSTAND

(Written after the first performance)

ONSIEUR ROSTAND, thanks to his rapid
and brilliant career, and to the colossal success
of *Cyrano de Bergerac*, is certainly the French
author of the present day who attracts the greatest
amount of public attention in France, whose talent is
the most keenly debated, whose claims are supported
and disputed with the greatest vehemence. His
popularity in France is as great as that of Mr.
Kipling in England; and in France, as with Mr.
Kipling in England, there are not wanting many and
determined advocates of the devil. Some deny to
M. Rostand the title of poet, while admitting that he is
a clever playwright; some say that he has no talent
whatsoever. In the case of poetical plays the public
is probably in the long-run the only judge. Never in
the world's history has it been seen that the really
magnificent play (in verse) has proved a lasting failure,
or a really bad poetical play a perennial success. Of
course there are plays which, like other works of art,
come before their season; the public may perhaps
take years to appreciate them; while, on the other
hand, the public have often patronised plays of surprising mediocrity and vulgarity; these works, however,
have never resisted the hand of time. But in the
main, the public has been right, and those who take

the opposite view generally belong to a class alluded to
by Pope :

> " So much they scorn the crowd, that if the throng
> By chance go right, they purposely go wrong."

Certainly, in M. Rostand's case, whatever may be the
exact " place " of his plays in the evolution of the world's
poetical drama, one thing is quite certain, and that is
that his plays are triumphantly successful. This for a
play is a merit in itself. After the triumph of *Cyrano*,
it was difficult to believe that *L'Aiglon* would attain
the same level of merit and success ; and never was a
success more discounted beforehand. For weeks before,
L'Aiglon was the main topic of conversation in Paris,
and provided endless copy for the newspapers. Another
thing is certain : however the æsthetic value of *L'Aiglon*
may be rated in the future, it constitutes for the present
another gigantic success. Never did a play come at a
more opportune moment. At the time when the French
are thinking that their country has been playing too
insignificant a part in European politics, when it is
still convalescent and suffering from the vague discomfort subsequent on a feverish crisis, and fretting
and chafing under the colourless mediocrity of a régime
which falls short of their flamboyant ideal, M. Rostand
comes skilfully leading a martial orchestra and sets their
ears tingling and their hearts beating to the inspiring
tunes of Imperial France. M. Rostand's play is certainly
a forward step in his poetical career. *L'Aiglon* has the
same colour and vitality as *Cyrano*, the same incomparable instinct for stage effect, the same skill and
dexterity in the manipulation of words which amounts
to jugglery, the same fertility in poetical images and
felicitous couplets that we find in his earlier works ;

but, besides this, it has something which they have not
—a graver atmosphere, a larger outlook, a deeper note ;
the fabric, though the builder's skill is the same, is less
perfect as a whole, more irregular ; but in it we hear
mysterious echoes, and the footfall of the Epic
Muse. They compensate for the unevenness of the
carpentry.

In *L'Aiglon* we breathe the atmosphere of the epic of
Napoleon. Although the scenes which M. Rostand
presents to us deal only with the sunset of that period,
the glories and vicissitudes of its noon are suggested
to us ; we do not see the things themselves, but we are
conscious of their spirit, their poetic existence and
essence. M. Rostand evokes them, not by means of
palpable shapes, but, like a wizard, in the images of his
phrases and the sound of his verse, and thus we see
them more clearly than if they had been presented to
us in the form of elaborate tableaux and spectacular
battle-pieces.

The existence of Napoleon II. was in itself a tragic
fact. Yet more tragic if, as Metternich is reported to
have said of him, he had " a head of iron and body of
glass." And a degree more tragic still is M. Rostand's
creation of a prince whose frail tenement of clay is
consumed by ambition and aspiration, and who is
conscious at times of the vanity of his aspiration and
the hopelessness of his ambition. Thus tossed to and
fro, from ecstasy to despair, he is another Hamlet, born
not to avenge a crime committed against his father,
but to atone for his father's crimes. Perhaps the most
poetical moment of the play is that in which the Prince
realises on the plain of Wagram that he himself is the
atonement ; that he is a white wafer of sacrifice offered
as an expiation for oceans of blood. M. Rostand has

chosen this theme, pregnant with intense pathos, as his principal *motiv*, and has brought into relief the pity and the sadness of it by weaving round it music instinct with military ardour and patriotic fire. . . . It is needless to relate the play in detail. The close of the fifth act is perhaps the finest in conception of the whole play ; in it we see Napoleon, after the failure of an attempted escape to France, alone on the battlefield of Wagram, pale in his white uniform on the great green moonlit plain, with the body of the faithful soldier of the Old Guard, who killed himself rather than be taken by the Austrians, lying before him. Gradually in the sighing winds Napoleon imagines he hears the moan of the soldiers who once strewed the plain, until the fancy grows into hallucination, until he sees himself surrounded by regiments of ghosts, and hears the groans, the call and the clamour of phantom armies growing louder and louder till they culminate in the cry of " Vive l'Empereur, vive l'Empereur." He hears the tramping of men and the champing and neighing of chargers, and the music of the band ; he thinks " the Grande Armée " has come to life, and rushes joyfully to meet it ; the vision is then dispelled, and the irony of the reality is made plain to him, for it is the white uniforms of the Austrian regiment (of which he is colonel) that appear in the plain. The scene is almost Shakespearean in its effect of beauty and terror. Finally, in the last act we see the Roi de Rome dying in his gilded cage while he listens to the account of the pomp of his baptism in Paris, which is read out to him as he dies—he who as a child " eut pour hochet la couronne de Rome " is now an obscure and insignificant Hapsburg princeling, dying forgotten by the world, without a friend and under the eye of his imperturbable enemy.

The play has already been accused of incoherence, lengthiness, and inequality ; of too rapid transition, and of a clashing in style of preciosity and brutality ; of affectation and noise. It has been compared unfavourably with *Cyrano*, but it must be said that if it is less finished and coherent than that play, less compact and artistic, it is also more human, it has more *epische Breite*, and it is less like a marionette show. Fault is found now, as it was before, with the form of M. Rostand's verses ; they are no doubt better heard on the stage than read in the study, and this surely shows that they fulfil their conditions. His verses are not the verses of Racine, of Alfred de Vigny, of Leconte de Lisle (just as Mr. Kipling's verses are not the verses of Milton or Keats) ; but they have a poetical quality and a poetical value of their own ; and while their clarion music is still ringing in my ears I should think it foolish to quarrel with them and to criticise them in a captious spirit ; possibly on reading *L'Aiglon* the impression produced may be different. For the present, still under the spell of the enthusiasm and shouts of applause which his stirring couplets inspired on the memorable first night of the performance, I can but thank the author who brought before my eyes, with the skilful and clamorous music of his harps and his horns, his trumpets and fifes and drums, the vision of an heroic epoch and the shadows of Homeric battles—the red sun and the cannon balls shivering the ice at Austerlitz, the Pope crowning another Cæsar in Notre Dame, Moscow in flames and the Great Army scattered on the steppes of Russia, and the lapping of the invisible tide round St. Helena.

PARIS, 1900.

ELEONORA DUSE. 1905-1923

I

LA FEMME DE CLAUDE

THÉOPHILE GAUTIER once said that there were four kinds of plays : good plays acted by good actors, good plays acted by bad actors, bad plays acted by good actors, and bad plays acted by bad actors. He said that he preferred the second category, and that his ideal was a play by Shakespeare performed by amateur ladies and gentlemen. Madame Duse's performance of *La Femme de Claude* would not then, according to this profession, have been to his taste. For it comes under the third category, that of a bad play pervaded and transfigured by a woman of genius. But we must distinguish ; compared with excellence *La Femme de Claude* may be said to be a bad play, compared, for instance, with *Othello* or *Bérénice* ; but compared, on the other hand, with many modern plays, it is a very good play indeed. Madame Duse has been reproached for composing her repertory solely of such pieces ; she is said also to complain of the necessity of being limited to such a repertory ; but it is doubtful whether she would show to a greater advantage in a more exalted repertory. She is not a tragic actress in the sense that one imagines Mrs. Siddons

or Rachel were tragic. She is not the incarnation of
the Tragic Muse ; the gorgeous pall overwhelms her ;
when she plays Cleopatra, for instance, her peculiar
force seems to fade away into air. What is needed for
her is something between high comedy and tragedy ;
and this is precisely what she finds in certain parts of the
modern repertory of Dumas fils, Ibsen, and Pinero,
which she is now giving us. It can never be a source of
regret to any lover of the drama that she plays *La Femme
de Claude* because it affords her opportunities of doing
certain things and revealing certain facets of her genius
which one could scarcely have believed existed. At
first sight, one would have thought Madame Duse's
genius was too refined and too noble to render the snake-
like, feline, insinuating, feverish, treacherous, panther-
like, savage temperament of Dumas' she-monster.
Sarah Bernhardt is the person who at once leaps into
the mind as being pre-eminently suited to the part ; the
part, indeed, might have been written for her, and certainly nothing could exceed the superb manner in which
she interprets it. Nevertheless Madame Duse's interpretation is equally fine, and perhaps still more amazing
because it is more unexpected. Sarah Bernhardt carries
you right off your feet at certain moments. Duse plays
on the nerves till they vibrate like beaten strings, in the
same manner as she herself is tremulously vibrating. It
is a gradual process, which begins from the first moment
she walks on to the stage until she falls forward at the
end with outstretched hands, when she is shot by her
husband. Her art is like that of a subtle violinist ; the
music, consisting of simple themes, delicately inter-
woven, progresses until the catastrophe is reached, and
then we attain to that height when all style disappears
and only the perfection of art, in which all artifice is

concealed, remains.   In general, when we see Madame
Duse in parts such as La Dame aux Camélias or Magda
we feel almost as if we ought not to be there ; as if we
were peeping through a keynole at scenes of too intimate
and sacred a nature.   Again in such scenes as that when
Armando hurls money and hisses vituperation at her in
the fourth act of *La Dame aux Camélias*, we feel as
though the police ought to interfere and prevent such a
noble and magnificent creature of God from being outraged in this dastardly fashion.   We begin to doubt
whether she is an artist or even an actress in the
true sense of the word, and whether all she affords us
is not a glimpse of the extraordinary nobility of her
private character, so that the play is entirely beside the
question, and she might just as well appear on the
stage in her everyday clothes and tell us a few confidences,
her joys and her sorrows.   But if she is unable to present
us a plastic poetical creation such as Sarah Bernhardt
builds for us in *Phèdre* or *La Princesse Lointaine*, her
performance of *La Femme de Claude* proves that in the
subtle and objective interpretation of a definite character entirely alien to her nature she can rival, if not
surpass, any artist in the world.   Of course she trans-
figures Cesarina—that is to say, she raises the scale of
everything she touches ; she does not make Dumas'
heroine a better woman than he intended her to be ; but
she makes her a greater woman than he can ever have
hoped she would appear.   She is wicked to the core, not
thoughtlessly non-moral and invincibly ignorant in
her wickedness, but consciously and deliberately destructive ; and this extreme pitch of evil is so delicately
and subtly rendered by Duse that its effect is tenfold ;
she is like the wife of Nero as described by Tacitus, who
professed virtue and practised vice, and whose demeanour

was the perfection of modesty. Her attitude towards the unfortunate young man, Antonino, in the first act when, Circe-like, she charms him, gives the impression that she herself is a victim of ingenuous and involuntary love ; her impassioned supplication to her husband in the second act would deceive the elect ; the notes ring out with the passionate indignation of sincerity, with the agony of one who is smarting from the wounds of unjust and iniquitous circumstance ; she does conquer the frigid Claudio at one moment, and surely if ever wickedness seemed justified by the unattractiveness of priggish austerity this seems to be a case in point, so utterly uninteresting is Claudio. Nothing could be more magnificent than Madame Duse's rendering of the whole of this long and arduous scene, which is a duel fought inch by inch between the desperate woman and the unrelenting man. And, at the last, when she sees her case is hopeless, and she allows her true nature to display itself, nothing could exceed the intensity of her frank exhibition of hatred and ferocity. But still finer was her definitive and final capture and subjugation of the feeble Antonino ; when she bids him follow her, it was as if one had beheld some demi-goddess, such as Circe, swoop gently on her prey, calm in the swift certainty of her triumph. Nobody can ever act better than Madame Duse does in that moment.

1895.

II

ADRIENNE LECOUVREUR

THE story of the first production of *Adrienne Lecouvreur*, as it is related in M. Legouvé's *Soixante Ans*

20

de Souvenirs, is one of the most interesting episodes in
the annals of the French stage. The part was written
for Rachel, but when Scribe read it out to the Committee of the Comédie Française it was unanimously
rejected. A little time later M. Legouvé persuaded
Rachel to let him read out the play to her privately, before
a limited audience of friends. This was done, and
Rachel, who began by clapping out of civility, ended in
a transport of tears. All that can be said for the play
now is that it gives an actress an opportunity of saying
the beginning of La Fontaine's perfect fable, of reciting
a speech out of *Phèdre,* and of dying by poison. The two
recitations lose half their value by being translated into
Italian ; in fact, the scene where Adrienne hisses Phèdre's
famous lines :

> " Je sais mes perfidies,
> Oenone, et ne suis pas de ces femmes hardies,
> Qui, goûtant dans le crime une tranquille paix,
> Ont su se faire un front qui ne rougit jamais,"

fell quite flat on Saturday night. It is true that the
speech loses all its directness and half its force in the
Italian version. It is also true that Madame Duse
failed to strike a note of tragic passion, but had she done
so it would not have made any great difference ; the
fault lies in the play. We are utterly indifferent to the
doings of the puppets on the stage. We do not care a
button what happens to them, as we are never made
to feel why things are happening to them. Therefore,
if an angel from Heaven were to descend and wither
these creatures of tinsel with scorn, it would leave us
cold. What are the opportunities, then, which the part
affords Madame Duse ? A brief love scene in the
first act, in which she suddenly inserts a little poignant
piece of real life into the encircling unreality, and the

death-scene at the end, where she reveals new phases of her genius :

" Silver lights and darks undreamed of."

The sight of her bewilderment when she feels the first effects of the poison, her delirium when she imagines herself once more on the lighted stage, and then when, coming back to her senses, she battles with death, with the " black minute," and " the fiend voices that rave," was one of the most terrible spectacles we have ever beheld. You felt yourself gasping for breath when she experienced the first throes, and when she became delirious the surroundings seemed to fade ; we were face to face with a ghost, we felt the icy wind blowing from the dark river. Magnificent as is this scene, thus interpreted, it seems a shocking waste of genius that Madame Duse should act such plays as *Adrienne Lecouvreur*. It is as if Whistler had painted sky effects for the Drury Lane pantomime. We are not allowed to see Madame Duse in Maeterlinck. Could we, then, not have a little more Dumas fils or Ibsen, or, better still, Goldoni, instead of Scribe ? There is only one man in the world who, we imagine, could write a play in which Madame Duse's genius could find a perfectly adequate scope, and that is Tolstoy. Anna Karenina and La Maslova are made of the same stuff as Eleonora Duse ; but it seems to be unlikely that such a dream will ever be realised.

1905.

III

LA GIOCONDA

It is a relief and a comfort to see Madame Duse in an Italian play after a course of the hackneyed and somewhat threadbare examples of her cosmopolitan repertory. Moreover, *La Gioconda* has the advantage not only of being Italian, but of being a play written by a man who is certainly the greatest living master of the Italian language, and one who is worthy to rank with the greatest writers of Italian prose. To see Madame Duse in such a play is like seeing a work of art, say a statue or a picture, in its proper setting, after having seen it in an exhibition among tawdry and discordant surroundings. The talent of Gabriele D'Annunzio and the fascination it exercises would form the subject of an interesting study. What one generally feels to be lacking in his work is the " fundamental brain-work " : a solid framework, either of thought or feeling. Yet, in everything that he writes, be it poetry, narrative, or drama, we are dominated, almost hypnotised, by the power he has over his language, the passion with which he moulds it, the modulation he extracts from it, the values which he creates and blends with words. You may say you dislike it ; you may call it empty, lacking in ideas ; enervating and oppressive as the atmosphere of a hothouse. In spite of all this—and this fact is confirmed by the avowal of the most rigid classicists in Italy—any lover of the Italian language, whoever appreciates the language of Dante, of Boccaccio, of Petrarch, and of Leopardi, cannot fail to feel the spell of this wonderful artist in words. It is not a case of juggling with words. It is not a trick, any more than the fascination of Wagner's music or Swinburne's poetry is due to trickery. It is something more than dexterity ; he seems to add another element to language—something compounded of music and of light.

One may dislike his style, just as one may dislike Wagner's music, but the fact remains that his production

V

ODETTE

ODETTE is a play which belongs, roughly speaking, to Sardou's second manner, to the period in which he wrote dramas dealing with modern life, such as *Dora* and *Fernande*. Sardou may be reproached with many things; but there is one quality which everybody is bound to concede him, namely, that he is rarely boring. To the hardened, jaded playgoer this quality is probably the most important of all. Whether Sardou writes comedy or farce, domestic drama, historical drama, or unvarnished melodrama, he generally manages to arrest the attention and lead it firmly along the ingenious pathways of his labyrinth by a golden skein of interest or wit.

In the case of *Odette* the path is straightforward and plain. The plot is not one of M. Sardou's feats of legerdemain. It depends for its interest on plain human emotions. We are not breathless to know what will happen, but we are eager to see how it will happen. The story is simple. A husband discovers the infidelity of his wife—Odette—and turns her out of the house on the spot, having previously removed her daughter out of her reach. This is the first act, and it is so effective in itself that it dwarfs the rest of the play. Fifteen years elapse. The daughter grows up believing her mother to be dead. Odette drifts into a vortex of dissipation and squalor. The daughter becomes engaged to a young man, but his parents refuse to give their consent unless Odette promises to leave France for eve[r]. A common friend of Odette and her husband infor[ms]

is something new and something big. Just as to many Wagner never seems to reach the heights of the great classical composers, nor to create melodies which soar up into heaven, but rather to drag you down into a mood in which you drown with pleasure, so, confronted with D'Annunzio, we seem to come under the domination not of Ariel, but of some unscrupulous Prospero. His sentences are intoxicating, and it is not merely a question of " sound and fury signifying nothing," he has a gift of evoking pictures which remain for ever branded on the mind. There are examples of it in this play. The want of backbone and solidity in his work would have led one to suppose that the necessities of the stage would have revealed his defects to an alarming degree. But the form of the drama has a salutary effect on his art; it chastens and concentrates his powers; the colour, the splendour, and the music remain; the same absence of fundamental grip is felt, but the screws are tighter; there is less that is superfluous. Moreover, *La Gioconda*, it cannot be denied, is in parts powerfully dramatic, if by dramatic we mean capable of stimulating, arresting, and holding the attention of a large audience. The third act is dramatic according to any standard, be it that of Sardou or Ibsen. And in no part of the play is there anything which the glare of the footlights renders impossible or tedious.

Madame Duse in the part of Silvia was sorrow incarnate. She might have been De Quincey's " Our Lady of Sorrow." And in her grief she was majestic, an Empress of grief. At the end of the third act, when to save her husband's statue she lets it crush her arms, owing to the reality (not the realism) of her acting, her gift of making one feel present before a piece of real life, the scene was intolerable; one longed for the curtain to come down. In the last act, when she is seen without her arms (she now wears a long robe, which is a great improvement) her expression of the quiet intensity of suffering was miraculous. M. Rosaspina played the part of the husband magnificently; and a full house received the play with tumultuous enthusiasm, and called Madame Duse before the curtain many times, which tends to show that the public prefers a play such as *La Gioconda* to the stock pieces of a stagy and worn-out repertory.

1905.

IV

LA LOCANDIERA AND *UNE VISITE DE NOCES*

ELEONORA DUSE'S *La Locandiera* remains what it was, incomparable and entrancing. Pascal said that had the dimensions of Cleopatra's nose been slightly modified, the history of the world would have been different. Had he seen Madame Duse in this part, he would probably have been grateful that she had nothing to do with affairs of state, for the raising of her eyelid and the magic in her eye when she calls Fabrizio would have wrought still greater havoc than Cleopatra's nose among the great ones of the earth. The whole of her company seem more at their ease, and show to greater advantage, in this delightful and essentially Italian play than in the cosmopolitan repertory in which they have lately been seen.

La Locandiera was followed by *Une Visite de Noces*, by Alexandre Dumas fils. To say that this play is Dumas' masterpiece would be to overstate the case, in the same way as it would be an exaggeration to say that Dickens's masterpiece is *The Christmas Carol*, or that Shakespeare's

masterpiece is Sonnet CXXIX. It i that Dumas never wrote anything m incisive, and more bitterly potent. and has the taste of bitter aloes; o the dose is restricted; or rather, it is lik clean-tasting, bitter alcohol such as v only be taken in small quantities and stantaneous sense of exhilaration. The gave to Madame Duse the opportunit triumph. Here is a case of a good play a wonderful actress; and after a plentif tinsel it is comforting now and then to cor true metal. Madame Duse reminded one Arnold's saying about Wordsworth's poetry, seemed to take the pen from him and writ She was nature itself. And what has been s the play applies equally well to the acting. her most obviously important achievement; b has she done anything more perfect, more f and more subtle. There were moments when h seemed like the " gate of a hundred sorrows." were intonations in her voice charged with intol pathos, when she speaks, in the words of her gre countryman:

" Come colui che piange e dice."

In leaving the theatre, after having seen how Madam Duse as the Locandiera gaily twists all men round he little finger, playing on their weaknesses as a harper on his strings, and how as Lydie, with despair in her soul, she unravelled the skeins of man's falseness, cowardice, and infamy, and spat out her disgust at it, one felt ashamed of being a man.

1905.

her of the situation. She refuses to communicate with
any one except her husband. He arrives just as a man
(for Odette's house is a nest of card-sharpers) is detected cheating at cards. He explains the situation to
her. She begs to be allowed to see her daughter. He
refuses. She in her turn refuses to leave France.
Finally, the husband consents to allow her to see her
daughter in his presence ; she is to figure as a friend of
the family. The interview comes off, and constitutes
Act IV. The daughter does not recognise her mother,
and Odette, condemned out of her daughter's own lips
and utterly heartbroken, goes away, signifying her
intention to remove all obstacles, which she does effectually by drowning herself.

When one sees Madame Duse the play fades into
insignificance. All we care about are the opportunities
it affords of seeing and realising new phases of the
temperament and the talent of this wonderful artist.
Odette gives her fine opportunities for expressing unutterable scorn, the courage of despair, and finally the
capitulation to despair. At the end of the first act,
when Odette left the room, branding her husband with
the word *viliacco* (coward), one felt, what one so often
feels in seeing Madame Duse, that she is made of something so noble and so true that all who are around her,
especially those whom she withers with scorn, seem
like plaster casts, and one wonders they do not crumble
to pieces. She calls to mind Dante's apostrophe to
Sordello :

> " O anima lombarda,
> Come ti stavi altera e disdegnosa,
> E nel muover degli occhi onesta e tarda ! "

1905.

VI

THE RETURN OF ELEONORA DUSE

GREAT acting, really great acting, of the first magnitude, is a rare phenomenon, and nothing receives more abundant lip-service from the world. And yet the artistic life of the great actor or actress, like that of most artists, is one long Calvary, and tangible recognition often comes when the career is almost over. Eleonora Duse played in London in 1893 ; she played in *La Dame aux Camélias*, in *La Locandiera*, and other plays, and the world agreed that she was a very great artist, but they did not crowd the theatre.

In 1895 she was with us for another season ; she played *Magda*, and the critics praised her to the skies. In 1905 she came back again and revealed new facets of her genius ; she played in D'Annunzio, she played *Adrienne Lecouvreur, Fédora, Odette, Une Visite de Noces*, and *La Femme de Claude*. Never had her art been greater. She was in the full force of her powers ; she had achieved the ripeness of experience without having lost the buoyancy of youth ; but she played for the most part to empty or half-empty houses. When she played Paula Tanqueray, never had her art seemed to be so great : the critics were loud in her praise, but the theatre was seldom full.

Of course, there was the barrier of language. It is only fair to remember that it is a great deal to expect an audience to follow a play in a language that they do not understand, and in certain parts the greatness and point of the acting depends often on the intonation that is given to certain phrases, the way a single word is given a special value, the inflection that charges a word with a world of feeling, power, pathos, irony, or fun.

These things are lost upon those who cannot follow a play in the original. But the fact remains that for many years, and when she was at the zenith of her fame, Duse received, in England, lip-service in plenty, but little else. And now, fifteen years later, she comes back to us, playing the parts of old women, such as Mrs. Alving in *Ghosts*, and the theatre is so crowded that the theatrical agencies have waiting lists for " returns," and people advertise seats for sale at five pounds each in the agony column of *The Times*; the audience so enthusiastic that they rise, as one person, after the plays, and cheer and weep, and insist upon remaining until the weary actress can hardly bear the strain of it all. And yet she is still playing in the Italian language. Such are the vicissitudes in the career of the artist.

The younger generation, who knew of Duse only by hearsay, were, of course, anxious to see her and to know whether they agreed with the dithyrambs they had read by an older generation of critics. They were not disappointed. " She can never," I heard one of the youngest and most brilliant of Oxford undergraduates say, " have been as beautiful as she is now." Duse appeared in three plays, *The Lady from the Sea*, *Ghosts*, by Ibsen, and in *Così Sia* (Thy Will be Done), an Italian mystery play by Gallarati-Scotti. The first play she appeared in was *The Lady from the Sea*, and she had not been on the stage a minute before all doubts were at an end.

Yes, she looked older, considerably older ; her face seemed to have been ravaged by sorrow, but she appeared to be more, instead of less, beautiful ; and time, which had whitened her hair and hollowed her cheeks, had added, it seemed, further mystery to the depth of her eyes, and had enlarged and enriched the range and the tones of her voice. The movements, the grace, the super-subtle skill with which every point was made, were as wonderful as ever, and there was something more : a greater depth, a greater breadth, something, perhaps, that only the years can give.

After Duse had been on the stage talking and moving for a few minutes, you no more bothered to think whether she was young or old than you questioned the presence of the footlights or the stage properties. What she was doing was right, inevitably, and she held the whole great audience in the hollow of her hand. And yet the play itself was tedious enough if you knew Italian, and must have been insufferable to those who looked on at it through the mosquito-net of non-comprehension. But it gave her great opportunities. You forgot about Ibsen. What did he mean when he wrote this play about the enigmatic lady who is the victim of a sea-change, who is haunted by the thoughts of the sea ? Was he laughing at himself, at his own heroines, his Rebeccas, his Noras ? Did he mean his Ellida to be pilloried as a warning to show how absurdly people could behave in Norway ? or was he preaching a sermon on liberty or writing a dramatic poem ? Or was he expressing the reaction that he felt after writing *Rosmersholm?*

The " Lady from the Sea " is the daughter of an Inspector of Lighthouses ; she married Doctor Wangel, who is twenty-five or thirty years older than she, and the father of two grown-up daughters. It was not a love marriage ; she feels sincere friendship for her husband and nothing more. Her heart belongs to another, to a mysterious sailor, whom she had met by chance. He had to leave the country in a hurry, as he was (justly) suspected of having stabbed the captain of his ship, but before going he had taken a ring from Ellida, and a ring from his own finger, slipped them both on a larger ring, and flung them into the sea, saying that he and Ellida now were both wedded to the sea.

The sailor went away, but Ellida heard from him later and he told her that she must wait for him. He would let her know when he was ready, and then she must come to him at once. For ever after this Ellida is haunted by the thought of the sea and tormented by the desire for it. She feels herself suffocated in the landlocked fjords. One day, the stranger comes back and recalls her promise and claims its redemption. He will come back in twenty-four hours, he says, to fetch her, only, if she is to go away with him, it must be of her own free will. He comes, and Wangel, her husband, gives her back her liberty—she is to choose as she pleases ; the moment that Ellida feels that she is free to choose, the spell is broken, and she no longer wants to go. She will never leave her husband now. The moral of the play is, perhaps, that nothing is so sacred as liberty, that laws become binding only when we have accepted them of our own free will.

Out of this rather uneven drama, which, in the Italian version, was rendered still more uneven by half of the play being left out, Duse fashioned a wonderful poem of dream, yearning, sorrow, and fear. She showed us a woman who had suffered greatly, and who lived in a world of dreams which had once been delicious but which had become terrible, not only through its tyranny but through its unknown possibilities. She is for ever haunted by the obsession of the sea, and she does not know what her dream will lead her to. She wants to be saved from herself, from her dream. When the stranger

from the sea actually appears in the flesh, her first movement is one of perfectly natural joy at the arrival of a
long-expected friend, and the manner in which this
involuntary expression of joyful recognition escaped
from the lips of Duse, the way she said the words,
" Eccoti ! " was an unforgettable piece of the very rarest
acting. It had about it the stamp of divine simplicity.

This fleeting moment of joy is immediately succeeded
by the shadow of terror, and Duse, as she cowered
behind her husband imploring him to save her, cast one
of those spells over the audience that seem to be
almost palpable. But before this moment the climax of
the play was reached, and indeed from the first moment
she came on the stage, she conveyed a sense of suffering,
and of suffering deep down in the soul ; suffering, too,
from an intangible unearthly cause in so poignant a
fashion that it was almost unbearable to watch her and
listen to her.

In *Ghosts*, Duse transfigured the part of Mrs. Alving,
and she changed the middle-class Norwegian " highbrow " woman, who had so painfully thought out for
herself perplexing questions of conduct and morality,
into an imperial figure. The great effects of her acting
in this play, like all her great effects, differ from those of
other great actors and actresses in this : that when they
happen they seem to transcend the limits or limitations
of the stage and to reach what belongs only to the innermost regions of real life. In real life human beings,
when faced by catastrophe, are dramatic not by what
they do and say, but by what they do not do and do not
say ; by their silence, their reticence, the way in which
they go on with whatever has to be done.

That is a difficult thing for an actor to express on the
stage, which demands, as a rule, a certain amount of

is something new and something big.　Just as to many
Wagner never seems to reach the heights of the great
classical composers, nor to create melodies which soar
up into heaven, but rather to drag you down into a
mood in which you drown with pleasure, so, confronted
with D'Annunzio, we seem to come under the domination not of Ariel, but of some unscrupulous Prospero.
His sentences are intoxicating, and it is not merely a
question of " sound and fury signifying nothing," he
has a gift of evoking pictures which remain for ever
branded on the mind.　There are examples of it in
this play.　The want of backbone and solidity in his
work would have led one to suppose that the necessities
of the stage would have revealed his defects to an
alarming degree.　But the form of the drama has a
salutary effect on his art ; it chastens and concentrates
his powers ; the colour, the splendour, and the music
remain ; the same absence of fundamental grip is felt,
but the screws are tighter ; there is less that is superfluous.　Moreover, *La Gioconda*, it cannot be denied,
is in parts powerfully dramatic, if by dramatic we mean
capable of stimulating, arresting, and holding the
attention of a large audience.　The third act is dramatic
according to any standard, be it that of Sardou or Ibsen.
And in no part of the play is there anything which the
glare of the footlights renders impossible or tedious.

Madame Duse in the part of Silvia was sorrow
incarnate.　She might have been De Quincey's " Our
Lady of Sorrow."　And in her grief she was majestic,
an Empress of grief.　At the end of the third act, when
to save her husband's statue she lets it crush her arms,
owing to the reality (not the realism) of her acting, her
gift of making one feel present before a piece of real
life, the scene was intolerable ; one longed for the

curtain to come down. In the last act, when she is
seen without her arms (she now wears a long robe, which
is a great improvement) her expression of the quiet
intensity of suffering was miraculous. M. Rosaspina
played the part of the husband magnificently ; and a
full house received the play with tumultuous enthusiasm,
and called Madame Duse before the curtain many times,
which tends to show that the public prefers a play such
as *La Gioconda* to the stock pieces of a stagy and worn-
out repertory.

1905.

IV

LA LOCANDIERA AND *UNE VISITE DE NOCES*

ELEONORA DUSE'S *La Locandiera* remains what it was,
incomparable and entrancing. Pascal said that had the
dimensions of Cleopatra's nose been slightly modified,
the history of the world would have been different.
Had he seen Madame Duse in this part, he would probably have been grateful that she had nothing to do
with affairs of state, for the raising of her eyelid and
the magic in her eye when she calls Fabrizio would
have wrought still greater havoc than Cleopatra's nose
among the great ones of the earth. The whole of her
company seem more at their ease, and show to greater
advantage, in this delightful and essentially Italian play
than in the cosmopolitan repertory in which they have
lately been seen.

La Locandiera was followed by *Une Visite de Noces*, by
Alexandre Dumas fils. To say that this play is Dumas'
masterpiece would be to overstate the case, in the same
way as it would be an exaggeration to say that Dickens's
masterpiece is *The Christmas Carol*, or that Shakespeare's

masterpiece is Sonnet CXXIX. It is true, nevertheless, that Dumas never wrote anything more complete, more incisive, and more bitterly potent. It is like a tonic, and has the taste of bitter aloes ; one is thankful that the dose is restricted ; or rather, it is like some colourless, clean-tasting, bitter alcohol such as vodka, which can only be taken in small quantities and produces an instantaneous sense of exhilaration. The part of Lydie gave to Madame Duse the opportunity for a fresh triumph. Here is a case of a good play interpreted by a wonderful actress ; and after a plentiful supply of tinsel it is comforting now and then to come across the true metal. Madame Duse reminded one of Matthew Arnold's saying about Wordsworth's poetry, that nature seemed to take the pen from him and write for him. She was nature itself. And what has been said about the play applies equally well to the acting. It is not her most obviously important achievement ; but never has she done anything more perfect, more finished, and more subtle. There were moments when her face seemed like the " gate of a hundred sorrows." There were intonations in her voice charged with intolerable pathos, when she speaks, in the words of her greatest countryman :

" Come colui che piange e dice."

In leaving the theatre, after having seen how Madame Duse as the Locandiera gaily twists all men round her little finger, playing on their weaknesses as a harper on his strings, and how as Lydie, with despair in her soul, she unravelled the skeins of man's falseness, cowardice, and infamy, and spat out her disgust at it, one felt ashamed of being a man.

1905.

V

ODETTE

ODETTE is a play which belongs, roughly speaking, to Sardou's second manner, to the period in which he wrote dramas dealing with modern life, such as *Dora* and *Fernande*. Sardou may be reproached with many things ; but there is one quality which everybody is bound to concede him, namely, that he is rarely boring. To the hardened, jaded playgoer this quality is probably the most important of all. Whether Sardou writes comedy or farce, domestic drama, historical drama, or unvarnished melodrama, he generally manages to arrest the attention and lead it firmly along the ingenious pathways of his labyrinth by a golden skein of interest or wit.

In the case of *Odette* the path is straightforward and plain. The plot is not one of M. Sardou's feats of legerdemain. It depends for its interest on plain human emotions. We are not breathless to know what will happen, but we are eager to see how it will happen. The story is simple. A husband discovers the infidelity of his wife—Odette—and turns her out of the house on the spot, having previously removed her daughter out of her reach. This is the first act, and it is so effective in itself that it dwarfs the rest of the play. Fifteen years elapse. The daughter grows up believing her mother to be dead. Odette drifts into a vortex of dissipation and squalor. The daughter becomes engaged to a young man, but his parents refuse to give their consent unless Odette promises to leave France for ever. A common friend of Odette and her husband informs her of the situation. She refuses to communicate with any one except her husband. He arrives just as a man (for Odette's house is a nest of card-sharpers) is detected cheating at cards. He explains the situation to her. She begs to be allowed to see her daughter. He refuses. She in her turn refuses to leave France. Finally, the husband consents to allow her to see her daughter in his presence ; she is to figure as a friend of the family. The interview comes off, and constitutes Act IV. The daughter does not recognise her mother, and Odette, condemned out of her daughter's own lips and utterly heartbroken, goes away, signifying her intention to remove all obstacles, which she does effectually by drowning herself.

When one sees Madame Duse the play fades into insignificance. All we care about are the opportunities it affords of seeing and realising new phases of the temperament and the talent of this wonderful artist. *Odette* gives her fine opportunities for expressing unutterable scorn, the courage of despair, and finally the capitulation to despair. At the end of the first act, when Odette left the room, branding her husband with the word *viliacco* (coward), one felt, what one so often feels in seeing Madame Duse, that she is made of something so noble and so true that all who are around her, especially those whom she withers with scorn, seem like plaster casts, and one wonders they do not crumble to pieces. She calls to mind Dante's apostrophe to Sordello :

> " O anima lombarda,
> Come ti stavi altera e disdegnosa,
> E nel muover degli occhi onesta e tarda ! "

1905.

VI

THE RETURN OF ELEONORA DUSE

GREAT acting, really great acting, of the first magnitude, is a rare phenomenon, and nothing receives more abundant lip-service from the world. And yet the artistic life of the great actor or actress, like that of most artists, is one long Calvary, and tangible recognition often comes when the career is almost over. Eleonora Duse played in London in 1893 ; she played in *La Dame aux Camélias*, in *La Locandiera*, and other plays, and the world agreed that she was a very great artist, but they did not crowd the theatre.

In 1895 she was with us for another season ; she played *Magda*, and the critics praised her to the skies. In 1905 she came back again and revealed new facets of her genius ; she played in D'Annunzio, she played *Adrienne Lecouvreur*, *Fédora*, *Odette*, *Une Visite de Noces*, and *La Femme de Claude*. Never had her art been greater. She was in the full force of her powers ; she had achieved the ripeness of experience without having lost the buoyancy of youth ; but she played for the most part to empty or half-empty houses. When she played Paula Tanqueray, never had her art seemed to be so great : the critics were loud in her praise, but the theatre was seldom full.

Of course, there was the barrier of language. It is only fair to remember that it is a great deal to expect an audience to follow a play in a language that they do not understand, and in certain parts the greatness and point of the acting depends often on the intonation that is given to certain phrases, the way a single word

is given a special value, the inflection that charges a word
with a world of feeling, power, pathos, irony, or fun.

These things are lost upon those who cannot follow
a play in the original. But the fact remains that for
many years, and when she was at the zenith of her fame,
Duse received, in England, lip-service in plenty, but
little else. And now, fifteen years later, she comes back
to us, playing the parts of old women, such as Mrs.
Alving in *Ghosts*, and the theatre is so crowded that
the theatrical agencies have waiting lists for " returns,"
and people advertise seats for sale at five pounds each
in the agony column of *The Times*; the audience so
enthusiastic that they rise, as one person, after the plays,
and cheer and weep, and insist upon remaining until
the weary actress can hardly bear the strain of it all.
And yet she is still playing in the Italian language.
Such are the vicissitudes in the career of the artist.

The younger generation, who knew of Duse only by
hearsay, were, of course, anxious to see her and to know
whether they agreed with the dithyrambs they had read
by an older generation of critics. They were not disappointed. " She can never," I heard one of the
youngest and most brilliant of Oxford undergraduates
say, " have been as beautiful as she is now." Duse
appeared in three plays, *The Lady from the Sea*, *Ghosts*,
by Ibsen, and in *Così Sia* (Thy Will be Done), an Italian
mystery play by Gallarati-Scotti. The first play she
appeared in was *The Lady from the Sea*, and she had
not been on the stage a minute before all doubts were
at an end.

Yes, she looked older, considerably older ; her face
seemed to have been ravaged by sorrow, but she appeared
to be more, instead of less, beautiful ; and time, which
had whitened her hair and hollowed her cheeks, had

added, it seemed, further mystery to the depth of her eyes, and had enlarged and enriched the range and the tones of her voice. The movements, the grace, the super-subtle skill with which every point was made, were as wonderful as ever, and there was something more : a greater depth, a greater breadth, something, perhaps, that only the years can give.

After Duse had been on the stage talking and moving for a few minutes, you no more bothered to think whether she was young or old than you questioned the presence of the footlights or the stage properties. What she was doing was right, inevitably, and she held the whole great audience in the hollow of her hand. And yet the play itself was tedious enough if you knew Italian, and must have been insufferable to those who looked on at it through the mosquito-net of non-comprehension. But it gave her great opportunities. You forgot about Ibsen. What did he mean when he wrote this play about the enigmatic lady who is the victim of a sea-change, who is haunted by the thoughts of the sea ? Was he laughing at himself, at his own heroines, his Rebeccas, his Noras ? Did he mean his Ellida to be pilloried as a warning to show how absurdly people could behave in Norway ? or was he preaching a sermon on liberty or writing a dramatic poem ? Or was he expressing the reaction that he felt after writing *Rosmersholm* ?

The " Lady from the Sea " is the daughter of an Inspector of Lighthouses ; she married Doctor Wangel, who is twenty-five or thirty years older than she, and the father of two grown-up daughters. It was not a love marriage ; she feels sincere friendship for her husband and nothing more. Her heart belongs to another, to a mysterious sailor, whom she had met by chance. He had to leave the country in a hurry, as he was (justly) suspected of having stabbed the captain of his ship, but before going he had taken a ring from Ellida, and a ring from his own finger, slipped them both on a larger ring, and flung them into the sea, saying that he and Ellida now were both wedded to the sea.

The sailor went away, but Ellida heard from him later and he told her that she must wait for him. He would let her know when he was ready, and then she must come to him at once. For ever after this Ellida is haunted by the thought of the sea and tormented by the desire for it. She feels herself suffocated in the landlocked fjords. One day, the stranger comes back and recalls her promise and claims its redemption. He will come back in twenty-four hours, he says, to fetch her, only, if she is to go away with him, it must be of her own free will. He comes, and Wangel, her husband, gives her back her liberty—she is to choose as she pleases ; the moment that Ellida feels that she is free to choose, the spell is broken, and she no longer wants to go. She will never leave her husband now. The moral of the play is, perhaps, that nothing is so sacred as liberty, that laws become binding only when we have accepted them of our own free will.

Out of this rather uneven drama, which, in the Italian version, was rendered still more uneven by half of the play being left out, Duse fashioned a wonderful poem of dream, yearning, sorrow, and fear. She showed us a woman who had suffered greatly, and who lived in a world of dreams which had once been delicious but which had become terrible, not only through its tyranny but through its unknown possibilities. She is for ever haunted by the obsession of the sea, and she does not know what her dream will lead her to. She wants to be saved from herself, from her dream. When the stranger from the sea actually appears in the flesh, her first movement is one of perfectly natural joy at the arrival of a long-expected friend, and the manner in which this involuntary expression of joyful recognition escaped from the lips of Duse, the way she said the words, " Eccoti ! " was an unforgettable piece of the very rarest acting. It had about it the stamp of divine simplicity.

This fleeting moment of joy is immediately succeeded by the shadow of terror, and Duse, as she cowered behind her husband imploring him to save her, cast one of those spells over the audience that seem to be almost palpable. But before this moment the climax of the play was reached, and indeed from the first moment she came on the stage, she conveyed a sense of suffering, and of suffering deep down in the soul ; suffering, too, from an intangible unearthly cause in so poignant a fashion that it was almost unbearable to watch her and listen to her.

In *Ghosts*, Duse transfigured the part of Mrs. Alving, and she changed the middle-class Norwegian " highbrow " woman, who had so painfully thought out for herself perplexing questions of conduct and morality, into an imperial figure. The great effects of her acting in this play, like all her great effects, differ from those of other great actors and actresses in this : that when they happen they seem to transcend the limits or limitations of the stage and to reach what belongs only to the innermost regions of real life. In real life human beings, when faced by catastrophe, are dramatic not by what they do and say, but by what they do not do and do not say ; by their silence, their reticence, the way in which they go on with whatever has to be done.

That is a difficult thing for an actor to express on the stage, which demands, as a rule, a certain amount of exaggeration and where, if a point is to be made, it must be made clearly. Duse achieves this very thing. At the end of the first act of *Ghosts*, when Mrs. Alving sees through the open door her husband's history repeating itself, and the hidden sins of the father blossoming in a terrible fashion in the son, a look comes over Duse's face, as though she had received the crowning and final blow of calamity ; and yet there came into her eyes also, and into the lines of her mouth, a set expression of determination, a courage to go on, and to face whatever had to be faced, and not to show it, not to betray what she was feeling and suffering, not to reveal for one second the torture of the hidden wound ; and this experience which she conveyed, Heaven knows how, although common enough in real life, needs for its presentation and manifestation on the stage, and behind the footlights, a command of consummate craftsmanship, and an infallible certainty of instinct : a divine authority.

Così Sia, the mystery play, was the only Italian work in which Duse appeared. It is not a great work of art, and I do not think it is a work of art at all. It exploits some of the qualities of the Italian artist just as Sardou's melodramas exploited the electric shocks which the genius of Sarah Bernhardt was capable of giving. But those who saw Madame Duse in the part will never forget it. They may even hesitate before seeing it a second time, as it is an experience that harrows the feelings beyond all bounds.

During the whole first act we see a mother watching over the sick-bed of her little boy, her little boy who is dying, and when the father comes in, and makes unreasonable remarks, she tells him to go away and to leave her alone. I saw two of the performances of this play, and in the first performance, Madame Duse, when she played that scene, dismissed the husband with a sudden authoritative gesture and an imperative accent that one felt came from the Holy of Holies of Motherhood. The second time I saw her, she played the scene and said the words " Go away " in a different fashion. She said them to herself without looking up, too deeply drowned and submerged in her misery to rise to the surface ; too far away to listen, almost too sad to mourn, out of reach of all consideration, and reason, and attention, only wanting to be left alone like a wounded animal.

I do not know which of these two renderings was the finer. Both of them seemed to be sublime. In both of them she revealed what Anatole France, in talking of Marie Antoinette during her trial, calls " La majesté d'une mère." In *Ghosts*, Duse had already shown what she could do when dealing with motherhood, but in this Italian play she revealed fresh aspects of the theme and new facets of her genius. In *Ghosts* she gave us the infinite sympathy, the profound suffering, the tigerish courage, of motherhood ; ready to do everything for a suffering son, capable of understanding everything, ready to face and to dare all, however impossible, however dreadful.

In the Italian play she showed us motherhood *au grand complet*, over the cradle when the mother whispers and argues with the Mother of God ; motherhood outraged in its dignity, when her son thinks she is begging, and offers her broken heart, that is crying for the balm of one word of love, a purse of gold ; and, finally, broken motherhood, imploring God that her son may not be punished for the wrong he had done her, and taking the blame upon herself and offering all she has left of her life.

It is a terrible spectacle, and were it not for the great

beauty of Madame Duse's acting, it would not be bearable.

I am told that the Italian public did not bear it. In seeing it I felt once more, what I have so often felt in looking at Duse's acting, that one was looking through a keyhole at things too sacred and too intimate for mortal inspection, and that her acting made one feel like a cad.

One had no right to be there; one was violating the sanctuary of sacred things, and listening at the curtain of a forbidden confessional. So tremendous, so intimate and so rare is the artless art of Eleonora Duse.

1923.

SARAH BERNHARDT IN *PHÈDRE*

IF *Phèdre* is not Racine's masterpiece (French critics generally concede that honour to *Athalie*), it is undoubtedly his most important play from a theatrical point of view : the *Hamlet* of the French stage. It moreover contains what is perhaps the most powerful and exacting woman's part in the whole range of dramatic literature. Two salient facts strike one in this play, and they have sometimes been noted as objections. The first is, that whereas the framework and machinery of the play and the central idea which informs it are Greek, its spirit is Christian. Phèdre herself is no Pagan. She is a victim of involuntary and irresistible passion ; but she is full of remorse and reveals the consciousness of her guilt in her fear of Heaven, as manifested in the Sun-god and Minos, the judge of the dead. But this apparent discord in reality increases the poignancy of the drama, for in rendering Phèdre morally innocent the tragedy of her plight is heightened. The second fact, which is sometimes brought forward as an objection not only to *Phèdre* but to all Racine's plays, is akin to the first, namely, that the personages talk the language and express the sentiments of the epoch and surroundings of Louis XIV., whether the action takes place in Rome, Turkey, Greece, or Jerusalem. But it is really only the superficial and external forms of manner and speech which belong to the seventeenth century in these plays ; the passions which these forms clothe are eternal and for all time, because they are human. And just as in *Bérénice*, Racine gives us the unchanging drama of the unwilling separation of willing lovers, so in *Phèdre* he presents us with the eternal drama of the woman who is the involuntary prey of an insuperable passion for a man whom she is debarred by circumstances from loving unless she would be criminal. And nowhere has this passion been more powerfully delineated, nor the gradations and phases of the martyrdom more subtly traced. Every touch tells ; nothing is omitted ; so that no modern psychologist could possibly add anything to the delicacy and reality of the study. For instance, Phèdre is haunted by the image of her stepson in her husband's features :

> " Je l'évitais partout. O comble de misère !
> Mes yeux le retrouvaient dans les traits de son père."

In addition to the interest which the play derives from this masterful and moving analysis of passion, there is also the charm and the divine beauty of the diction in which the passion is clothed. It contains not only Racine's most majestic and noble utterance, but also lines which have never been surpassed by any French poet for haunting melody of cadence. These qualities can only be realised to the full by those who have seen Madame Bernhardt in this part. Here she moves in the dominion which she has made her own : that of poetry and imaginative creation. She is equal to the part, and on the same scale. She seems to create it : to find always the unexpected, and yet the absolutely right intonation and rendering. There are two separate excellences in her interpretation of Phèdre ; the first is its plastic beauty, and the second is its spiritual significance. The plastic beauty is a miracle in itself. Even if she acted the play in dumb show, it would still be a marvel of expressiveness. Her gestures are like phrases of silent music, and obey an invisible rhythm to which even her most violent outbursts of passion and anger are subordinate. Again, so varied and so artfully controlled, so ravishingly melodious are the modulations of her diction, that were she to read the play in an arm-chair, the evocation of passionate action would still be magically present. Just as Emerson says that Napoleon enlarged our conception of the capacity of man for business, so does Madame Bernhardt in this part enlarge our conception of the possibilities of the human being in dramatic art.

There is the mark of men and the mark of gods. Madame Bernhardt in *Phèdre* is superhuman : a super-woman. And had Racine seen her in this part he would have been compelled to adhere to the stage, and had Shakespeare seen her after writing *The Tempest* he would have spent the years of his retirement at Strat-ford in writing a woman's part for her, for, like Dante's Siren, she, and only she, could say :

> " ' Io son,' cantava, ' io son dolce sirena
> Che i marinari in mezzo il mar dismago.' "

1905.

PELLÉAS AND MÉLISANDE

IN writing about Maeterlinck's plays it is difficult to avoid the use of a word which has been hackneyed to an almost nauseating extent, and which has become a part of an irritating literary jargon, namely, " atmosphere " ; for in Maeterlinck's plays the human figure is more important than the clash of events, and the atmosphere in which the figures and events are plunged is more important still ; both the figures and the events are subservient to the circumambient poetry. The atmosphere of this play is one of " wizard twilight." It is a drama written in poetical algebra, and it proceeds by glimpses, hints, and delicate psychic asides. The drama, nevertheless, is present, and is none the less poignant for being reduced to its simplest terms, and to terms of poetry. The love story of *Pelléas and Mélisande* has a profound mystery and simplicity which belong to the kingdom of childhood. It is a tragic fairy-tale : a *Paolo and Francesca* transposed into Limbo and played by children. This is what makes its symbolism so poignant ; because the childishness of the characters is symbolic of the childish helplessness of the human race blundering and groping on the darkling chessboard of fate. It all happens in a land of shadows, in an abstract landscape of grey cardboard towers, which allows the spectator to concentrate on the mere feeling. We behold the kind of visions, so distinct and so marvellously strange, which we find in the poetry of Coleridge.

Madame Bernhardt and Mrs. Campbell are ideal artists for the rendering of these citizens of the " vague land." Poetry—the understanding and expression of the spirit of poetry—is the strong point of both these artists. That Mrs. Campbell must needs play in French is, in this case, no handicap, and quite beside the mark ; because the words are nothing ; the talk is a kind of bird-language, a speech made up of sighs and tears and plaintive tremors and half-articulate cries ; and Mrs. Campbell would render these with equal success were she to play the part in Chinese or Malay. She is at home in this dreamland, and native to this region of glamour and mystery. The beauty and the pathos of her performance—especially in the last act—are so great that one is left despairingly wondering why we so seldom have an opportunity of appreciating her talent. Madame Bernhardt's interpretation of Pelléas was likewise fraught with poetry, and in the tragic moments touched us with the very thrill of eerie magic. There was no trace of mannerism or exaggeration in her playing. It was like everything she does, genial in conception and consummate in execution.

1905.

TOLSTOY'S LAST PLAY

WHEN the moral crisis occurred in Count Tolstoy's life which led him to abjure literature in favour of manual labour, fortunately for the world, the consistent vein of inconsistency which distinguished this great man from his childhood onwards prevented the entire realisation of his new ideal in practice. That is to say, although he sometimes used the spade he did not altogether abandon the pen. It may be a lie that the pen is mightier than the sword, but in Tolstoy's case there is no doubt that the pen was mightier than the spade. As a husbandman he was an unconvincing amateur ; as a writer he was the prose Homer of his time.

Tolstoy, fortunately for us, never ceased to write, and when he died he left behind him a mass of unpublished MSS. Among them was a play, *The Living Corpse*, which is at this moment being acted in the " Art Theatre " at Moscow.

The play was written in 1900. The subject was one of those stories which happen in real life, which we read in the law reports of the Press—those slices of raw life— and of which we say when we read them : " What a good subject for a book or a play ! " or rather the usual phrase is : " If you put that into a play all the critics would say it is impossible."

The story was taken whole from an actual lawsuit which occurred some years ago. Tolstoy took the facts, changed the surroundings, the *milieu* in which they happened, and the characters as well, and made a play. The play was never produced during Tolstoy's lifetime, because some of the actual actors in the real drama were still living, and their relations asked Tolstoy not to have the play staged.

The story is as follows : Liza Protasova leaves her husband Theodore, whom she had loved, because he is

> " A little slovenly in dress,
> A trifle prone to drunkenness."

Not a bad man ; but weak, extravagant, and given to periodic outbreaks when he spends the night listening to gipsies singing, and drinking champagne. You must know Russia to understand what listening to gipsies means, and you must be well inoculated with gipsy music before you understand its tyrannical spell. It is in a lesser—or greater—degree like smoking opium.

Apart from these more or less venial failings, Theodore is not a bad man, nor is he even an unfaithful husband. Nevertheless, his wife, after one of these periodic outbursts, leaves him and returns to her mother, who thoroughly approves of such a course. But no sooner has Liza taken this step than she repents herself of it, and she sends Theodore a message by one Karenin asking him to come back to her. Karenin is an honest prig and a bore. He is in love with Liza. He executes the commission, but Theodore is away, listening to the gipsies and especially to one of them called Masha, and he refuses to go back.

Weeks go by and then months. Karenin loves Liza ; Liza loves Karenin. Masha loves Theodore. Liza's mother wishes her daughter to be divorced and to marry Karenin. An embassy with this proposal is dispatched to Theodore. But according to the Russian law, in such a case, in order to get a divorce, when a wife has left her husband because she no longer wishes to be his wife, the husband must take the guilt on himself. He must declare himself a guilty, unfaithful husband ; and if he is not one, he must concoct sham evidence to show that he is, and swear to it. This Theodore refuses to do, because he is not guilty ; he has not been unfaithful. He says : " I have been a bad husband, I am a worthless man, but there are things which I cannot do, and one of them is quietly to tell the necessary lie in order to make this divorce possible." He seeks another solution. He finds a simple one : suicide. But when the revolver is at his temple he hesitates, in an agony, and at that moment Masha the gipsy intervenes, sees what is happening, and suggests yet another solution : that he should let the world think he has killed himself, and in reality escape with her, leaving his wife free to marry Karenin. He does this. He writes a letter to his wife saying he is about to kill himself ; he leaves his clothes by the river. The plan succeeds ; by chance a corpse is found ; Liza says it is that of her husband (and it is no use saying that this is improbable, because it all happened) ; Theodore and Masha disappear, and Karenin marries Liza. All is for the best, for them.

Theodore sinks deeper into the mud, and one fine day when he is telling his story to a friend in a squalid tavern he is overheard by a tramp, who, quickly perceiving the possible profit in such a situation, suggests to Theodore a scheme of joint blackmail ; that they should blackmail Liza. Theodore tells him to go to what I see now is prettily called " the underground world " ; and the tramp, in a rage, calls a policeman and

gives Theodore in charge for bigamy. But not only
Theodore but his wife and Karenin too are all of them
had up for bigamy ; they are charged with conspiracy—
if that be the right term—for having, that is to say, been
privy to the scheme, and for having paid Theodore to
get out of the way and become a " Living Corpse." The
maximum penalty of the law for bigamy is exile to
Siberia, the minimum what is called " Church con-
trition " ; but in any case the second marriage is can-
celled ; and if Karenin, Theodore, and Liza were acquitted
of conspiracy, Liza and Theodore would nevertheless
be bound to resume their interrupted married life. The
lawyers do not believe a word of the true story as it is told
by the witnesses, and Theodore, to prevent Liza from
being bound to him once more, commits suicide in the
corridor of the law court during the trial. That is the
story ; and these are the facts as they actually happened
in real life.

Now, how has Tolstoy dealt with the story ? He has
not bothered to write acts at all. He has written a series
of scenes, twelve in all, in which the things which happen
are those which in other plays we presume have occurred
during the *entr'actes*. Thus, in Scene 1, we see the
Protasov family after Liza's return, when Liza sends
Karenin to her husband. In Scene 2, we see Theodore
listening to the gipsies. In Scene 6, we see Liza's
younger sister paying a visit to Theodore on her own
account and trying to arrange matters. In Scene 8, we
see Karenin's mother, who is strongly opposed to the
marriage of her son with Liza, and we see her receiving
Liza for the first time. In Scene 9, we see the tavern
where Theodore tells his story. In Scene 10, we see
the home of the Karenins when they receive the summons
of the law court. In Scene 11, the preliminary ex-

amination of the three actors in the drama by the *juge
d'instruction* ; and in Scene 12, the corridor of the law
court (" *La salle des pas perdus* ").

It is exactly as if Mr. Kipling's *Story of the Gadsbys*
were put on the stage. The scenes are short, so short
that they sometimes seem long, because you are not
given time to enter into the atmosphere. The characters are so real that it is difficult for the best actors
not to diminish their reality. This is why perhaps the
play is better to read than to see.

The " Art Theatre " of Moscow (which in a few
weeks' time is going to do *Hamlet*, with Gordon Craig's
setting) is justly considered at the present moment to
possess the most complete, the most carefully disciplined, the most harmonious, artistic, and capable company
of actors in Europe. The " production " on this stage,
whether for the fantasy of Maeterlinck (as in *The Blue
Bird*) or the realism of Tchekov, is unrivalled. In
Tolstoy's play, the scene in which Theodore is listening
to the gipsies is typical of the production. It is a miracle
of detail and realism, a triumph of artistic interpretation.

It is curious to look on at such a scene from the stalls ;
to look on, in cold blood, at what is generally shared
through a mist of glamour. (Gipsies in this case are not
ragged people in picturesque clothes : they are a chorus
of men and women in everyday dress who, though
swarthy in complexion, look like the audience in the
upper circle at a Queen's Hall concert.)

Sitting in the stalls we notice first of all the extreme
boredom and fatigue of the gipsies. They yawn ; one
of them has got toothache and a swollen face ; they carry
on an undercurrent of irrelevant conversation among
themselves, like people behind the wire-netting in the
telegraph office, while they automatically sing. We

notice, above all things, the mechanical side of the gaiety and the poetry they are paid to express. We see the guttering candles ; the empty champagne bottles ; the lieutenant in uniform beating time semi-consciously to the music ; while the sun, which has just risen, streams through the windows of the cheerless, shabby, and gaudy private room of the restaurant. But although we see all this we also see by the expression on Theodore's face that were he in that room in real life we should be sharing the glamour he feels ; we should be oblivious of every sordid detail and of all the mechanism ; we should only be aware of the poetry, the romance, the passion evoked by that wailing concord of piercing, discordant sounds which play on the nerves like a bow upon strings. First you tremble all over as with a fever ; then you are aware that the fever is pleasant. Then you forget all this ; you are far away amid white dawns and sleepless nights, and the light and laughter of wild black eyes ; and a barking chorus as of a pack of unearthly wolves ; and when you are brought back to reality, you demand, you insist, on one more glimpse of that sweet and bitter, that discordant and melodious fairyland.

Moscow, 1911.

HAMLET AT THE " OLD VIC "

A TRAGEDY written by Shakespeare, called *Hamlet*, has lately been acted on the stage in London for the first time for very many years—at the " Old Vic." It is true that versions and portions of Shakespeare's *Hamlet* have been frequently put on the stage at various theatres ; but it is a long time, perhaps fifty or a hundred years, since the whole play has been performed as it was written—from beginning to end. Mr. Poel, it is true, produced it (in two parts, I believe), and produced it, so I am told, beautifully ; but Mr. Poel's enterprises are, so to speak, private views, and are not faced by the British public. At the " Old Vic," Shakespeare's play was face to face with the best of all publics : the public which wanted to see the play, and were ready to sit listening to it from one to six p.m.— on hard seats and on a stuffy afternoon. The public enjoyed it ; they listened with absolute attention, and they applauded enthusiastically at the right moments throughout, and deliriously at the end. I think if Shakespeare's ghost was there he must have been pleased. Any one seeing that performance could tell what the author was about, and could follow the story he had to tell without difficulty. There was no elaborate scenery to distract him, but just enough to suggest the colouring of the circumstances ; there was no noise of hammering behind the scenes to drown the speech of the players ;

and the words of the play were spoken and not mouthed, and spoken as they were written.

I don't wish to decry the Hamlets that, given the time allotted by the County Council or whatever gods there be to an evening performance, are all we usually get. Nobody who has ever seen Sir Johnston Forbes-Robertson's Hamlet will forget the courtly grace of his bearing, the cunning melody of his delivery, the perfect understanding of rhythm which he gave to the utterance of such speeches as " O what a rogue and peasant slave am I " ; the naturalness of his conversation with the gravediggers ; the noble dignity of his death scene. In the last thirty years there have been many memorable Hamlets : Mr. Martin Harvey's, Mr. H. B. Irving's, Mr. E. H. Sothern's (a brisk, sharp American Hamlet), Madame Sarah Bernhardt's, an inspired performance ; and the Art Theatre at Moscow contributed, under the guidance of Mr. Gordon Craig, at least two new unforgettable pictures : the play scene, with a stiff, gold King and Queen facing the audience, high on two golden thrones, and the picture of Hamlet being borne away on a broad shield in a pale, rosy, and azure dawn by silver-armoured captains to the sound of clarions.

But in none of these productions was it possible to see the whole play, although Sir Johnston Forbes-Robertson gave us much that is usually left out, and allowed us the final entry of Fortinbras. But at the " Old Vic " you have it all, and consequently you understand the story and you enjoy the poetry. There isn't time for the ranting that delays the action, nor for the shifting, setting, resetting, and manipulation of portentous accessories ; what is left is the play—*le spectacle*. It is the rarest thing in the modern world to be able to go to *le spectacle*. As far as I know, the only two theatres where this is possible at the present moment are the " Old Vic " and the Hammersmith Theatre. Everywhere else it is the accessories that count ; and if they are not the chief they are, at any rate, an indispensable factor in the production.

Years ago, in the 'fifties, Théodore de Banville, the poet, who was at that time a dramatic critic, wrote a startling prophecy ; he said that he foresaw that the stage would develop into two diverse channels : one in which scenery would be the paramount object—real waterfalls, dazzling squadrons of spangled nymphs, processions and here he foresaw the cinema, because he said *the eye grows swiftly weary of all stationary spectacle, however spectacular*, and demands motion.

The second channel, he said, would be an intense indulgence in realistic detail ; and here he foresaw the Théâtre Libre, Antoine, the Art Theatre of Moscow, Granville Barker, and the Stage Society.

He made the discovery that nobody can look at a *tableau vivant* for more than one minute without feeling miserably bored ; and that therefore no scenery, however gorgeous or various, would suffice unless it was in per- petual motion (the cinematograph). The logical con- clusion, which is proved to-day by the " Old Vic " and by *Abraham Lincoln* at the Hammersmith, is that if the play and the players are interesting the scenery does not matter one fig ; because no audience looks at scenery for more than a minute (unless it changes), and the moment the players interest them they forget the scenery—they become unaware of its existence. If managers could only realise this they would save themselves millions of money, and we should have some interesting plays. Because both the developments that Théodore de Ban- ville foresaw have proved failures, the spectacular theatre has made Shakespeare spell ruin, and has been easily outrivalled by the cinema, the realistic theatre has only been successful if its plays have been interesting, the mounting has never mattered. It matters not two straws if Ibsen is acted, with every match a Swedish match, on the stage—or in a barn ; all the care of the Art Theatre didn't succeed in making you think you were looking at a cherry orchard in the dawn (as the mechanical birds were not the least like real birds), and it was the *play*, and the *actors*, not the mounting, that held the audience.

So now, perhaps, the time has come, or will come shortly, when the theatrical world, in a wholesome wave of realism, will go back to *plays* and to acting. There is the " Old Vic," and there is its production of *Hamlet*, a performance lasting five hours with the briefest intervals, holding a huge audience breathless, to prove that the thing can be done.

Now that I have delivered myself of this perilous argument, I can say something about the play and the performance. In the first place, the mounting, which was reduced to the simplest terms, was more effective than any Shakespearean mounting I have ever seen in London. Effects were suggested by small details. A jester gambolled about in the Court Scene (Act I.), and stood looking ghastly with his painted clown's cheeks while Hamlet fought Laertes. The play scene was a revelation. It was done with the dumb show first, and one felt the suspense and the gradual enlightenment of the audience on the stage. Mr. Russell Thorndike, who played Hamlet, achieved an effect which I have seen no one else playing Hamlet achieve save Sarah Bernhardt. He carried on the excitement of the play scene into the following scene with Rosencrantz and Guildenstern.

You felt (though less acutely than in Sarah's performance) that Hamlet was still vibrating with excitement ; that his nerves were all jangled and tingling ; and Mr. Thorndike's delivery of the " can-you-play-upon-this-flute " speech was one of the triumphs of the afternoon ; and the audience felt this and applauded unanimously. Mr. Thorndike's performance was satisfying throughout, never stagey and never exaggerated, and at times quite admirable. What struck me most of all in the production was Mr. Charles Warburton's King, who, instead of giving us Maclise's scowling cardboard counter of melodrama, was a human, energetic, dignified King who made us thoroughly sympathetic with the arrangement he was making for the dispatch to England (and farther) of his troublesome, talkative nephew. Polonius (not cut), Mr. Orlando Barnett, became as lifelike as a Cabinet Minister, and Ophelia (Miss Saunders) was really mad and not just pretty. All the parts were well played ; and Shakespeare's ghost, who I am sure must have haunted many actor-managers, will now, I am sure, be appeased.

He is an honest ghost.

1919.

22

PETER IBBETSON

IN *Peter Ibbetson*, the book, there are two magics,
or perhaps three. There is, first, the gift Du
Maurier had of evoking his past. With this gift
he laid the foundations of three books. *Trilby* is
based upon his youth, *The Martian* on his schooldays,
and *Peter Ibbetson* on his childhood ; and I know of no
other book in the language where the enchanted hours
and dreams of childhood are evoked and represented
with a more subtle and delicious blend of *Wahrheit* and
Dichtung.

The second magic is his style. What constitutes the
charm of that style I do not know, and I have often
wondered, but it is a style that has accent and intonation
like a charming voice, so that it does not matter in the
least what he says ; and a style that calls up pictures,
sights, sounds, and smells—and especially the sights,
sounds, and smells of the past.

Just taste a piece of it which I take at random : " Moreover, Mimsey and I had many tastes and passions in
common—music, for instance, as well as Bewick's wood-
cuts and Byron's poetry, and roast chestnuts and domestic
pets ; and above all the Mare d'Auteuil, which she preferred in the autumn, when the brown and yellow leaves
were eddying and chasing each other round its margin, or
drifting on its troubled surface, and the cold, wet wind
piped through the dishevelled boughs of the forest, under
the leaden sky.

" She said it was good to be there then, and think of home and the fireside ; and, better still, when home was reached at last, to think of the desolate pond we had left ; and good, indeed, it was to trudge home by wood, and park, and avenue at dusk, when the bats were about, with Alfred and Charlie and Mimsey and Madge and Médor ; swishing our way through the lush, dead leaves, scattering the beautiful, ripe horse-chestnut out of its split, creamy case, or picking up acorns and beech-nuts here and there as we went."

Then there is in this book a third magic. Du Maurier in all his books had a leaning towards not exactly the supernatural but a kind of psychical fairyland. Hence we get Trilby mesmerised by Svengali, and singing his interpretation of the music, and the messages from Mars in *The Martian*. In *Peter Ibbetson* we have the " dreaming true " *motiv*. Peter Ibbetson meets the companion of his childhood in his dream, and together, night after night, they are able to reconstruct the past : not only their childhood, but anything and everything either of them has ever seen or experienced.

Charm of style, the magic of the past, the sights and sounds and dreams of childhood, moreover a French childhood in the France of Louis Philippe . . . a dream world . . . little Mimsey grown up into the divinely beautiful Duchess of Towers—these are perilous elements out of which to concoct a play for the London stage. Nevertheless, it has been done and done sufficiently well to make a successful play, a good marketable, actable play, " straight, paying stuff " with just enough whiffs of Du Maurier, and a sufficient suggestion of the pathos and beauty of the book to pacify and to please its lovers.

Think for a moment what it means to adapt a play

from a book. When an author sits down to write a play he can at least choose and-invent scenes and circumstances suitable to his plot and to his characters, but the author who is adapting a play from a book has to " get " certain things " in," as boys at school, when they write Latin verses, are determined to " get " certain words and phrases " in," regardless of the sense or of their appropriateness. And besides this, he has to do his best to let the audience know who all the characters are, and that as soon as possible, and also to provide enough ordinary dramatic fare to make the play go down.

At the Savoy Theatre it has been done like this : we have a first act at Mrs. Deane's house in the country, and in this house all the characters are marshalled at an evening party.

The characters are dressed in the costumes of 1870, and this every one enjoys . . . and what we enjoy still more are the dances of that epoch : the Varsovienne (and was the other a Schottische ?). Several characters in the book appear ; among others, Colonel Ibbetson, the villain, " created " and " composed " with infinite finish by Mr. Gilbert Hare, and here the Duchess of Towers, very handsomely impersonated by Miss Constance Collier, meets Peter Ibbetson.

Then we have a second act at Saint Cloud, where Peter Ibbetson is revisiting the scenes of his childhood. Here he is made to meet some old friends and to catch sight of the Duchess of Towers driving past with the Empress Eugénie, and to fall asleep in the inn parlour, and enter the dream world of the past. The walls of the inn fade away, and we are in the sunlit garden. " It was on a beautiful June morning in a charming French garden, where the warm, sweet atmosphere was laden with the

Doctor Johnson's appreciative summing up of the opera is as much to the point now as when it was written. " It was refused by one of the houses," said the sage, " but I should have thought it would succeed, not from any great excellence in the writing, but from the novelty, and the general spirit and gaiety of the piece, which keeps the audience always attentive, and dismisses them in good humour " ; and Boswell's opinion is " that there is in it so much of real London life, so much brilliant wit, and such a variety of airs, which, from early association of ideas, engage, soothe, and enliven the mind, that no performance which the theatre exhibits delights me more."

To the present generation of playgoers and lovers of music it has an added and priceless value. It is English, as English as a landscape by Constable, or eggs and bacon, and is full of ravishing English music. With the exception of the recent revival of Gilbert and Sullivan's operas we have rarely had the chance of hearing a note of English music. In the world of opera, again with the exception just mentioned, there is little English music to hear. The music in the musical comedies and revues is mostly American or foreign in inspiration, but in *The Beggar's Opera* the songs are not only English but they are songs of the people ; traditional tunes that were born nobody knows how and were whistled in the streets and the country lanes and sung in taverns and on board ship —songs which in all times have been the wonder and despair of composers ; of Beethoven, who set " Sally in our Alley," the tune of which occurs in the third act of *The Beggar's Opera* ; of Handel, who is reported to have said he would rather have composed " The Girl I left behind Me " than any tune in the world. Has this music left England for ever ? one asks, or is it buried

scent of lilac and syringa, and gay with butterflies and dragon-flies and humble-bees, that I began my conscious existence," where under the apple-tree is sitting the beautiful Madame Pasquier, and Gogo and Mimsey are doing their lessons, and talking of the two invisible fairies that attend them : Le Prince Charmant and La Fée Tarapatapoum : and there is the dog Médor, the dog we have seen so often in old numbers of *Punch*, who would " wag his three inches of tail and utter soft whimperings of welcome in his dream " while Mimsey said, " C'est le Prince Charmant qui lui dit : Médor, donne la patte ! " I thought this scene beautiful on the stage ; very cleverly stage-managed and lighted, for although the lighting was brilliant, one had the impression that one was looking at a dream-world, and the children played their parts delightfully. For the sake of this scene alone, which was really moving and had the true Du Maurier flavour and charm, the play is worth seeing.

Peter wakes up ; and events have for the play's sake to be so tightly telescoped that he has to meet the Duchess of Towers in the same act, and they have to recognise each other as Gogo and Mimsey on the spot. This scene was likewise moving and touching, but it was a slight strain on one's credulity to believe that the Duchess had gone to sleep in the carriage, as it had shortly before been stated that she was driving with the Empress Eugénie. Then we get a third act of good sterling drama, where Peter kills Colonel Ibbetson. The scene is very well played both by Mr. Rathbone and Mr. Hare. Mr. Hare has some of the finish of his incomparable father. There is just this difference. He lights a match and a cigarette in this scene, and you say to yourself how well and how naturally he did that ; if it had been Sir John Hare playing the part the cigarette would have lit before you would have had time to notice how he lit it, however carefully you were waiting and watching for it.   In Act IV., after a not very (to me) interesting emotional prison scene, we get back once more into the dream-world, and see Gogo and Mimsey catching the water-beetles and the newts at the Mare d'Auteuil, and here the Duchess of Towers explains to Peter that his new dream-life has only just begun, and the possibility of reconstructing any moment of the past.   In the darkness of the glade they summon up a vision of the opera, and the voice of Adelina Patti is heard singing for them.   And there the play should end.   Unfortunately, there is an anti-climax in the shape of an epilogue forty years after, in which the Duchess of Towers returns with white hair after her death.   But one need not stay for it, and I didn't.   There is plenty of good acting in the play on the part of Mr. Rathbone, Miss Bateman, and others, and the only real cavil I have to make (apart from the question of the epilogue) is, why should the English proprietor of the Tête Noire, whom Peter recognises as an old London friend, be spoken to in French ?   But if it must be, for Heaven's sake let it be correct French.   The sentence about the *sauce verte* must make Du Maurier turn in his grave nightly, not only because *sauce* is there alluded to as " Il."

1920.

THE BEGGAR'S OPERA

" WE were all at the first night of it," P reported to have said when *The Be Opera* was given for the first time, at the Linc Inn Fields Theatre, on 29th January 1728, great uncertainty of the event, till we were much e couraged by overhearing the Duke of Argyll say, ' It w do, it must do !   I see it in the eyes of them.'   This wa a good while before the first act was over, and so gave us ease soon. . . .   He was quite right in this as usual ; the good-nature of the audience appeared stronger and stronger every act, and ended in a clamour of applause." These words are singularly appropriate to the perform-ance of *The Beggar's Opera* at the Lyric Theatre, Hammersmith, on 5th June 1920.   One was conscious of a slight frigidity in the audience during the prologue and the opening scene ;   the audience were not quite at home in the unfamiliar atmosphere, in that world where people unblushingly called things by their names, but we felt (just as the audience had felt in 1728) as soon as Polly had sung her first couplets that *The Beggar's Opera* was *une bataille gagnée*, as Sainte-Beuve said about *Monte Cristo*.   " The audience," said Boswell, " were much affected by the innocent looks of Polly," and the other night, when she sang

"   But he so teaz'd me
And he so pleas'd me,
What I did, you must have done,"

the modern audience rapturously encored her.

temporarily and not deeply beneath the mass of semi-educated slush ? It still exists. It was heard in France during the war. When our troops marched into Metz, or one of the towns taken from the Germans, they did it to a beautiful and entirely English tune. Unfortunately, the words of " Rollicking Bill the Sailor " could not have been sung in an opera even in Gay's time ; but the musicians of his time could not have bettered the tune, with its sudden change of rhythm, its buoyant vitality, its rippling gaiety, and warm joyousness.

Such music was heard on many a march. Indeed, there was one regiment where the commanding officer found out that so long as he did not censor the words of songs, the soldiers preferred morris-dance tunes to any others to march to. English music still exists among the people, hidden away and obscured under the music that education or semi-education has produced. It sometimes comes to the surface in the music-hall. It blossomed once more gloriously in the whole of the Gilbert and Sullivan series, and since then it was heard again in Dr. Ethel Smyth's *Boatswain's Mate*. Otherwise, it has been banished from the academic schools of music and divorced still more rigidly from the concert room and the stage.

But now once more we have the opportunity of hearing it at its best and sunniest at the Hammersmith Theatre. Song after song was encored on Saturday night, and, as the evening went on, the applause increased in volume and in warmth. The performance was admirable. Mr. Frederic Austin, not content with arranging the settings of the music, played Peachum excellently. Mr. Frederick Ranalow was perfectly suited to the part of Macheath, the highwayman, and he sang the airs inimitably. Miss Sylvia Nelis was an ideal Polly, demure and quiet, and she warbled like a bird, and Miss Elsie French aroused the enthusiasm of the audience by her acting as Mrs. Peachum. The dances were effective and not overdone, and the whole production, the mounting, the setting, the scenes, and the songs (not forgetting the conducting of Mr. Goossens), revealed unsparing work, as well as discretion, knowledge, and taste.

The opera has been cut, as it would be too long to give in an ordinary evening's performance, but it has not been bowdlerised. Gay's words, however plain they are at times, do not produce that sensation of acute discomfort we sometimes experience in the theatre when witnessing the plays of our prudish modern dramatists. The fact is that the opera, the words, the jokes, the lyrics are natural. *The Beggar's Opera* was written in ridicule of the musical Italian drama, and not even Gilbert ever satirised more comically the sad plight of opera heroes than Gay does in the scene in Newgate, where Macheath, the highwayman, having successfully arranged matters with the slighted Lucy, is confronted in the presence of Lucy by Polly, his wife, and gets out of the difficulty by singing :

> " How happy could I be with either,
>   Were t'other dear charmer away !
> But while you thus tease me together,
>   To neither a word will I say :
>   But tol de rol ! "

No quarrel could last long, and no situation, however tense, could fail to relax to the strains of this ditty, which intoxicated the audience. When *The Beggar's Opera* made all England go mad in the eighteenth century, the principal topic it raised was whether or not it would increase crime by encouraging people to be highwaymen.

That is no longer our concern, or at least that concern belongs now to the world of movies and of crook adventures on the films. The topic this performance will, one hopes, raise will be the revival of English opera and English music. That there is no English opera at present is every one's fault, not the fault of this or that impresario or of this or that syndicate. Opera cannot live without subsidy, and subsidy will only be forthcoming when the people demand opera and insist on having it.

That audiences appreciate it when they get it has been proved by the experiences of the " Old Vic," the recent season at the Surrey Theatre, and the reception of *The Beggar's Opera* on Saturday last. But if English opera is to be written and performed, the requisite machinery for producing operatic works old and new must be created and supported. At present it does not exist.

Ventures such as those made at the Surrey Theatre, however large and enthusiastic the audiences, cannot be made permanent without financial support. The maintenance of an orchestra and a troupe is too expensive. The receipts cannot cover the expenses. But there are signs now of the demand for opera becoming more widespread and imperative. I feel certain the production of *The Beggar's Opera* will intensify this craving. Nobody will be able to come away from this performance ill-humoured, for its airs are, as Boswell said, very soft and " associated with the warm sensations and high spirits of London."

Purcell's music was heard not long ago at Cambridge. The Glastonbury Players are at the " Old Vic." One swallow does not make a summer, but it seems as if shoots were appearing first in one place and then in another, heralding what may possibly be a spring in the arid desert of English musical production. In the meantime, here is *The Beggar's Opera*. Not a word more will I say but : " Tol de rol ! "

1920.

SIR JAMES BARRIE AND THE GUITRYS

SIR JAMES BARRIE has proved once more that
all the orthodox canons which are enunciated by
hundreds with regard to theatrical art are nonsense.
The framers of all such theory probably had instances
of particular successful plays in their minds. All
that is really vitally essential in a play, a performed
play, is that the audience should want to know what is
going to happen next and remain in their seats—in
other words, that they should be diverted.

This is no doubt what Goethe meant when he said
that in a play everything should be symbolic and lead to
something else. In *Mary Rose* everything is significant
and does lead to something else. In the first act we are
in a deserted house, opened by a shivering caretaker to
an Australian soldier. The feeling of damp, disuse, and
decay is subtly wafted across the footlights, and when
we are told that " she " was seen on the staircase and
drew back to let the caretaker pass, and still more when
the door slowly opens and slowly shuts itself, we feel an
unmistakable thrill. The Australian falls asleep, and
sees in his dream the life that went on in the same house
when his parents lived in it, before he was born.

There is great dramatic originality in this idea, because, as we know beforehand that this happy life which
we now watch is finished and done with, and sadly done
with ; that the daughter of the house whom we see in all
her freshness and bloom, and in the untouched ecstasy of

349

first love is now a shivering ghost, we savour an ironic thrill of the first quality.

The house that we have seen silent, empty but haunted, we now see full of life and talk : the apple-tree is in blossom ; Mrs. Morland is knitting on the sofa ; Mr. Morland is discussing prints with his friend Mr. Amy, and Mary Rose (Miss Fay Compton) appears from the apple-tree, and confides that Harry, the father of the Australian in the first scene (both parts played by Mr. Loraine) has proposed to her. There is a drawback, and the parents (the parents and their old friend are admirably played by Mr. Norman Forbes, Mr. Whitby, and Miss Mary Jerrold) think it is only fair to tell the young man. Years ago when they were on an island in the Hebrides—an island shunned by the natives, and called in Gaelic the island that wants to be visited—one day when Mr. Morland was fishing, Mary Rose, quite a little child then, disappeared. A search was made everywhere, and she was not to be found. In ten days' time she reappeared, nor was she conscious of having been away for more than a moment. Nor did they ever tell her that she had been away for more than a moment. Mary Rose has grown up unconscious of her unearthly experience, and the parents have never spoken to her about it. But now they feel bound to tell the young man who wants to marry her. The young man, of course, does not regard this strange story as an obstacle, and in the next act we find Mary Rose, who has been married two years and has a son, on the very island with her husband, having a picnic. Why they go there I did not quite understand. It would have been more satisfactory if inevitable chance had led them there. But there they are, and after a conversation with a gillie, an Aberdeen student (played by Mr. Thesiger) who is doing

scent of lilac and syringa, and gay with butterflies and
dragon-flies and humble-bees, that I began my conscious
existence," where under the apple-tree is sitting the
beautiful Madame Pasquier, and Gogo and Mimsey are
doing their lessons, and talking of the two invisible
fairies that attend them : Le Prince Charmant and La Fée
Tarapatapoum : and there is the dog Médor, the dog
we have seen so often in old numbers of *Punch*, who
would " wag his three inches of tail and utter soft whimperings of welcome in his dream " while Mimsey said,
" C'est le Prince Charmant qui lui dit : Médor, donne la
patte ! " I thought this scene beautiful on the stage ;
very cleverly stage-managed and lighted, for although
the lighting was brilliant, one had the impression that
one was looking at a dream-world, and the children
played their parts delightfully. For the sake of this
scene alone, which was really moving and had the true
Du Maurier flavour and charm, the play is worth seeing.

Peter wakes up ; and events have for the play's sake
to be so tightly telescoped that he has to meet the Duchess
of Towers in the same act, and they have to recognise each
other as Gogo and Mimsey on the spot. This scene was
likewise moving and touching, but it was a slight strain
on one's credulity to believe that the Duchess had gone
to sleep in the carriage, as it had shortly before been
stated that she was driving with the Empress Eugénie.
Then we get a third act of good sterling drama, where
Peter kills Colonel Ibbetson. The scene is very well
played both by Mr. Rathbone and Mr. Hare. Mr. Hare
has some of the finish of his incomparable father. There
is just this difference. He lights a match and a cigarette
in this scene, and you say to yourself how well and how
naturally he did that ; if it had been Sir John Hare playing the part the cigarette would have lit before you

would have had time to notice how he lit it, however carefully you were waiting and watching for it.   In Act IV., after a not very (to me) interesting emotional prison scene, we get back once more into the dream-world, and see Gogo and Mimsey catching the water-beetles and the newts at the Mare d'Auteuil, and here the Duchess of Towers explains to Peter that his new dream-life has only just begun, and the possibility of reconstructing any moment of the past.   In the darkness of the glade they summon up a vision of the opera, and the voice of Adelina Patti is heard singing for them.   And there the play should end.   Unfortunately, there is an anticlimax in the shape of an epilogue forty years after, in which the Duchess of Towers returns with white hair after her death.   But one need not stay for it, and I didn't.   There is plenty of good acting in the play on the part of Mr. Rathbone, Miss Bateman, and others, and the only real cavil I have to make (apart from the question of the epilogue) is, why should the English proprietor of the Tête Noire, whom Peter recognises as an old London friend, be spoken to in French ?   But if it must be, for Heaven's sake let it be correct French.   The sentence about the *sauce verte* must make Du Maurier turn in his grave nightly, not only because *sauce* is there alluded to as " Il."

1920.

THE BEGGAR'S OPERA

"WE were all at the first night of it," Pope is
reported to have said when *The Beggar's
Opera* was given for the first time, at the Lincoln's
Inn Fields Theatre, on 29th January 1728, " in
great uncertainty of the event, till we were much en-
couraged by overhearing the Duke of Argyll say, ' It will
do, it must do ! I see it in the eyes of them.' This was
a good while before the first act was over, and so gave
us ease soon. . . . He was quite right in this as usual ;
the good-nature of the audience appeared stronger and
stronger every act, and ended in a clamour of applause."
These words are singularly appropriate to the performance of *The Beggar's Opera* at the Lyric Theatre,
Hammersmith, on 5th June 1920. One was conscious of
a slight frigidity in the audience during the prologue and
the opening scene ; the audience were not quite at home
in the unfamiliar atmosphere, in that world where people
unblushingly called things by their names, but we felt
(just as the audience had felt in 1728) as soon as Polly
had sung her first couplets that *The Beggar's Opera* was
une bataille gagnée, as Sainte-Beuve said about *Monte
Cristo*. " The audience," said Boswell, " were much
affected by the innocent looks of Polly," and the other
night, when she sang

> " But he so teaz'd me
> And he so pleas'd me,
> What I did, you must have done,"

the modern audience rapturously encored her.

Doctor Johnson's appreciative summing up of the opera is as much to the point now as when it was written. " It was refused by one of the houses," said the sage, " but I should have thought it would succeed, not from any great excellence in the writing, but from the novelty, and the general spirit and gaiety of the piece, which keeps the audience always attentive, and dismisses them in good humour " ; and Boswell's opinion is " that there is in it so much of real London life, so much brilliant wit, and such a variety of airs, which, from early association of ideas, engage, soothe, and enliven the mind, that no performance which the theatre exhibits delights me more."

To the present generation of playgoers and lovers of music it has an added and priceless value. It is English, as English as a landscape by Constable, or eggs and bacon, and is full of ravishing English music. With the exception of the recent revival of Gilbert and Sullivan's operas we have rarely had the chance of hearing a note of English music. In the world of opera, again with the exception just mentioned, there is little English music to hear. The music in the musical comedies and revues is mostly American or foreign in inspiration, but in *The Beggar's Opera* the songs are not only English but they are songs of the people ; traditional tunes that were born nobody knows how and were whistled in the streets and the country lanes and sung in taverns and on board ship —songs which in all times have been the wonder and despair of composers ; of Beethoven, who set " Sally in our Alley," the tune of which occurs in the third act of *The Beggar's Opera* ; of Handel, who is reported to have said he would rather have composed " The Girl I left behind Me " than any tune in the world. Has this music left England for ever ? one asks, or is it buried

temporarily and not deeply beneath the mass of semi-educated slush ? It still exists. It was heard in France during the war. When our troops marched into Metz, or one of the towns taken from the Germans, they did it to a beautiful and entirely English tune. Unfortunately, the words of " Rollicking Bill the Sailor " could not have been sung in an opera even in Gay's time ; but the musicians of his time could not have bettered the tune, with its sudden change of rhythm, its buoyant vitality, its rippling gaiety, and warm joyousness.

Such music was heard on many a march. Indeed, there was one regiment where the commanding officer found out that so long as he did not censor the words of songs, the soldiers preferred morris-dance tunes to any others to march to. English music still exists among the people, hidden away and obscured under the music that education or semi-education has produced. It sometimes comes to the surface in the music-hall. It blossomed once more gloriously in the whole of the Gilbert and Sullivan series, and since then it was heard again in Dr. Ethel Smyth's *Boatswain's Mate*. Otherwise, it has been banished from the academic schools of music and divorced still more rigidly from the concert room and the stage.

But now once more we have the opportunity of hearing it at its best and sunniest at the Hammersmith Theatre. Song after song was encored on Saturday night, and, as the evening went on, the applause increased in volume and in warmth. The performance was admirable. Mr. Frederic Austin, not content with arranging the settings of the music, played Peachum excellently. Mr. Frederick Ranalow was perfectly suited to the part of Macheath, the highwayman, and he sang the airs inimitably. Miss Sylvia Nelis was an ideal Polly, demure and quiet, and

she warbled like a bird, and Miss Elsie French aroused the enthusiasm of the audience by her acting as Mrs. Peachum. The dances were effective and not overdone, and the whole production, the mounting, the setting, the scenes, and the songs (not forgetting the conducting of Mr. Goossens), revealed unsparing work, as well as discretion, knowledge, and taste.

The opera has been cut, as it would be too long to give in an ordinary evening's performance, but it has not been bowdlerised. Gay's words, however plain they are at times, do not produce that sensation of acute discomfort we sometimes experience in the theatre when witnessing the plays of our prudish modern dramatists. The fact is that the opera, the words, the jokes, the lyrics are natural. *The Beggar's Opera* was written in ridicule of the musical Italian drama, and not even Gilbert ever satirised more comically the sad plight of opera heroes than Gay does in the scene in Newgate, where Macheath, the highwayman, having successfully arranged matters with the slighted Lucy, is confronted in the presence of Lucy by Polly, his wife, and gets out of the difficulty by singing :

> " How happy could I be with either,
>   Were t'other dear charmer away !
> But while you thus tease me together,
>   To neither a word will I say :
>   But tol de rol ! "

No quarrel could last long, and no situation, however tense, could fail to relax to the strains of this ditty, which intoxicated the audience. When *The Beggar's Opera* made all England go mad in the eighteenth century, the principal topic it raised was whether or not it would increase crime by encouraging people to be highwaymen.

That is no longer our concern, or at least that concern belongs now to the world of movies and of crook adventures on the films. The topic this performance will, one hopes, raise will be the revival of English opera and English music. That there is no English opera at present is every one's fault, not the fault of this or that impresario or of this or that syndicate. Opera cannot live without subsidy, and subsidy will only be forthcoming when the people demand opera and insist on having it.

That audiences appreciate it when they get it has been proved by the experiences of the " Old Vic," the recent season at the Surrey Theatre, and the reception of *The Beggar's Opera* on Saturday last. But if English opera is to be written and performed, the requisite machinery for producing operatic works old and new must be created and supported. At present it does not exist.

Ventures such as those made at the Surrey Theatre, however large and enthusiastic the audiences, cannot be made permanent without financial support. The maintenance of an orchestra and a troupe is too expensive. The receipts cannot cover the expenses. But there are signs now of the demand for opera becoming more widespread and imperative. I feel certain the production of *The Beggar's Opera* will intensify this craving. Nobody will be able to come away from this performance illhumoured, for its airs are, as Boswell said, very soft and " associated with the warm sensations and high spirits of London."

Purcell's music was heard not long ago at Cambridge. The Glastonbury Players are at the " Old Vic." One swallow does not make a summer, but it seems as if shoots were appearing first in one place and then in another,

heralding what may possibly be a spring in the arid desert of English musical production. In the meantime, here is *The Beggar's Opera*. Not a word more will I say but : " Tol de rol ! "

1920.

SIR JAMES BARRIE AND THE GUITRYS

SIR JAMES BARRIE has proved once more that all the orthodox canons which are enunciated by hundreds with regard to theatrical art are nonsense. The framers of all such theory probably had instances of particular successful plays in their minds. All that is really vitally essential in a play, a performed play, is that the audience should want to know what is going to happen next and remain in their seats—in other words, that they should be diverted.

This is no doubt what Goethe meant when he said that in a play everything should be symbolic and lead to something else. In *Mary Rose* everything is significant and does lead to something else. In the first act we are in a deserted house, opened by a shivering caretaker to an Australian soldier. The feeling of damp, disuse, and decay is subtly wafted across the footlights, and when we are told that " she " was seen on the staircase and drew back to let the caretaker pass, and still more when the door slowly opens and slowly shuts itself, we feel an unmistakable thrill. The Australian falls asleep, and sees in his dream the life that went on in the same house when his parents lived in it, before he was born.

There is great dramatic originality in this idea, because, as we know beforehand that this happy life which we now watch is finished and done with, and sadly done with ; that the daughter of the house whom we see in all her freshness and bloom, and in the untouched ecstasy of

first love is now a shivering ghost, we savour an ironic thrill of the first quality.

The house that we have seen silent, empty but haunted, we now see full of life and talk : the apple-tree is in blossom ; Mrs. Morland is knitting on the sofa ; Mr. Morland is discussing prints with his friend Mr. Amy, and Mary Rose (Miss Fay Compton) appears from the apple-tree, and confides that Harry, the father of the Australian in the first scene (both parts played by Mr. Loraine) has proposed to her. There is a drawback, and the parents (the parents and their old friend are admirably played by Mr. Norman Forbes, Mr. Whitby, and Miss Mary Jerrold) think it is only fair to tell the young man. Years ago when they were on an island in the Hebrides—an island shunned by the natives, and called in Gaelic the island that wants to be visited—one day when Mr. Morland was fishing, Mary Rose, quite a little child then, disappeared. A search was made everywhere, and she was not to be found. In ten days' time she reappeared, nor was she conscious of having been away for more than a moment. Nor did they ever tell her that she had been away for more than a moment. Mary Rose has grown up unconscious of her unearthly experience, and the parents have never spoken to her about it. But now they feel bound to tell the young man who wants to marry her. The young man, of course, does not regard this strange story as an obstacle, and in the next act we find Mary Rose, who has been married two years and has a son, on the very island with her husband, having a picnic. Why they go there I did not quite understand. It would have been more satisfactory if inevitable chance had led them there. But there they are, and after a conversation with a gillie, an Aberdeen student (played by Mr. Thesiger) who is doing

a little gillying, and who seems to have strayed into this play from the works of Mr. Shaw, Mary Rose hears voices and a full orchestra calling her and disappears a second time.

I wished the voices and the orchestra away. As Sir James Barrie had been able to frighten us at the beginning of the play without any music, I cannot help thinking he would have frightened us again, and a great deal more, without these sounds. For there is nothing uncanny about stage music. This time Mary Rose remains away twenty-five years, and comes back to find her parents very old, her husband a grizzled captain, and her son not there ; he has run away to sea and is in Australia. And once more she is not aware of having been away more than a moment. Her entry, ending with her rushing away to look for her child, is one of the most strange and poignant things I ever remember seeing on the stage. So is the " curtain," namely, the father asking whether Mary Rose has done wisely to come back.

The next act we are back again in the haunted house, and Mary Rose appears as a ghost and talks to her son, the Australian, who takes her on his knee. He knows who she is, but she does not know and cannot guess who he is, and, finally released from her haunting, she disappears to the sounds of the island voices and the full orchestra into the starry night.

I confess I found the last scene far less impressive than the rest of the play, and when Mary Rose, the ghost, appeared and talked she lost for me her power of making me feel a little bit cold down the spine.

I would rather she had not appeared, but that somehow or other (how I don't know, that is Sir James Barrie's business) we had been made to feel that the spell was

broken and that the house was no longer haunted, without seeing her in the ghostly flesh walk through the window into the stars. (One of the stars fell down, on purpose.)

As I was coming out of the theatre I heard some one say to a lady, " Did you enjoy it ? " " Yes," said the lady, " very much ; but what does it mean ? " *Mary Rose* was probably written, as Dr. Johnson said of *The Beggar's Opera*, " to divert without any moral purpose " ; but, consciously or unconsciously, it points one moral which is, curiously enough, the same moral which lies at the root of M. Sacha Guitry's play, *Mon Père avait Raison*. " Il faut vieillir ensemble," says the hero with regard to married lovers. And if you disappear on a fairy island it is better not to come back.

> " Life's night begins, let her never come back to us ;
> There would be doubt, hesitation, and pain."

That might be the moral of *Mary Rose*. There is some excellent acting at the Haymarket (Miss Fay Compton looks as if she were born for the part), but Mr. Loraine, although, of course, extremely competent, seems more at home in Mr. Shaw's world or in Rostand's bold and coloured kingdom of romance than in the whimsical, homely, eerie, pathetic fairyland of Sir James Barrie.

At the Aldwych we had a French season. Slices from the biography of Pasteur, superbly acted by M. Lucien Guitry, one serious comedy, *Jean de la Fontaine*, and three light comedies.

Of these the most interesting as a play was *Jean de la Fontaine*. In it the author tells a moving story with many sidelights and many glimpses of mortal things, and many drops of human tears, but unfortunately he tries

to do too much. It was an ambitious thing in itself to put the *sublime bonhomme* on the stage. The story of his unhappy married life is a good subject for a play, and if M. Sacha Guitry had confined himself to that the result would have been more satisfactory. As it is, he tries to crowd into the play too many sides of La Fontaine's life —if so many there are not enough—his friendship with Madame de la Sablière, his love for the little *rossignol* who runs away with Lully, the composer, his attempted reconciliation with his wife, her attempted reconciliation with him, his enmity with Ninon de Lenclos, his literary career.

There is much, too much, local colour, and the local colour does not conceal the complete modernity of the play. One feels that the story is happening on the boulevards ; that is quite right, and as it should be, only one does not believe that it also happened to La Fontaine in this way. M. Sacha Guitry acted La Fontaine with infinite charm. But he did not show himself a great actor in the part, nor did the part seem to be that of a great man.

The real La Fontaine was more squalid and more sublime. And when M. Guitry read out the first lines of the fable of *Le Coche et la Mouche* I did not for one moment believe that I was listening to the author of that masterpiece, although I did think that was just the way in which authors read out their poems.

One of the most entertaining of the plays was *Mon Père avait Raison*, and it had the advantage of containing parts for M. Lucien Guitry and for his son Sacha as well. This play, written like all the rest by M. Sacha Guitry, reveals all the qualities and all the limitations of its high-spirited author. It is witty, extraordinarily lifelike at moments, revealing a gift of acute and pene-

23

trative observation and tailing off into farce at the end. M. Sacha Guitry has not yet by the writing of a masterpiece entered the first class of French writers of comedy, but his work is always irresistible and sometimes moving. His father, on the other hand, as an actor has reached the top rung of the ladder. Years of hard work and unflagging devotion to his art, incessant care and an infinite capacity for taking pains, have met with their reward, and combined with his natural talent and vigorous temperament have sealed his reputation in such a way that he can now boldly claim to be the first of living actors.

1920.

THE GUITRYS AND LA FONTAINE

WHEN Henry James in a letter from Paris, written after he had been living with the literary giants of his epoch, Flaubert, Zola, and Daudet, said that the French men of letters were like the Chinese in their total ignorance and disdain of what was taking place in the world of barbarians outside the Great Wall, he was, whether consciously or not, paying them a compliment.

For what does such a sentence imply ? It implies that the standards of perfection are so high and the classic models are so exquisite within the wall, that it takes a man all his lifetime to know them, to study them, and to try and live up to them. He has neither time nor inclination to bother about what is happening outside the wall. It takes a Frenchman all his time to write and appreciate the French language, without troubling himself about foreign languages, because he knows how well it can be written : the infinite variety of what there is to appreciate, the immensity of the field of work before him, and the intensity of the effort that will be required of him.

In the last month we have been favoured with a manifestation of French art at its best in the shape of M. Lucien Guitry's acting, and with a delicious expression of French wit in the plays of M. Sacha Guitry. But the former is in an infinitely higher category than the latter. M. Lucien Guitry belongs to the great race of French actors. His name will be written in letters of gold with the names of Delaunay, Frédéric Lemaître, Coquelin, and Got. During his long career, from the time when he played the Armand Duvals and the *jeune premier* parts with Sarah Bernhardt, and the lovers in Maurice Donnay's comedies, until the period when he impersonated the more robust characters in Rostand's poetical drama and the dynamic heroes of M. Bernstein, his talent, his art, and his complete mastery over the means at his disposal have continued to develop and to ripen until they attained the absolute perfection that we have lately had the joy of witnessing. Unfortunately, I missed his *Pasteur*, but one has only to see M. Guitry in the first act of *Mon Père avait Raison*, only indeed in the last sentence of that first act, when he gives his son a push after a sudden, abrupt, and broken-off embrace, to realise that he is the first actor now alive.

Every detail, every gesture, every intonation, every look is perfect ; but so quickly is each nuance indicated that it has happened before you know how it has happened, just as in real life. Nothing brings out the perfection of his acting more subtly and more clearly than the juxtaposition of M. Lucien Guitry and his son Sacha. M. Sacha Guitry acts well. He has charm, grace, talent, and wit in abundance ; but his art is not too swift for the eye. You see—sometimes in any case—how it is done. With the father, never. And what the father leaves undone ! There is never the millionth part of a shade of anything too much. He knows so surely when not to move his hands and when to keep the expression of his eyes under control. His art is an example of supreme reserve and rigid economy, and it reminds one of the sentence of one of the younger French writers that " la langue Française est un piano sans pédale." M. Lucien Guitry plays the pianoforte without a pedal, and yet his *crescendos* are tremendous and his *forte* overwhelming.

So much for the art as revealed in the acting. Now as to the plays. That they are witty, as light as the smoke-ring of a cigarette, goes without saying. Are they anything else ? *Pasteur* I leave out, as there is no very great art in piecing together slices of life from a great man's biography, and if you have a superb actor to impersonate these slices you achieve your end easily. But in *Jean de la Fontaine* M. Sacha Guitry attempted something far more ambitious. He aimed at putting on the stage perhaps the greatest figure in French literature and one of the most charming and the most rare personalities of all time.

He attempted to give us, to show us, the quintessence of the life of the poet who said :

" Un vain bruit et l'amour ont occupé mes ans."

He attempts to give us an echo of that *vain bruit* and to penetrate into the heart of that *amour*. Does he succeed ? Only partially. He does not give the sense of that quality in La Fontaine which made him sum up his life in such a line. The beginning (as is generally the case with M. Sacha Guitry's plays) is perfect. La Fontaine is asleep in a chair near the fire with his back to the audience. Madame de la Fontaine is sitting at her work. Her lover calls through the window, not seeing La Fontaine, " Es-tu seule ? " " Oui," answers La Fontaine, and keeps up the conversation, as if the lover had meant to address him, and then, without his wife suspecting anything, he goes out to fight the lover and returns wounded, explaining, with consummate naturalness, that he has met with an accident. He then leaves

his home for good, and in the next act we see him in
Paris, in his lodgings, making love to the entrancing
rossignol impersonated by Mademoiselle Yvonne Prin-
temps, who is the living goddess of charm. She lives
next door and sings Lully's songs.

All this is exquisite and there is a lilt in the scene like
that in one of Browning's love poems :

> " It might have been, once only :
>   We lodged in a street together,
> You, a sparrow on the housetop lonely,
> I, a lone she-bird of his feather.
> .   .   .   .   .
> My business was song, song, song :
>   I chirped, cheeped, trilled, and twittered . .

But the she-bird flies away with Lully, and the sparrow
is left lonely.

And then there is a little too much. Too many
episodes of La Fontaine's life are brought in. They
crowd the too-slender canvas of the play. There is
Madame de la Sablière, and there is Ninon de Lenclos,
and there is La Fontaine's wife, who wants him to come
back to her. She goes to see him in Paris after his historic
visit to Château Thierry, when he went back to her and,
on being told that " Madame est aux vêpres," left Château
Thierry never to return. That is what happened actually.
What happens in the play is that his wife returns the
visit, and begs him to come back to her, and reveals
incidentally two things : one, that her lover is married
— giving M. Sacha Guitry the opportunity for a
wonderful gesture and look—and, secondly, that she
knows his works by heart. He is so charmed with this
second revelation that he at once begins to recite to her
the fable of *Le Coche et la Mouche*, which he has just
composed. It is a touching scene and a human scene

and a dramatic scene, moving, in that La Fontaine never lets her see for a moment that he has known all along of her infidelity, and he plays up to her sincere claim to irreproachability, but one cannot help feeling that it is the life, the Bohemian life of Paris in the twentieth century that is being depicted, and not the Bohemian life of the *Grand Siècle*. In other words, we feel that this La Fontaine is a charming, engaging, witty, delightful person, but he is not the *sublime bon homme* : he has neither the necessary sublimity nor the necessary squalor.

There is one well-known story which sums up the whole character of La Fontaine. When he was ill, and had just lost his best friend and patron, one of his friends hurried to him, to offer him the hospitality of his house. " J'y allais," said La Fontaine. The La Fontaine of the play, although he says many witty and pretty things, never says a thing like this.

The fact is, that La Fontaine, as a man as well as a writer, rightly deserved the epithet which his contemporaries gave to him of *l'inimitable*, and to make him move and live in a play would require another La Fontaine. M. Sacha Guitry is not another La Fontaine. His work as playwright is not in the first class of French art of this kind—in the first class of French light comedy. It is scintillating, engaging, amusing, original, but it does not descend, as does, for instance, a comedy like Maurice Donnay's *Amants*, directly from Racine. M. Lucien Guitry's art does belong to the first class of French acting. His name can be boldly affiliated to and compared with the greatest names in the French temple of Thespis.

June 1920.

MACBETH

THE essence of drama is speed. The greatest of all dramas, the Mass, is also the most rapid. The words of it, Newman says, " hurry on as if impatient to fulfil their mission. Quickly they go, the whole is quick, for they are all parts of an integral action. Quickly they go, for they are awful words of sacrifice ; they are a work too great to delay upon ; as when it was said in the beginning, ' What thou doest, do quickly.' "

The words which Newman quoted here might be a fitting motto for *Macbeth*. It is the most rapid of all Shakespeare's plays. " What thou doest," whisper the witches to Macbeth, " do quickly." Macbeth is like a man whose soul is caught in the wheels of a supernatural machinery, and he is whirled on in dizzy revolution of crime, remorse, and further crime, necessitated by previous crime, to his doom.

He is hurried on, and never for one moment is he allowed to enjoy the fruits of his crimes in peace. It is the most moving of spectacles ever devised by a mortal poet, for we feel from the beginning that the tragedy is inside him. It is his particular soul, and no other, which has just those elements which make it the inevitable prey of the metaphysical machine. Œdipus would have listened to the weird sisters and walked on heedless. Macbeth's tragedy was in his own soul. Ambition spins the plot, and he is betrayed by what is false within. And in the helter-skelter catastrophe of events that succeed one another more breathlessly and more violently than the pictures of a film, Shakespeare has inserted his gravest and weightiest words — words of brooding melancholy and infinite retrospect, so that the violent action is constantly opening doors on calm regions of boundless and unfathomable speculation.

We speculate as we gaze on the soaring leap of vaulting ambition and the shipwreck of a kingly nature too violent for peace, too slender for his dizzy dreams, and we pity. *Mentem mortalia tangunt*

How much of all this was conveyed to the audience in Mr. Hackett's production at the Aldwych Theatre ? A certain amount ; just so much as the play itself was given a free hand ; and certainly a good deal more of the play was allowed a free hand than in the productions of *Macbeth* that we have been accustomed to during the last ten years.

If *Macbeth* is mounted elaborately, as it was at the Lyceum, and more recently at His Majesty's Theatre, the frequent changes of scene, involving complicated changes of scenery, delay the action and diminish its dramatic effect. If musical interludes are added, the action is still further delayed, and not only delayed, but deadened. If, in addition to elaborate mounting and titillating music, you add fireworks, air-craft alarms, maroons, stage thunder, stage lightning, ballets, floating witches, and choruses of winged elves singing and dancing, you end by giving not the effect of a tragedy, but that of an opera comique and a pantomime. You may amuse and delight the audience, but you no longer move or terrify it. The words of the weird sisters are frightening, but add a stage cauldron, stage-fire, and thunder, " like a tea-tray in the sky," and the fright vanishes.

In Mr. Hackett's production the mounting is not on the whole over-elaborate, and at moments it is beautiful. The colour effects are harmonious and cleverly planned ; the dresses are effective, the lighting is good, and the play is allowed to move on. It is true that the blasted heath is like a Gustave Doré illustration ; it is true that the stage thunder is unmistakably like a crashing of tea-trays, and it is true that the incidental music reminds one of *Mary Rose* with its " harps in the air," and has certainly nothing either sinister or eerie about it ; but, on the whole, the action is little impeded by the accessories, and the stage effects, as in the banquet scene and the sleep-walking scene, are often beautiful. But I think it is true to say that, whenever there was most bustle and *acting* going on on the stage, the interest of the audience flagged, and whenever there was less bustle, less acting, and the words were spoken quietly, the audience were gripped, interested, and moved.

Mr. Hackett is a sound Macbeth and, above all, a *manly* Macbeth. And if one has to choose between the actor who interprets Macbeth as a neurotic dreamer who commits murder to become a king, and the actor who interprets him as a kingly man who commits a murder to win the crown which he thinks his by right of nature, I personally prefer the latter, which is Mr. Hackett's interpretation. Irving, Sir Johnston Forbes-Robertson, and the late Sir Herbert Tree, gave us interesting versions of the former interpretation, and necessarily so, because such was their temperament.

Mr. Hackett, as Hazlitt said about Kemble, stands at bay with fortune and maintains his ground solidly against " fate and metaphysical aid " ; Irving and Tree reeled and staggered against the powers of darkness. But Mr. Hackett delivered the soliloquies finely and soberly, and

in the " My way has fallen into the sere," and the
" To-morrow and to-morrow " speeches, his tone had,
as Hazlitt said again on another occasion about
Kemble, " something retrospective in it—an echo of
the past."

Mr. Hackett's Macbeth made you feel that Macbeth
was born to be a king, and if the crown did not come to
him naturally he would be bound to seize it forcibly. He
spoke well, he fought well, and he died well, but he is
not a harrowing Macbeth. You did not feel, as Steven-
son said of Salvini, that when he spoke of his hangman's hands he seemed to have blood in his utterance.
You never felt that he was on wires and that he would
in fact sleep no more. You felt, if he did feel inclined
to brood in the night hours on the unfortunate occur-
rences, he would take a good sleeping-draught and wake
up fresh for the next day's fight and the next day's
murder.

But in his reflective soliloquies the dignified manliness
of his utterance moved the audience and let them feel
what Shakespeare is capable of, and that is a thing to be
thankful for. It was a joy to see Mrs. Patrick Campbell
again in any part ; to enjoy her grace, the swift sureness
of her movements, and to see her haunting eyes and to
hear her faery speech. How beautiful her eyes looked
right at the back of the stage in the banquet scene !
Lady Macbeth is a tremendous part, a crushing part, and
to make the audience realise it fully you need tragic
sublimity. " Mrs. Siddons's Lady Macbeth," said
Hazlitt, " is little less appalling in its effects than the
apparition of a preternatural being." And, talking of
her sleep-walking scene, he says : " She glided on and
off the stage almost like an apparition."

It is no disparagement to Mrs. Campbell to say that

tragic sublimity is not the keynote of her peculiar power any more than it is that of Eleonora Duse, who, when she played Shakespeare's Cleopatra, used to sink and dwindle under the greatness of the part, just as she would expand and rise, and exalt and magnify the part, in a D'Annunzio or a Sudermann play. Mrs. Campbell is always interesting, always beautiful and impossible to stop watching, and in the sleep-walking scene she gives an exquisitely moving performance. But it is not tragic. Just as in the murder scenes you do not feel that here is a dæmonic, dynamic personality who is going to stop at nothing and compel everything and everybody to give way to her, so in the sleep-walking scene you do not feel confronted with the awful spectacle of a mind and character so strong that nothing can break it in life, and only during sleep can nature take its revenge on it, but you do feel in the presence of a vision of surpassing beauty ; you do see a soul in pain, wandering in the twilight of Purgatory and wistfully moaning for its release.

Mrs. Campbell made one feel that Maeterlinck was lineally descended from this sleep-walking scene : that this one scene was enough to beget a Maeterlinck. Mrs. Campbell, one felt, belonged to the world of Maeterlinck rather than to that of Shakespeare ; but, however that may be, it was delightful to see her once more in scarlet and gold and other coats of many colours, acting always interestingly and quite admirably in the retrospective scenes.

Mr. Leslie Faber gave a fine performance of Macduff, and the whole company were sound and competent. One wished that " execution " could be pronounced as a word of five syllables instead of four syllables in the second scene of the first act. And one could not help thinking that the place where Macbeth first meets the witches is of such a nature as to take away any possible surprise on the part of Macbeth, or indeed of any one else, either at their presence there or at their sudden disappearance.

1920.

THE CENCI

*T*HE CENCI was first printed at Leghorn in 1819, and published in England in the spring of 1820. The Shelley Society organised a private performance of the play in 1886, but it was then still under the ban of the Censor. *The Cenci* was produced in Prague in honour of the Shelley Centenary; but the first public, unbanned London performance took place last Monday afternoon, 13th November, one hundred and three years after the play was written.

All this gives us food for ironic thought; it makes us wonder at a great many things : at the attitude of Shelley's contemporaries towards his work, at the curious workings of the Censorship, at the blindness of people in general to possible dramatic effect (there was nothing to prevent the play being produced abroad by a Duse or a Salvini), but, after all, the play's the thing. Let us talk about the play. I believe when it was acted in 1886 it was thought dull, and that the performance took four hours. The other day at the New Theatre it was played with sufficient speed and without unnecessary intervals, and I do not think the audience was for a moment bored. The first impression that struck me was this : here we were confronted with some evidently big thing; we were in the presence of a great mind; the "fundamental brain-work" of the poet hit one in almost every line. The language was not only beautiful but restrained, and dramatically magnificent.

Shelley truly says in the preface to *The Cenci* that he has avoided in the composition of the play what is commonly called " mere poetry." There is only one descriptive passage, as he himself points out, in the play ; that about the chasm where Cenci is to be murdered, and that is necessary to the action of the drama. And yet in the simple and straightforward lines of the play we hear the unmistakable accent of poetry and of greatness. It was unnecessary for Shelley, in this case, to " load every rift with ore," as Keats advised him to do. Indeed, it would have been more than unnecessary. It would have been wrong, for the rifts in this case were the lines of a great and terrible tragedy which needed no gleam of gold to enhance its terror and its pity. It is a drama of which the keynote is resistance—resistance to evil and injustice, and the divine retribution that follows revenge, however justifiable such revenge may seem to be. And resistance was the *strongest* fibre in Shelley's genius, and the situation in which he is greatest is that in which Prometheus resists Zeus and Beatrice Cenci resists her father. The resistance of a " pard-like spirit, beautiful and swift," against the evil and injustice of the world ; a resistance which is calmly ready to dare everything and to suffer, uncomplaining, the utmost penalty and extremest suffering for what is dared and done in protest. That retribution is the keynote of the drama is a fact which is sometimes lost sight of. Some people are blinded by the great qualities in the character of Beatrice, the nobility of her resistance, the depth and nature of her sufferings, the courage with which she endures her punishment ; and others, on the other hand, are outraged by her conduct, and revolted when she allows her mother and her relations to be tortured and the unfortunate Marzio to die on the rack, sooner than confess the truth, namely, that she had planned her father's murder. Such a complaint would be justified were Beatrice represented as being a saint. She is not a saint, nor does Shelley represent her as one. She is Beatrice Cenci, the daughter of Count Francesco Cenci (such as Shelley read about her in such documents as were available in his time), and as a lady in the audience said : " That girl takes after her father." She is not a saint, because when persecuted she retaliates. She hits back, instead of enduring and submitting passively and meekly. And she has to pay the inevitable punishment for retaliation. She plans the murder and insists on the silence of her family with so terrible a calm that some people murmur " fiend ! " ; she pays the final penalty and suffers her doom at the end with so sublime a courage that the unthinking murmur " saint." She is neither : she is a woman, and therefore a sinner, and therefore a fit subject for the tragic stage.

As one heard the lines spoken, one became aware of a high sculptural simplicity and of the indefinable invasion of poetry into the language of everyday life, as we in the lines of the Greek dramatists and in Racine :

> " O God ! that I were buried with my brothers,
> And that the flowers of this departed Spring
> Were fading on my grave ! "

Or, again :

> O ! Before worse comes of it
> 'Twere wise to die : it ends in that at last."

Who is there now, one thought, who can write like this ? And is there perhaps some one among us now writing masterpieces which we are unaware of and poetry to which we are deaf ?

The drama had not proceeded far before one realised

that *The Cenci* was more than a great piece of literature.
The banquet scene at the end of Act I. was drama, and
drama which would be recognised as such at any time,
in any place, and before any audience—(why were the
guests dressed as Christmas crackers in the style of the
Russian Ballet ?)—and the impression of drama increased
as the play proceeded.

The arrangements for the murder of Cenci (how
beautifully Miss Thorndike spoke the Chasm speech !),
the murder itself, the ironic arrival of the Papal authority
for the arrest of Cenci when it is too late, and then the
unforgettable scenes of the trial and the prison, were
given their full effect. But I should like to protest
with all my strength against the introduction of the
tortured Marzio's screams at the beginning of the trial.
There is no sanction in the text for any such thing, and
even as a Grand Guignol thrill they miss their effect,
since there is no preparation for them. They are
merely an ugly blot. As the play drew to a close, its
greatness, and the greatness of Shelley as a poet and as a
dramatic poet, seemed to be revealed to us with a great
sweep as of opening wings. When Beatrice in the prison
says to Lucretia :

" Your eyes look pale, hollow and overworn,
With heaviness of watching and slow grief.
Come, I will sing you some low, sleepy tune,
Not cheerful, nor yet sad ; some dull old thing,
Some outworn and unused monotony,
Such as our country gossips sit and spin,
Till they almost forget they live."

As these beautiful and simple words were spoken in
their situation, so dramatically right, so scenically effective, one felt that it was true that Shelley has been so far
the only meet successor of the Elizabethan dramatists.

24

With regard to the acting, I am in agreement with what has been said about Miss Thorndike by the majority of the critics, that at the beginning there were mannerisms and a want of harmony ; but from the moment Beatrice sees her course clear, Miss Thorndike's interpretation became clear also, and not only clear but inexpressibly dignified, grave, and moving, and at the end magnificent. Opinions differed widely about Mr. Farquharson's exceedingly interesting performance, with the exception of his banqueting scene. I was not carried away by it, but I am quite ready to dub myself a fool, as we were advised to at school if we didn't appreciate Horace. I have not dwelt at length on the acting, because to me the important thing about this performance is the vindication of Shelley as a great dramatic poet it has brought about ; yet, but for Miss Thorndike's courage in producing the play, and but for the manner of acting, the vindication would not have been made. When Miss Thorndike spoke the final lines :

> " Here, mother, tie
> My girdle for me, and bind up this hair
> In any simple knot ; aye, that does well.
> And yours, I see, is coming down. How often
> Have we done this for one another ; now
> We shall not do it any more. My Lord,
> We are quite ready. Well, 'tis very well,"

it was clear that not only was Shelley a great poet and that we had lost in him a great dramatist, but that we had found in Miss Thorndike an actress who knew how to speak tragic verse.

1922.